Sport and Society

Series Editors
Benjamin G. Rader
Randy Roberts

Books in the Series Sport and Society

The Brawn Drain

JOHN BALE

THE
BRAWN DRAIN

Foreign Student-Athletes
in American Universities

University of Illinois Press

Urbana and Chicago

© 1991 by the Board of Trustees of the University of Illinois
Manufactured in the United States of America
C 5 4 3 2 1

This book is printed on acid-free paper.

Library of Congress Cataloging-in-Publication Data

Bale, John.
    The brawn drain : foreign student-athletes in American
universities / John Bale.
        p. cm.—(Sport and society)
    Includes bibliographical references.
    ISBN 0-252-01732-3 (alk. paper)
    1. College sports—United States.   2. Athletics—Recruiting.
3. Students, Foreign—United States.   I. Title.   II. Series.
GV351.B35 1991
796'.071'173—dc20   90-32829
                                                                CIP

To my mother
   and
to the memory of my father

Contents

Preface

Once upon a time it might have been quite appropriate to say, as Shakespeare did, that all the world is a stage. Today a more satisfactory metaphor might be that all the world's a stadium. A frantic form of internationalization has been associated with the world of sport in recent years; not only has international sporting competition mushroomed as more countries adopt the *citius, altius, fortius* model of sports, but so too has the international migration of skilled sports talent. Although talent migration has been a feature of the global scene for many centuries, the internationalization of the composition of domestic sports teams and clubs is a relatively recent phenomenon. Modern trends will invariably have their antecedents but it is undoubtedly the case that the widespread international migration of sports personnel is a postwar occurrence. It is this particular form of talent migration, set in the context of the American collegiate sports system, that this book addresses.

Despite the migration of athletic talent to American universities, we know relatively little about it in comparison with academic-talent migration, and Neil Amdur has gone so far as to state that "the foreign-athlete situation remains one of the most complex, covert and least understood problem areas of intercollegiate athletics."[1] As Bruce Kidd observed from a Canadian perspective: "Take the US athletic scholarships. Why do some athletes head south unquestioningly while others pay their way to study in Canada? What backgrounds do they come from? What considerations are foremost in their minds? What is the result of this experience on their subsequent behaviour? If they return to Canada, do they lobby for similar opportunities in Canada, or do they become part of the conduit for Canadian athletes to US colleges?''[2] Answers to these questions would increase our understanding of the processes involved, and it is these and other questions about the international recruiting game that will be explored in the following chapters in an attempt to help to demystify the foreign student-athlete situation.

Chapter 1 sets the stage upon which the drama of American intercollegiate sport is played, giving evidence of the global nature of sports competition and organization. Chapter 2 looks at the evolution of the present system, the role of the governing bodies in intercollegiate sport and the conferences, and also explores the present-day system, interpreting sport in academia in various ways—as part of the educational process, as a form of entertainment, and, perhaps, as a kind of exploitation. There is more than a suggestion that the uneasy relationship between sport in the American university and respect for the individual is an exploitive and hence a dehumanizing relationship.

Chapter 3 considers the overall pattern of international recruitment of scholars and student-athletes by the American higher education system. Attention is drawn to the broad trends, both historical and geographical, and to the sports involved. Secondary and previously unpublished data are used in this chapter to provide, for the first time, a realistic estimate of the number of foreign student-athletes on US campuses in the late 1980s. A detailed case study is presented for one sport—track and field athletics—in chapter 4. Here, again using previously published and unpublished data, the geographical origins by continent and nation as well as the destinations by state and college are traced for the period since World War II. Data for the past decade or so are used to identify the patterns of supply and demand.

Chapter 5 explores the experience of being a foreign student-athlete in the United States. The role of the coach is highlighted and the background of students is identified, as is the way in which cheating may work its way into the initial stages of migration. The college experience is dealt with more fully in chapter 6, which identifies the sporting, educational, and social experiences, including problems, of being a foreign student-athlete. These chapters adopt a much more qualitative approach. Journalistic and previously published and unpublished research sources are used to express the views of the various "actors" on the international recruiting stage, while in chapter 7 the experience of foreign sojourn is explored in an even more personal way by presenting transcriptions of in-depth interviews with student-athletes. These approaches present a clear picture of the personal experiences of foreign student-athletes in America. Prospective recruits and administrators should therefore be better informed of foreign student-athletes' experiences in the United States. The book concludes with an interpretation and an evaluation of the international recruiting game and explores some of the controversies, both at home and abroad, which have accompanied it.

Acknowledgments

This book's title, *The Brawn Drain,* was suggested to me by Tony Mangan and I must thank him for it. I adopted this title because it is a handy counter to the much more heavily documented "brain drain." But I do not use the word "brawn" in a derogatory sense; I am too well aware that all student-athletes are not brawny, just as I know that many academic migrants may not be especially brainy.

The Brawn Drain grew out of my decades-long fascination with American college sports. I am not sure whether this fascination was born when I saw Burt Lancaster playing the title role in the early-fifties biopic *Jim Thorpe—All American* (titled *Man of Bronze* for British audiences) or nurtured by my avid reading of surface-mailed copies of *Track and Field News* while at high school, but my interest in college sports only began to assume an academic angle when, in 1969, I encountered for the first time (in "Up from the Mines and Out from the Prairies," in *The Geographical Review*) the seminal work of American sports geographer John Rooney. Of course, I always knew college sports in the States were different from those in Britain, but what Rooney stressed was the geographic dynamic in American sports— the frantic recruitment of high school talent nationwide. Later he produced his fascinating study *The Recruiting Game,* but a reviewer, Alvar Carlson, writing in the *Journal of Geography,* noted that the foreign dimension had been omitted. It was that review which sowed the seeds of the present book.

As my interest in American sports grew, people who had simply been academic contacts became acquaintances and friends. It is very difficult to overstate the debt I owe to John Rooney. His hospitality and cooperation, while I was on fleeting visits to Oklahoma State, led to a lasting friendship. At Stillwater I was able to see what a big-time sports campus was really like and what college and high school sports meant to local people. I saw at first hand aspects of US sport which Americans take for granted but which confirmed what I had known from afar — that American college sport is unique. In Stillwater I saw campus sports facilities that would be lacking in British cities of 250,000 people or more. And I could see from the billboards and welcoming signs in the vernacular landscape what sport meant in terms of place-pride. At OSU I was also able to share my ideas on international athletic recruiting with research students and faculty members.

From Atlanta, Dick Pillsbury and John Ball led me along fascinating byways of American sports, from Fulton County Stadium to Lanier Raceway. Their hospitality and friendship are fondly recalled and greatly appreciated. I must thank Tom Hollander for very generously providing me with access to his dissertation on foreign athletic recruiting. I am also grateful to Ted Goudge for reading an early version of the manuscript — and for early-morning running with me through downtown Phoenix. A version of the text was also read by Howard Stidwill, who I must also thank for help with the interviews which form the basis of chapter 7 and for access to his doctoral dissertation. Japhet Muita was kind enough to provide me with some insights into sports and education in Kenya. Carl Ojala, Joe Arbena, Rankin Cooter, Harry Harvey, and Derek Benning also gave up valuable time in order to help with my inquiries.

I must also thank the many sports information directors from university athletic departments across the United States who were generous in their responses to my requests for team rosters and other information; their support was invaluable. The second half of this book could not have been written without the help of a large number of student-athletes, some of whom became my friends. Many did much more than simply complete my questionnaires and agree to be interviewed; they added insightful comments and offered help with my research when encouragement was most needed. I must thank Joyce Randle and Agnes Fairclough, who assisted with the typing of the manuscript, and Andrew Lawrence, who, with imagination and flair, expertly converted my rough sketches into polished maps, graphs, and diagrams. The funding for the research that formed the basis of this book was provided by the Department of Education, University of Keele, assistance which I am pleased to acknowledge.

Finally I must thank my parents for instilling in me an interest in sports from an early age, and my wife, Ruth, for providing moral support over the years. Although many people have helped in this book's production, the usual disclaimer applies.

I CONTEXTS

That is the point about American sport; that it is not very sportive. It is because it is not very sportive that we sometimes say it is not very sporting.

G. K. Chesterton

ONE

The Global Arena

At a track and field meet a few years ago the men's 400 meters was won by a Jamaican, the 800 meters by a Brazilian, the 1,500 meters by an Irishman, the 5,000 and 10,000 meters by a Tanzanian, the 400-meter hurdles by a Swede, the pole vault by a Swiss, the triple jump and hammer throw by Englishmen, and the javelin throw by an Icelander. The women's 100 meters and 200 meters went to a Jamaican, the high jump to an athlete from Iceland, and the javelin throw to a Norwegian. The Olympics? The World Championships? No, the meet was the 1983 NCAA (National Collegiate Athletic Association) championships at Houston, Texas. Foreign student-athletes won fifteen of the thirty-five individual events and many others took part and gained placings.

A similar situation would be found in a number of other sports and in a number of other countries. Indeed, the internationalization of domestic sports activity is a phenomenon throughout the modern Western world. Foreign recruits in sports are restricted neither to college sport nor to Sportsworld USA. Professional baseball has long recruited players from the Caribbean and from Central America; from the mid-sixties to the mid-eighties about 10 percent of major-league baseball players came from overseas, the major sources being the Dominican Republic and Puerto Rico.[1] Of around twenty-three hundred soccer players registered with the ninety-two English League clubs in 1987, 1.9 percent were recruited overseas. When we consider the two most successful postwar clubs, Liverpool and Manchester United, however, fourteen of their seventy-five players—or 18.7 percent—were foreign recruits.[2] Americans are employed in professional basketball in many countries, and in 1986 over 33 percent of the Division I players in the English Basketball League were foreign, the majority Americans.[3]

Sixty percent of the players representing Denmark and Uruguay in the 1986 soccer World Cup played for clubs in countries other than their own. In both the United States and the United Kingdom, professional ice hockey is manned by sporting migrants from Canada; each of the top eighty rugby clubs in France has, on average, one foreigner on its books; in England 8 percent of registered county club cricketers were, in 1987, deemed ineligible to play for England— clubs employing Indians, Pakistanis, West Indians, Australians and other nationals.[4] Professional cyclists frequently cross national boundaries to compete for foreign teams (a tendency especially common among cyclists from the Netherlands and France) and even tiny Switzerland had eighty-two foreigners playing in its national soccer league in 1987.[5]

The developments in Eastern Europe in late 1989 are likely to produce a much greater flow of sports talent from East to West. Talented Romanian soccer players will move to the West and similar tendencies will emerge in other countries and in other sports. Restrictions on sports migration from Eastern Europe were being eased in the mid-1980s, the export of sports talent seen as a useful means of obtaining hard currency. Soviet soccer players are now employed by British and Italian clubs and Czech ice hockey talent is today found in Scotland. It is clear, therefore, that the world, rather than the nation, has become the recruiting oyster for those organizations whose prime aim is sports success.

The international recruitment and migration of sports talent is but part of the widespread interaction among members of different nations in what is an increasingly interdependent and shrinking world. Such movement, and the resulting "culture shock" and problems of adjustment, is the outcome of a world of shared values and aspirations. One subset of such skilled international migrants is the large number of foreign student-athletes going to American universities and colleges; it is this "brawn drain" that forms the subject of this book.

Foreign-student migration has been well documented within the substantial literature on brain drain,[6] cross-cultural interaction,[7] and student adjustment to foreign sojourn.[8] Likewise, the domestic recruiting of American high school athletic talent has been described in both sober and sensational terms.[9] But we know relatively little about those foreign student-athletes who, over the years, have been recruited to American academe. The subject of foreign student-athletes is not featured in a volume of annotated references to over 540 publications on foreign students in American universities,[10] nor in a bibliography on international students and study abroad programs.[11] Neither do data included in the publications of the Institute of International Education[12] contain any references to foreign student-athletes in the United States. The present book therefore fills something of a lacuna in the literature on both sports in the USA and international talent migration.

What is the extent of foreign recruiting to the athletic departments of American universities? Have the numbers involved grown over time? Where do such recruits come from? And which institutions act as the hosts? How are student-athletes recruited? Why do they come to America? What are their backgrounds? How do they adjust to life in the United States? Are they exploited—or do they do the exploiting? What are their experiences, educational, social, and athletic? What happens to them after they complete their eligibility? The purpose of this book is to answer these questions. It is about foreign student-athletes in the American educational and sporting milieux.

Geographies and the World Sports System

Inasmuch as the following pages are concerned with the movement of groups of young people from one location to another, this book is essentially a geographical study of sports. Traditionally, sports-geographic studies have focused on the national level of scale[13] and where international-scale studies do exist they have tended to be concerned with either sports diffusion[14] or with geographic variations in participation or achievement.[15] Typically, the geographic treatment of sports has exemplified "a research style where description takes precedence over interpretation";[16] too often the human beings involved, their emotions, feelings, and perceptions, are buried beneath a welter of per capita indices; people have tended to be reduced to dots on maps or parts of flow lines between places. There is considerable incentive to undertake studies such as this because of the intrinsically geographical nature of much of the readily available data generated by sports. But it is only rarely, as in Rooney's use of the recruiting diary of a head football coach,[17] that the feelings and emotions of real people involved in the world of sport begin to surface. The present book builds on that more humanistic approach. It not only examines the historical and geographical patterns involved in the international recruiting game but also explores the experiences of the people involved, the motives for their geographic behavior, and the social networks which contributed to that behavior.

Our opening paragraph described a track and field meet. But track is not the only sport to have attracted foreigners to the athletic departments of America's more sports-oriented universities and colleges. To different degrees, swimming, ice hockey, golf, basketball, tennis, gymnastics, soccer, wrestling, and even gridiron football have been involved. However, this book's purpose is not to "explain" the phenomenon of international recruiting. Instead, such recruiting can be regarded as an "explanation" or proof of the interactions of the ideological structures which pervade the spheres of sport and education in the world of American intercollegiate sports, a realm which must be distinguished clearly from recreational sports activity, which tends to characterize British universities and the institutions of higher education in most countries. NCAA Division I sports, and, it could be argued, American intercollegiate sports in general, form part of what German sports sociologists term *Leistungssport*—literally "performance sport," which might be better rendered as either "highly competitive sport" or, as Allen Guttmann[18] prefers, "top-level sport." *Leistungssport* is global in organization in the sense that there are internationally agreed-upon rules and regulations, and international bureaucracies to administer these rules. World records and international competitions are ratified and organized by international committees of various kinds (e.g., the International Olympic Committee, the International Athletics Federation, etc.). Such transnational bodies operate, as far as possible, without regard to international frontiers, reflecting the fact that international relations encompass much more than the conventionally "political."[19] At this level, sport is undeniably highly commercialized and influenced, if not dominated, by market operations. Players can be bought and sold; big sports events are increasingly produced, packaged, and sold like any other commodity on the mass consumer market and can be regarded as "expressing the quintessential ideology in capitalist society: egoistic, aggressive individualism, ruthless competition."[20]

A major feature of sport, like capitalism, is that it is a world system, and movement and interaction are necessary for its survival in its present form. Ron Johnston's description of capitalism applies almost equally to *Leistungssport:* "Goods, capital and labour must be shifted around to realise potentials as they are perceived. The movement of labour [i.e., athletes] brings cultures into contact and provides a potential basis for tension and conflict."[21] It has been recognized by Johann Galtung that "there is an isomorphism between the competitive sport system and the world system."[22] By a "system" is meant a collection of discrete elements which are linked in such a way that no one element is altogether independent of all other elements. Nation-states are the elements of the global sports system which is obviously geographical in the sense that (a) the elements of the system are spatial units which are described in geographic terms,[23] and (b) the units have a spatial arrangement in relation to each other. It is the world system which, at root, allows sport as we know it to exist, and reproduce itself.

Although some elements of the world's sports system have, until relatively recently, been weakly linked (e.g., Maoist China and some "Third World" countries which have operated as virtual independent subsystems), there can be little doubt that it is today a global system. Soccer, volleyball, and track and field are perhaps the world's most widespread sports, though minority interest activities like American football are increasingly being communicated to a global audience via television.

The system was not always like this. It has come to dominate and in many cases replace previous sport-like systems which were much more geographically limited in extent. Sport may be simply one form of a whole family of "movement cultures" or "body cultures,"[24] but it is one that has colonized and imposed itself on many indigenous physical activities in Africa, Asia, and other parts of the underdeveloped world.[25] Folk games of quite specific types were highly localized and the modern world sports system as we now know it was associated with the development of colonialism, capitalism, technological industrialization, and urbanization. During the course of such events, indigenous games and sports were eroded, and very little resistance seems to have confronted the elimination of "traditional" sports-like activities in many countries of Africa, for example.[26]

An achievement-sport ideology typifies a set of values which act as a medium within which foreign student-athletes operate. This ideology, however, is also the product of the individuals whose activities perpetuate or modify it. Achievement sport focuses on winning, record breaking, and quantification[27] irrespective of global location, and in order for the global sports system to function, particular sports, at a basic level, must be the same the world over. Soccer played in Warsaw, Indiana, is to all intents and purposes the same sport as soccer played in Warsaw, Poland. The same rules and regulations apply to the four-hundred-meter relay if it is taking place in Moscow, Russia, or Moscow, Idaho. Indeed, record breaking can only exist as a meaningful aim in sport if the nature of the activity is identical among nations at the global scale. Ali Mazrui has suggested that "the first laws ever to be voluntarily embraced by men from a variety of cultures and backgrounds are the laws of sports."[28]

John Hargreaves has pointed out, however, that there are grounds for thinking that sport is *not* a homogeneous entity and that there are crucial differences between levels and types.[29] For example, intramural sports are different from bowl games in professional football. However, insofar as there is a global phenomenon whose organizations transcend political boundaries and permit international cooperation on the playing field and the international movement and migration of personnel, there *are* grounds for suggesting that degrees of homogeneity exist in sports.

Ideologies, Experiences, and Scales

Although modern sports can be conceptualized as a global spatial system, the *experience* of sport at the level of the stadium, swimming pool, gymnasium, or rink does vary from place to place. For instance, in the period of Maoist sport ideology, the faces of *defeated* Chinese international athletes "seemed to be lighted by smiles of exquisite amusement."[30] Under the same political regime players were reported not to be keeping score in unofficial basketball games in a deliberate effort to make the game fraternal and communal.[31] Such occasions were treated with surprise by Western athletes, who tend to experience disappointment (even agony) in defeat. A basketball game between different university teams in Britain is played according to the same basic rules as an NCAA Division I game in the United States but the experiences are totally different, the former being low-key with a handful of spectators and the latter typified by razzmatazz and boosterism.

American sports ideology reflects a number of aspects of American "national character," among them what Wreford Watson called "freedom to move," "the mixing of peoples," "individualism," and a sense of destiny.[32] In summarizing different national forms of motivation it has been stressed that on average, Americans tend to have high levels of achievement motivation, are generally assertive, and display high levels of extraversion.[33] As Peter Taylor has pointed out, "individual competition to achieve personal success—log cabin to White House [or Little League to Super Bowl]—is the basis of American liberal ideology."[34] To this add freedom of movement and the mixing of peoples and we have an ideology fully consistent with the recruitment of foreign athletic talent.

Hence, heterogeneity emerges at the *national* scale as a result of a national ideological filter which separates day-to-day experiences of sport at the *local* level from the reality (i.e., the *global* scale). John Hoberman claims that "*American* sport carries a very substantial ideological load of ideas about masculinity, femininity, celebrity, patriotism, heroism, narcissism, race, violence and more"[35] (italics added), whereas the sporting ideologies of say, Nazi Germany, Maoist China, or, until recently, East Germany are, each in their own ways, different. Sporting activities help to "bolster the ideological integrity of a nation"[36] and, incidentally, make the separation of sport from politics totally spurious.

In the context of this book, therefore, we have three geographical scales, namely the scale of *reality* (top-class sport as practiced in virtually every nation in the world according to an agreed set of rules which allow international cooperation in competition), the scale of *ideology* (the American sports ethos), and the scale of *experience* (the intercollegiate sports scene). These are not three different things happening at three different scales, but simply a single manifestation of achievement sport "within which the arrangement of the three scales is functionally important."[37] This idea is illustrated as figure 1, which is analogous to Peter Taylor's view of interdependence in world political geography.[38]

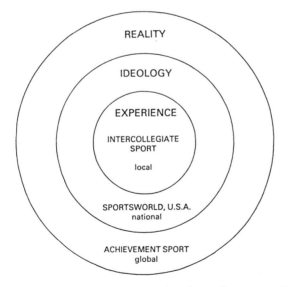

Figure 1. A three-tier model for the study of top-class sport. (Based on an idea in Peter Taylor, *Political Geography* [London: Longman, 1985], 25.)

The idea can be illustrated by an example. The implications of achievement sport at the college or local level can be felt when a foreign student-athlete is awarded an athletic scholarship at the expense of a local high-school student. Locally, this might appear frustrating or unjust, but according to national ideology it is acceptable because winning for the college is paramount. But recruitment of a foreigner could not exist if it was not for the existence of globally organized achievement sport. If sport was not *essentially* the same in Tanzania as in Texas, the local experience would clearly be quite different. In other words, our day-to-day experiences in today's world result from global rather than simply local pressures. The *explanation* of international recruiting is therefore sought in general structures which characterize and underpin sport everywhere. These structures (competition, record seeking, etc.) are interpreted here as "the properties which make it possible for discernibly similar social patterns (i.e., sport) to exist across varying spans of time and space."[39]

This chapter has conceptualized modern sport as a world system, a system which permits student-athletes from north, south, east, and west to be recruited to colleges and universities across the length and breadth of America. College and university sport in the United States is, in essence, the same as sport elsewhere. It possesses, however, its own historical and ideological characteristics, the distinctive nature of which forms the basis of the chapter which follows.

TWO

Sport in the American University

The recruitment of foreign sports talent cannot be understood without first considering its *context*. For this reason this chapter is devoted to a brief review of the historical background to the development of serious sport on U.S. campuses and to the ways such athletic activity can be interpreted. It examines the links between the desire to boost one's school and the growth of recruiting, and evaluates the extent to which intercollegiate sports can be regarded as education, entertainment, and exploitation. This consideration of the ethos of American intercollegiate sport will make it easier to understand the pressures which exist to recruit internationally, the subject of the chapters which follow.

Sports and Boosterism

This chapter does not provide a detailed review of either the growth of American sports or the history of American higher education, since each of these subjects has been dealt with in detail elsewhere.[1] The principal concern is to interpret developments over the past century with the phenomenon of international recruiting in mind. Particular attention is devoted to the most *distinctive* aspects of the US college sports scene, aspects which appear unusual to the foreign observer. One thing must be stressed from the outset: The character of American college sports is unique, its distinctiveness lying in the great stress which the Americans place on the use of sports in the boosting of place—the behavioral expression of place-pride. Boosterism, a central aspect of not only frontier life but American life in general (recall the earlier discussion of the fact that extraversion is regarded by social psychologists as part of the "American character"), manifested itself in university sports teams. Although a rudimentary form of competition may have taken place between local colleges as early as the 1820s, it was really in the mid-nineteenth century that the localized intramural traditions (in which many activities were more like "folkgames" than modern sports) gave way to more serious intercollegiate competition.[2]

The first recorded intercollegiate athletic contest, a rowing (crew) match between Harvard and Yale, was held in 1852. This inaugural event served to boost the economic interests of an Eastern railroad company who paid all the expenses of the crews, seeking to get people to use rail transport to the event.[3] It seems that other schools (Brown, Pennsylvania, Dartmouth, and Trinity) imitated the Harvard-Yale innovation, though social rather than competitive rowing remained more attractive for many years.[4] The first intercollegiate baseball match took place in 1859 (between Amherst and Williams) and the equivalent football game occurred between Rutgers and Princeton in 1869. Intercollegiate track and field—in the form of a two-mile footrace among teams from Amherst, Cornell, and McGill (Canada)—had its origins in 1873, while competitors from Pennsylvania, Columbia, and Yale took part in the first swimming meet four years later.

All of these contests featured *men's* sports. Although some antebellum schools provided young women with facilities for physical, as well as intellectual and moral education,[5] there was a forty-year time lag between the first intercollegiate event for men and that for women. The latter, which took place in 1896, was a basketball game between the University of California at Berkeley and Stanford. No men were allowed to attend except to repair the baskets.[6] As men's intercollegiate sports developed in seriousness, women tended to be relegated to a cheerleader role and it was not really until well into the second half of the twentieth century that women's sports began to even approach the importance of men's.

By the 1880s, associations had been created to conduct intercollegiate competitions in rowing, baseball, track, football, and basketball. Student-sponsored sports began to give way to full-time intercollegiate athletics; a sport-for-sport's-sake ideology was gradually being replaced by one which emphasized winning at all costs. In 1884 somewhat more than 3,000 spectators attended a Harvard-Yale football game; by the 1890s the same match-up was attracting 20,000.[7] In 1903 the

Harvard Stadium was built to accommodate 23,000 spectators while by 1921 the average football game attendance for 49 colleges was 30,700, rising to over 67,000 by 1930.[8]

These massive crowds reflected the increasingly ludic nature of society on the one hand and the distinctiveness of the American college system on the other. It is this distinctiveness that is now examined, with emphasis particularly on the place-boosting traditions associated with American academe.

The reasons why college sports in the United States developed differently from their European analogs lie in part in the differing historical contexts.[9] The sports historian Benjamin Rader argues that in America there were no traditions which inhibited the transformation of sports into serious activities and into commercial enterprises,[10] but sports geographer John Rooney may be equally correct when he notes that "the decision to adopt serious intercollegiate athletic programs was in large part prompted by what might be termed a 'glory of place,' place-boosting philosophy, combined with the growing commercial drive that in general characterized American society. . . . the 'team' became a vehicle of community and school pride."[11] Boosterism was not a uniquely American phenomenon but it did emerge as a highly distinctive feature of the United States at the end of the nineteenth century. Pride in boosting one's place (notably through sports—see page 15) has continued to the present time, as the billboards found at the edges of many small US towns so blatantly show[12] (fig. 2). The booster spirit emphasized community development and place loyalty; as such it is sometimes interpreted as being ideologically conservative since by stressing place-pride it blurs differences in class interests. Boosterism welds class differences and stresses local, regional, or international differences.

Boosterism, sports, and community were intimately linked to the growth of the American system of higher education. This system needs to be clearly distinguished from that of Europe and most other parts of the world. In 1880, England had four degree-granting institutions while the state of Ohio had thirty-seven. Today, institutions of higher education in the United States serve around 45 percent of the population while in Britain the respective figure lies around 10 percent. Such statistics reveal the different interpretations placed on the nature of higher education in North America and Europe. Whereas in Europe, the early (and present-day) universities and colleges possessed elitist overtones and were national institutions with strong, royal charters, in nineteenth-century United States "no community could be complete without its college or university."[13] With no ancient traditions

Figure 2. Many American towns have the Rotary Club, the American Legion, bird sanctuaries, and churches, but only Winder, in Barrow County, Georgia, has the state track champions for class AA. Such place-boosting vernacular icons, found frequently among the welcoming signs at the edges of many American towns, are virtually unknown outside North America.

of higher education, universities in America could flourish in fertile soil, in places whose "population and prosperity lay all in the future." No clear-cut definition of the purpose of a university existed in much of frontier North America, leading to a much more vocational curriculum than is found in universities in other countries. The missionary spirit of the westward frontier undoubtedly contributed to the rapid growth of institutions of higher education, but perhaps more important from our perspective was the American booster spirit which made every place consider itself an "Athens of the West."[14]

The growth of settlement in North America inevitably led to competition between settlements. Intense community spirit grew from the newness of the places on the advancing frontier. The presence of a college would help a town grow and prosper; it would attract able students and aid local investment. It was a community, not a national institution, and a college's success (indeed, its survival, since there were many "ghost colleges," like ghost towns) reflected a vibrant community. As James Frey comments, "If a social unit did not have the support of the booster element, it usually could not survive politically or economically. In the case of the colleges and universities, boosters gravitated to athletics because these elements were able to generate instantaneous visibility and support. The attachment of boosters to athletic programs, as opposed to their academic counterparts, gave the former significant power and a high degree of operational autonomy."[15]

One can argue that the strong link between community and college and the symbiotic booster relations between them were focal points of the desire of one college to defeat another on the sports field. The visibility of sports and the way in which sports could link the interest of college and community led to a tradition of high-pressure recruiting which was to grow from involving local students to those from regional, national, and, today, global origins.

Pressure to "produce" a visible sports program led to pressure to recruit. With recruiting came pressure to abuse the few unclear "rules" which existed in the early days of intercollegiate sports. In 1895 it was asserted that "men are bought and sold like cattle to play this autumn on 'strictly amateur elevens' "; also by the 1890s recruiting seems to have assumed a number of shady dimensions. Reportedly "no less than seven members of the University of Michigan varsity of 1893 had never bothered with the formality of matriculating."[16] The fact that no rules existed to cover such contingencies was to lead to the establishment of intercollegiate sports' governing bodies.

Until the 1920s many colleges recruited on a rather haphazard basis, if they recruited at all. Many athletes on university teams were still students first and athletes second, and even the dominant football power, Notre Dame, obtained half its football squad from students who simply tried out for the team. What talent was sought from outside the campus was solicited by writing letters and seeking alumni advice. Between the world wars, prospective student-athletes were visiting the university and some were promised various kinds of subsidy. Benjamin Rader summarizes the incipient "athletic scholarship" situation of the period thus: "The ingenious and devious methods employed to subsidize athletes were imaginative. Athletes, if they met the scholastic requirements of the college, thus technically qualified for scholarships. Furthermore, the athletic departments offered a wide variety of job opportunities to the 'needy' athletes. They might nominally work within the departments dispensing towels, giving rubdowns, supervising intramural sports, or pushing a broom. Numerous well-paying jobs, both on and off campus, seemed especially suited to athletes."[17]

Football especially, but also basketball and some other activities, had assumed a sport-oriented ethic and by the 1920s college sports were beginning to take on the form of substantial public entertainments. With football leading the way, the growth of stadiums and facilities characterized the interwar years. Such facilities also influenced the propensity to recruit. John Rooney explains:

> Most of the big-name schools felt compelled to erect a colossal structure to house their gridiron show. Because the majority of the colleges were located in small towns, the gigantic buildings could serve no other purpose. The schools built facilities with borrowed funds, planning to pay them off with gate receipts. Since attendance was markedly influenced by the quality of play, the stadium debt provided a powerful motive to field a successful team. With so many universities seeking the same goals, severe competition for the available talent resulted. The modern era of high-pressure recruiting had begun.[18]

In the days when Jesse Owens was recruited to Ohio State, the athletic scholarship was often "an informal remunerative arrangement made by the coach and his staff" in return for menial work undertaken in the stadium or locker room.[19] By the late 1940s, "under-the-table gifts" to student-athletes had become commonplace, and the logical extension to make money awards came in the early 1950s when, as Mabel Lee puts it, "Someone (or ones) came up with the idea of handing out money from gate receipts to players 'above board,' calling the payment an 'athletic scholarship.' The exact process that was gone through, and by whom, to procure a ruling, and from whom, so that this would not jeopardize an amateur standing, seems to this day to be still a deep, dark secret."[20]

The open acceptance of athletic scholarships in the early 1950s was known as the "sanity code." In essence, it stated that grants-in-aid and jobs had to be awarded solely on the basis of the student-athlete's *financial need*. However, given the pressures to succeed in sports, it is not surprising that the sanity code failed to prevent colleges and universities from awarding "full-ride" scholarships, irrespective of need. By 1952 the National Collegiate Athletic Association (the major governing body of intercollegiate sports) was forced to repeal the sanity code and allowed the awarding of full scholarships based solely on *athletic ability.*[21] Today many universities give such scholar-ships, though a few, notably the Ivy League schools, do not.

By the 1950s and 1960s recruiting had become highly systematized. Athletic departments employed recruiting coordinators, and coaches moved around the country looking for the elusive blue-chip athletes. The 1950s witnessed the logical extension of the recruiting game, initially local, then regional, until it took on an international dimen-sion. By the 1970s the recruitment of student-athletes had become global, with relatively few countries being immune (either directly or indirectly) from the encroaching coach. The world has now become the arena in which place loyalties are constructed through the re-cruitment of foreign gladiators representing communities large and small across America.

Like sports in all countries of the modern world, American inter-collegiate sports activity is characterized by a bureaucratic form of organization. A number of governing bodies exist to control and organize college sports. Moves for faculty control of student sport began in the 1880s but these and subsequent attempts to "foist a British-like amateur sport ideal on a fiercely competitive win-oriented system which had developed in American colleges"[22] had failed, and an 1898 conference at Brown University discussed the problem of tramp athletes who transferred with impunity from representing one college to another. Faculty were concerned about intercollegiate sports for a number of reasons. First, there was the nagging question con-cerning who was actually eligible to participate in intercollegiate ath-letics. Second, there was the question of which rules and regulations should be adopted. In attempting to resolve these problems the Amer-ican college sports scene gradually moved toward bureaucratic con-trol, typical of modern sports organizations.

An Intercollegiate Conference of Faculty Representatives (Big Ten) had been set up as early as 1895 but it was not until 1906 that the NCAA was established. In that year 38 institutions of higher education agreed to form an organization which has grown steadily ever since.[23] By 1921 it had 102 member institutions; by the early 1940s mem-bership had gone over 200; in 1987-88 the total membership stood at 900.[24] Today the NCAA acts as a regulatory body rather than an advisory association. Its member institutions are divided into three divisions, those in Division I being generally regarded as the most sport-oriented. The NCAA can impose severe rules, in some cases overruling the policy of national governments. For example, South African athletes can participate in NCAA competitions but are "banned" from many open events in the United States. Likewise, the

NCAA curtails the organizational mobility of student-athletes; an athlete who transfers to another university is ruled ineligible for one year of competition. Such legislation does not apply to coaches; hence the universities and the NCAA benefit at the expense of the student-athletes.

Two other intercollegiate sports organizations are worthy of brief mention. While the NCAA dominates college sport, the National Association of Intercollegiate Athletics (NAIA), set up in 1940 by small colleges not served by the major NCAA conferences was, in 1988, 527 strong. While NAIA champions are not regarded by the general public as the "real" champions, NAIA schools do offer athletic scholarships and in some cases have been able to outmaneuver the NCAA. For example, not having "overage" restrictions enables NAIA schools to recruit mature student-athletes from overseas. This applies also to the third important governing body, the National Junior College Athletic Association, a group responsible for administering sports in the nation's two-year colleges, though a separate organization administers the California junior colleges. These institutions also offer athletic scholarships, which are accepted by willing foreign athletes sometimes much older than those eligible for NCAA institutions.

Women in Intercollegiate Sports

For many years women's intercollegiate sports lagged considerably behind those of the men in the extent to which women were encouraged to participate widely and for which scholarships were given. Top-level women's sports were discouraged and sport tended to accommodate women in a strictly "cheerleader" role. Only sports which emphasized women's "femininity" were encouraged. University expenses for women's sports contrasted dramatically with those for men. For example, in the mid-seventies Ohio State University spent $43,000 on women and $6 million on men in its intercollegiate sports programs, and even in 1978 the University of Notre Dame had a total scholarship budget of $1 million for men but nothing at all for women.[25]

From the perspective of the present study, a more significant point is that in women's intercollegiate sports, recruiting was traditionally discouraged. One of very few places to offer women scholarships on the basis of athletic ability was Tennessee State University, an institution which "produced" the 1960 Olympic 100-meters champion, Wilma Rudolph, and a number of other outstanding athletes.

It is only really since the mid-seventies that women have emerged from the shadows of American college sports. With the more widespread recognition of the Education Amendment Act of 1972, discrimination on the basis of gender has been eroded. In 1973, for example, only 16 universities offered athletic scholarships to women; by 1976 the figure was 121 and has risen steadily ever since.[26] Whereas in 1966-67 women in intercollegiate sports accounted for only 9 percent of overall participation, the figure by 1985-86 was 32 percent, female participants having risen in number from 15,727 to 92,192,[27] though since the mid-eighties the number has begun to fall, mirroring the statistics for men (page 45). The growing emphasis on women's sport has resulted in its taking on many of the characteristics of men's sports. Among these characteristics has been the steady increase in the recruitment of women athletes, and, as will be seen in the next chapter, in some sports the relative contribution of foreign women almost matches that of men.

If sport in American higher education has become less like play and more a form of display, can it rightly be called part of the education process? Or is it better described as entertainment? Some observers prefer to regard intercollegiate sports as a form of exploitation. These varying interpretations of sport in American higher education are explored below, with emphasis once again on the implications for the foreign student-athlete.

Education

Sport pervades American education from the elementary school level up. The high school can certainly be regarded as a microcosm of the collegiate sports system. Interscholastic competitions are thoroughly organized, and a National Federation of High School Athletic Associations was established as early as 1920.

Detailed statistical analyses are made of the achievements of high school athletes and many of the trappings of college sports are found at the high school level. Extravagant use of resources (including steroids) often characterize high school sports. As Al Reinert put it, in the context of high school football in Texas, "Somehow, towns that don't need street-lamps have fifty thousand watts of cadmium Super Troopers to light their high school field a dozen times a year, while schools that can't afford microscopes have carpeted training rooms with exercise machines and, probably, a whirlpool bath, all of it paid for by boosters club subscriptions."[28]

Community identification with the local high school sports teams is very strong. As Robert Lynd and Helen Lynd pointed out in their classic *Middletown* over sixty years ago, "civic loyalty centers around basketball more than any other one thing. No distinctions divide the crowds which pack the school gymnasium for home games."[29] Basketball is an obsession in Indiana (Middletown was a description of real-life Muncie), where twenty-seven high school gymnasiums each have a seating capacity in excess of 5,000 while the state's largest accommodates 9,325.[30] In many small towns and communities throughout the nation, the high school football or basketball team assumes the status of entertainment rather than anything remotely approaching physical education. Schools possessing students with obvious sporting talent may feel the need to produce athletes who will qualify for athletic scholarships, and many will collude with universities in their use of unethical methods to secure blue-chip athletes.

It is clear, therefore, that (in contrast to many other countries where youth sports are organized at the club level) sport ideology is instilled into student-athletes in America well before they reach the level of the college or university. The US population seems to support such attitudes. According to a report published in 1983, 68 percent of the American public agreed that school and college rivalries are good because they foster school pride and loyalty.[31]

The Variety of Options

The American system of higher education accommodates more students, per capita, than any other country in the world. Whereas in much of the world, universities can pick and choose which students they select, the United States has a long tradition of universities competing for students. In 1987 the United States had 5,142 students per 100,000 inhabitants. We can contrast this with respective figures for other selected "developed" countries. That for Canada was 4,950; Sweden, 2,209; and the German Democratic Republic, 2,640. At the other end of the "development" spectrum the equivalent figure for Jamaica was 508; Nigeria, 239; Kenya, 107; and Ethiopia, 66.[32] In 1985, 32 percent of high school graduates who enrolled in college courses in the United States gained bachelors' degrees.[33] In absolute terms this represented just under one million graduates. It is difficult to make international comparisons but in Britain the 1986-87 percentage of school leavers taking degree courses amounted to 10 percent.[34]

It will be obvious from the figures in the previous paragraph that degree-level courses are much more widely available in America than in any other country in the world. However, it is somewhat misleading to compare the proportions of Americans going to college and those from other countries. Many American students follow courses that in Europe would be studied in technical colleges. Many jobs that "require" a degree in the United States do not in Europe. It can be argued that American students do not, by and large, attend university with a view to entering the professions. Boorstin suggests that instead the American institutions reflect the democratic ideal and aim at the fulfillment of the individual. In 1980 there were over 3,200 institutions of higher education in the United States, college enrollment totaling over 7.5 million people in the eighteen-to-twenty-four age range. These aggregate figures obscure a variety of institutions offering a bewildering variety of qualifications—associate, bachelor's, master's, and doctoral degrees. While a student can work for a B.A. or a B.Sc., Boorstin wryly notes that it is also possible in the United States to obtain a B.O. (Bachelor of Oratory).[35]

This information enables us to understand how foreign student-athletes can readily enroll in a vast range of courses which would simply not exist in degree-granting institutions in their own countries, even if their countries had such institutions in any number. What is more, student-athletes are awarded grants-in-aid (or athletic scholarships) in many junior (or community) colleges (two-year institutions often called JCs), as well as in many of the four-year institutions, be they public or private universities or colleges.

Although generous in dispensing athletic aid, certain American universities would likely pose more than the average amount of culture shock for the foreign visitor. Certain American universities exert a degree of control over students which would amaze those familiar with the freedom found on the European campus. An extreme case is Brigham Young University, an institution at which 98 percent of the students adhere to the teachings of the Church of Jesus Christ of Latter-day Saints. At BYU students "have to sign an honor code that makes it clear what you're *not* going to do. No drugs, alcohol, tobacco, coffee, or tea. No promiscuity, gambling, cut-off jeans, tank tops, beards or unkempt hair either."[36] Yet, as we will see, BYU manages to recruit foreign student-athletes who are not inevitably Mormon. Even more unusual (from a European perspective) is Oral Roberts University, which has begun to achieve some success in sports but has not yet made any significant impact on the international recruiting stage, though it *is* beginning to recruit overseas (five members of its 1988 tennis squad were foreign).

Athletes' Entry Requirements

In order to gain entry to the American university a student has to graduate from high school with satisfactory grades. The precise nature of the entry requirements differ from university to university. What concerns us here is the way in which the American university is able to accommodate student-athletes for whom normal academic entry requirements may prove problematic.

The academic requirements for non-athletes have traditionally been waived for talented athletes. For example, over a thirty-year period at Michigan State University, 50 percent of students on athletic scholarships were admitted regularly with special considerations (i.e., the high-school grade point average [GPA] was less than 2.49 or they had achieved poor test scores), whereas the respective figure for the rest of the student body was only 3 to 4 percent.[37] Extensive academic support schemes (remedial help) are provided for athletes. Not surprisingly the prospects of many student-athletes gaining a degree in the four-year period of athletic eligibility is slight. Although the overall number of graduating student-athletes compares favorably with that of non-athletes, it seems likely that substantial numbers of student-athletes graduate *long after* their freshman semester. At Michigan State University, for example, it was revealed that of the student-athletes who graduated between 1950 and 1980, only 28 percent did so within four years of entry, and for more than 20 percent it was between six and eighteen years after entry. It has been estimated that of former collegiate football players in the National Football League, only one-third had obtained a bachelor's degree.[38]

Of course, graduation rates vary considerably among sports and among universities. Student-athletes least likely to gain degrees are in the big-money sports of football and basketball. At the University of Utah the overall graduation rate of athletes between 1973 and 1982 was 49 percent, but this ranged from 62 percent for women's basketball to 34 percent for men's basketball. For the graduation of football players in 1975-76 the figures for seven universities ranged from 69 percent for Nebraska to 25 percent for Brigham Young.[39] Other examples are shown in tables 1 and 2.

Beginning in August 1986 the NCAA effected an important ruling that first-year students would not be allowed to compete in intercollegiate sports unless they had left high school with a GPA of 2.0 (out of a maximum of 4) in a core curriculum of math, English, and social and natural sciences. In addition, first-year students hoping to play Division I football or basketball must have scored at least 700 (out of a possible 1600) in the Scholastic Aptitude Test (SAT), which millions of school leavers take each year. Of course, the door is not shut to students with more modest academic backgrounds. Junior

Table 1. High and low graduation rates, selected NCAA Division I
basketball programs, 1972-82.

Graduation Rate	University
96.2%	Columbia
91.2%	Villanova
80.0%	Georgetown
77.5%	North Carolina
72.5%	St. Johns
•	
•	
•	
28.2%	Louisiana State
27.9%	Missouri
26.8%	Cincinnati
21.3%	Nevada-Las Vegas
10.7%	Memphis State
7.8%	West Texas State

Source: Stanley Eitzen, "The Educational Experiences of Intercollegiate Student-Athletes," *Journal of Sport and Social Issues* 11, nos. 1-2 (1987): 23.

colleges will willingly receive (and recruit) foreign student-athletes in whom they see athletic potential.

The GPA and SAT requirements could pose problems for the foreign student. Indeed, *within* the United States the SAT has been criticized as possessing a strong cultural bias favoring white students. Many black students, it has been argued, may be eligible for athletic scholarships but cannot accept them because of their high-school academic performance. For foreign student-athletes the NCAA identifies minimal academic qualifications from foreign schools which are necessary to satisfy the 2.0 rule.[40] Incoming British student-athletes, for example, would have to possess passes in five subjects at the Ordinary Level ("O"-level) of the General Certificate of Education—far below the requirement for entry into a British university. Similar cross-national equivalents are provided by the NCAA for other countries.

Degress of Comparability

Given the relative ease of entry to US universities, it is sometimes assumed that the resulting American degrees are inferior in quality to those from institutions of higher education in other countries. In view of the fact that "there would seem to be little doubt that the recognition and validation of studies pursued and qualifications acquired abroad constitute problems"[41] (both to the recipients of such

Table 2. Active NFL players and their degrees, 1988, high and low rates.

University	Players in NFL	Percent with degrees
Ivy League	33	91
Notre Dame	53	79
Duke	13	77
Penn State	77	66
Boston College	28	64
Virginia	19	63
Michigan	49	61
.		
.		
.		
North Carolina	22	5
Memphis State	21	5
Iowa	20	10
Wisconsin	35	14
Oklahoma State	28	14
San Jose State	37	16
Mississippi State	25	16

Source: John Rooney, "The Myth of Student-Athletes," Sport Place 2 (1988).

credentials and to their prospective employers), it is worth considering briefly the "problem" of cross-national comparability of degrees.

Mellor has unambiguously stated that for the teaching profession, for example, it is the American *master's* degree which "is generally considered to be the desirable qualification for appointment to, say, positions of responsibility in high schools and junior colleges . . . in the way that a first degree in most Commonwealth universities is the basic qualification required of secondary school teachers."[42] However, only master's degrees from a (seemingly arbitrary) list of American universities are considered by the British Department of Education and Science as approximating the British first- or second-class honors degrees, qualifications used for partly determining teachers' pay scales in the United Kingdom. While such discrimination does not occur in all countries of the world, many other examples could be quoted of British professions rejecting—or at least undervaluing—those possessing American degrees. For example, a study of American college degrees has stated that "a student following a degree curriculum in veterinary surgery in the United States may not enroll as a student member of the Royal College of Veterinary Surgeons in London."[43] Similar comments might also apply to accountancy, medicine, dentistry, and pharmacy. Associate degrees, awarded by junior or community colleges, are virtually worthless outside the USA.

In view of the bewildering array of institutions of higher education in the United States such caution is understandable, especially as the accreditation of some US colleges is subject only to the most perfunctory state provisions and there is a lack of any form of *national* accreditation. However, there is undoubtedly a good deal of snobbishness directed at American degrees from the European side of the Atlantic, and it might be desirable to move toward evaluating students' competencies rather than attempting to seek equivalence in degrees. Whatever the future situation, foreign student-athletes should be alerted to the fact that US degrees are not automatically recognized as being comparable in quality to those obtained in the countries from which they have come.

The Entertainment Business

Despite the fact that it is asserted that "competitive athletics programs are designed to be a vital part of the educational system,"[44] it is all too obvious that a blatantly commercial atmosphere surrounds big-time collegiate sports. In Rooney's words, many American universities "are in the entertainment business—a business separate in almost all respects from their primary educational purpose."[45] Indeed, "most of them are ill-equipped to manage the delicate balance required of a major entertainment operation within the confines of an academic institution."[46] The estimated aggregate revenues of the intercollegiate athletic programs of NCAA institutions for the 1985 fiscal year has been alleged to be just in excess of $1 billion. For the most sport-oriented of these institutions, over half such revenues came from football. The fact that estimated aggregate expenses in 1985 amounted to $1,153,292,000 continues to make college sports a losing business.[47]

Sport as entertainment draws in crowds; the crowds generate revenue; revenue serves to maintain a winning team; a winning team helps generate college and regional pride; such place-pride sustains the entertainment business. Indeed, given that much of such entertainment is loss-making, it is "the need of the community" which Chu and Segrave[48] view as the prime factor sustaining college sport in its present form.

In many towns too small to attract a professional sports franchise, the college or university teams perform the entertainment function provided by the pros in the larger places. The local economic impact of such college sports is significant. For example, it has been estimated that in 1975 the University of Wisconsin's football team generated expenditures from football fans originating outside Dane County to the extent of $4,680,000. If purchases by parent visitors and local patrons, and money paid directly to the university for tickets, parking, etc., was included, the figure was estimated at nearer $14,000,000.[49]

The entertainment function of big-time college sports can be exemplified by the attendance figures for football games for the period 1952-83. At Ohio State, for example, the *average* game attendance was 84,681; at Michigan it was 82,257; at Michigan State, 63,485. Three other universities had average attendance figures of over 60,000 and four more were over 57,000.[50] When the NCAA basketball championships were held in Dallas in March 1986, more than $7 million was injected into the local economy.[51]

College sports also provide television entertainment. Indeed, much intercollegiate sport has come to depend on revenues paid by TV networks and for many institutions broadcasting fees are the major source of revenue after ticket sales. Nand Hart-Nibbrig and Clement Cottingham have gone so far as to state that "television has in fact replaced universities and colleges as the producer of intercollegiate sports."[52] While football has traditionally been the focus of college sport entertainment, sports in which foreign recruits are more prominent seem to be increasingly used as vehicles for the business of entertainment rather than sport. Ice hockey and basketball are the obvious examples.

The college sport experience in the United States is often interpreted as a form of festival. Many facets of a big intercollegiate event are staged, spectators as well as teams contributing to the theatricality of the event. John Koval has described an intercollegiate football game at the University of Notre Dame as sharing the characteristics of Mardi Gras or the Seattle Seafair. "The electricity in the air is continuously being charged with music and marching bands, for the order of the day is enjoyment through common participation in an event which has evolved its own traditions and rituals."[53] Such an event is the apogee of a large number of similar confrontations, reaching down to the small high-school towns where football or basketball provides weekly entertainment as well as a focus for place-pride.

Festivity and entertainment may be one way of looking at US intercollegiate sports, but as early as the 1930s the Dutch historian Johann Huizinga described this kind of sport as a form of "puerilism" which he believed existed when "athletic rivalry assumes proportions tending to push intellectual interests into the background, *as is the case at some American universities*"[54] (emphasis added). For example, when the University of Louisville won the 1986 NCAA basketball competition, students were given a day off from classes. Such an emphasis on sports, Huizinga argues, reflects the attitudes of a community whose behavior is less mature than is warranted by the state of its intellectual and critical facilities (fig. 3).

Whatever way we interpret it, there can be little doubt that the life of a student-athlete at an American university is more than an educational experience. Festivity, entertainment, puerilism, theater, or whatever, this is a long way from the pursuit of learning and the other bases upon which the university was founded. Although observers such as James Coleman have suggested that interscholastic confrontations might assume forms more compatible with the academic aims of the institutions,[55] sports seem to have resolutely remained as the principal source of collective representation.

Figure 3. Place-pride or puerilism? Popular icons of the modern American university. Note the emphasis on "fighting."

In order to sustain the entertainment industries of American academia, alumni support has become crucial. The involvement of alumni in virtually running the athletic departments of many US universities is another unique attribute of American university life. Such involvement takes many forms. Alumni can act as agents informing the athletic department of potential recruits at local, national, and global scales. However, greater significance is placed on the way alumni generate substantial funding for the nation's most sport-obsessed institutions. These funds provide the financing of domestic and foreign recruits.

The following excerpt from the Wake Forest University Athletic Department Media Guide exemplifies the role of the booster club:

> There is no better example of the growth of Wake Forest athletics than the Deacon Club. The arm of Wake's scholarship program since the club's founding in 1950, this organization ranks among the nation's top collegiate booster clubs despite a comparably small membership.
>
> The figures speak for themselves. When the university moved to Winston-Salem in 1956, the Deacon Club consisted of 1,800 members and it raised $30,000 annually. Today, with 1,000 more members, this group raises over $1.8 million a year for Wake Forest's student-athletes. Wake Forest could not have the caliber of athletic programs it now enjoys if not for the Deacon Club.
>
> "The success of any intercollegiate athletic program is predicated on the ability of an institution to provide scholarship assistance," says Wake Forest director of athletics Dr. Gene Hooks.
>
> "Private schools with high admission standards and equally high tuition and fees find the need to provide scholarship to be even more acute because the walk-on athlete has become almost extinct at those schools. For the Wake Forests of the world to achieve any degree of success, we must give a maximum number of scholarships in any sport in which we have any competitive ambition. Our hope for this success is entrusted to the Deacon Club."

Alumni-supported booster clubs are independent organizations pledged to support the universities and their athletic departments. The money such groups raise and subsequently have at their disposal is considerable (table 3). For example, Auburn University's alumni association "purchased a $412,000 house as an added incentive for the football coach (Pat Dye) to stay at the university."[56] A detailed study of the Clemson University booster association, the IPTAY ("I pay thirty a year") Club, showed how contributions rose from $1,600 in its initial year, 1935, to $80,000 in 1952 and topped the half-million dollar mark in 1972, $1 million in 1977, $2 million in 1979, and $5 million in 1983. Paid membership grew from 162 initial

Table 3. The wealthiest collegiate coffers.

University	Amount of cash revenue raised, 1981-82 ($s)
Notre Dame	8,900,000
North Carolina	5,000,000
Missouri	4,887,168
Clemson	4,102,069
Stanford	3,489,000

Source: Hart-Nibbrig and Cottingham, *Political Economy of College Sports,* 66-67.

members to 6,000 in the early fifties and to about 18,000 in 1985. On the Clemson campus IPTAY has its own offices and paid officials. Generous ticket and parking priorities for college games are given to the larger contributors. About one-quarter of IPTAY members pay $100 per annum; "these are people who receive little more than an almost-weekly Clemson sports newspaper . . . and psychic rewards for their loyalty."[57] Although it is popularly believed that such alumni giving breeds sports success, this relationship appears vague and ill-defined when subjected to empirical analysis.[58]

Exploitation?

The recruiting of student-athletes has been commonplace for over half a century and it is in the realm of recruiting that abuses of the athletic system are most rampant. Despite early objections by the NCAA, out-of-state recruiting had become normal by the 1920s. However, objections continued to be raised after World War II. The University of Missouri head football coach went so far as to request the NCAA to stop universities in Arkansas, Kansas, Kentucky, and Mississippi from recruiting boys from Missouri.[59] Once given official status by the NCAA, however, any institution could recruit and subsidize athletes from any part of the country—or indeed, the world.

Recruiting actually helps to define the modern student-athlete. According to the NCAA, a student-athlete is "a student whose matriculation *was solicited by* a member of the athletic staff or other representative of athletics interests with a view towards the student's ultimate participation in the intercollegiate athletics program"[60] (emphasis added), or when the student reports for an intercollegiate squad under the jurisdiction of the college athletic department. The soliciting of athletes has become a rationalized activity. Patterns of recruiting are predicated upon the distribution of talent and the location of the "consuming" universities and colleges. American sports geographers have identified the marked spatial variations that exist in the origins of superior college athletes. One example will suffice. Basketball is a major US college sport but the interstate variations in "production" of good high-school basketball players range from states like Illinois and New York, which each produce over 200 percent of the needs of in-state institutions, to a state like Idaho, which produces only about one-fifth of its needs. The locational mismatch between supply and demand has resulted in a complex pattern of inter-regional migration of sports talent.[61]

Such a pattern of student-athlete migration is almost duplicated by the hectic movement of coaches in search of talent. The movements of one football coach between early September 1974 and mid-February 1975 extended from Texas to Chicago, his quest for Oklahoma State University football players demonstrating the importance of getting the right person on the team.[62] But even in the less glamorous nonrevenue sports the *national* dimension of recruiting is significant. At the 1981 Eastern States high school track-and-field championships, for example, head coaches from forty universities from Texas to Pennsylvania were in attendance, seeking blue chippers for the college squads.[63]

To these well-known national recruiting patterns has been added a global dimension. College representatives are now present at *world* championships and Olympic Games as their recruiting vistas have extended beyond national scales. The nature of such recruiting is described in chapter 5.

Associated with recruiting is exploitation, dehumanization, and alienation. Pressures on coaches to deliver the athletes required by boosters and community pride inevitably lead to cheating, only a small proportion of which is ever discovered by the NCAA. A short list of examples of cheating will prepare the way for the international examples discussed later. The following examples emerged from a report of the American Council on Education:

- altering high school academic transcripts;
- changing admission test scores;
- offering jobs to parents and other relations of a prospect;
- getting grades for student-athletes in courses they never took;
- firing from a state job the father of a prospect who enrolled at other than that state's university;
- threatening to bomb the home of a high school principal who refused to alter transcripts.[64]

In such cases parents, teachers, athletes, and the university itself are all clearly implicated in the exploitation generated by the collegiate athletic system.

Having enrolled at college the student-athlete receives a grant-in-aid (or athletic scholarship). The grants, which the NCAA permits students to receive, illustrate further the exploitive nature of top-class college sports. It has been estimated that at 1979 prices the cash value of NCAA scholarships averaged about $4,500, though by 1986 it was estimated that they ranged from $6,000 to $12,000. Compared with professional athletes—and many college athletes compare favorably with professionals—the student-athlete clearly suffers at the hands of the intercollegiate sports "cartel," since 1979 annual earnings were around $60,000 in the NFL and $76,000 in major league baseball.[65] Stanley Eitzen has pointed out also that while student-athletes are obviously not amateurs, they are hardly professionals when they risk their health for $2 to $4 per hour.[66]

In sports like golf, tennis, or track and field, in which open competition exists and where cash rewards are available on the open market, the NCAA ensures that allegiance to the college is paramount since it does not allow student-athletes to have access to trust funds or prize money. This applies to the foreign recruit as much as to the domestic student-athlete. Of course, should student-athletes command enough in appearance or prize money, they can use it to finance their way through college but not compete in NCAA meets. There is no possibility, however, of earning modest fees in open meets and continuing to compete in intercollegiate sports.

Because, strictly speaking, the ten thousand to twelve thousand athletic scholarships are earned on an annual basis (and can be withdrawn if the student-athlete does not perform to expectations), there is great pressure placed upon student-athletes to achieve consistently good results in sport. In some cases the pressure can become too great, and it is not uncommon for student-athletes to do poorly in classwork and fail to graduate. It has been suggested that college athletes make up a "proletarian class," ranking among the most exploited workers in American society, the "surplus value" produced by the student-athletes accruing to their collegiate "employers."[67]

The charge that top-level college sports are exploitive is one that is frequently made, sometimes by athletes themselves. For example, one-time football player Allan Bloomingdale claimed that "football used to be fun, but college has changed my mind about that. This university has stripped any love of football I ever had."[68] Given the pressure on big-time university sports teams to succeed on the field of "play," it is hardly surprising that universities are often accused of exploiting student-athletes for their own ends. Steven Figler unequivocally states that "college athletes are recruited to *work for* their respective schools."[69] Although the term "exploitation" is difficult to define precisely, it has been suggested that in the world of college sports it occurs when "the coach, the team, the athletic department, the school, or the governing associations use college athletes for their own purposes without providing for the need of the athletes."[70] Figler suggests that exploitation exists when a student-athlete is "impeded or counselled against taking courses that would lead to responsible and direct progress towards a degree" and when students are "recruited into the college setting without possessing the necessary abilities or background to have a reasonable chance of succeeding academically."[71] Indeed, radical sociologist Harry Edwards believes that this process of exploitation actually starts at the high school level, before athletes have even set foot on a college campus. At high school, Edwards avers, little but excellence in sport is expected of the blue-chip athlete. In some cases high school athletes are held back academically "for the purpose of enhancing their size, strength and athletic skills, thereby making them more attractive products for high school recruiters."[72] Anyone who has read James Michener's account of the pseudonymous running back Artemius Crandall will have sensed with sadness the very real chance that four years at college *can* mean nothing in educational terms to the outstanding athlete.[73]

It has been suggested that the young, talented athlete "is pressurized inordinately to accept society's goals, and thereby his [*sic*] course of conduct is limited."[74] The outstanding athlete at high school is "so besieged by forceful, hypocritical recruiting that it is not possible for him to choose intelligently between available alternatives."[75] Harry Edwards similarly observes that "athletic recruitment and development among major collegiate football and basketball institutions has degenerated into a spiraling 'athletic arms race' wherein student-athletes are both the most strategic material and chief casualties."[76]

At first sight it might appear that such abuses are irrelevant to the case of the foreign student-athletes who form the subject of this book. After all, how many foreign recruits play Division I college football and basketball—*the* American sports? This question is answered in chapter 4 as precisely as the available data permit, but here several points need to be stressed. First, foreigners *do* take part in football and basketball, the two revenue-generating sports, though admittedly in small numbers. But more important is the second point, namely that cheating and exploitation may *not* be restricted to the big-money sports. It has been suggested that minor sports in the big-time universities "are probably as intense for the athletes and coaches as are the moneyed sports."[77] For this reason, cheating and various other forms of pressure may be found in sports other than football and basketball and in institutions more renowned for their academics than their athletes. For example, "incredible as it may seem, Johns Hopkins and the NCAA sparred over the eligibility of lacrosse players."[78] It is also salutory to remember that much of Jack Scott's radical *The Athletic Revolution* (one of the most well-known of the left-wing critiques of 1960s and 1970s US sports) was frequently concerned, not with football or basketball, but with the nonrevenue sport of track and field and the exploitation and abuses that occurred therein.[79] Although not marketed and organized at the same scale of football or basketball, sports like track, tennis, golf, and others are nevertheless highly visible and status-generating. It can also be pointed out that while some sports may be relatively low-key compared with football, it does not mean that they are not characterized by the same deeper structural or ideological characteristics of the more well-known American sports. So in their *Political Economy of College Sports*, Hart-Nibbrig and Cottingham are able to apply, in varying degrees, many of their generalizations concerning "corporate athleticism"[80] (the influence of the business ethic on the college sports system) to the so-called minor sports—those in which foreign recruits are chiefly found.

Neither are we solely concerned with NCAA institutions. Small colleges belonging to the NAIA also break the rules. Philip Boshoff cites as typical the use of players who have not satisfied academic requirements or who have not sat out the required sixteen weeks after transferring,[81] while in 1989 the NAIA placed the Adams State indoor track program on probation for "multiple eligibility violations."[82] Though minor in comparison to activities within NCAA Division I, these examples from nonrevenue sports on the one hand, and from small colleges on the other, show how widespread cheating has become. It is this environment into which the foreign student-athlete is admitted. The extent to which foreign student-athletes perceive themselves as being exploited is dealt with in chapter 7.

If college sport is said to be so exploitive, why do students continue to accept athletic scholarships? A common answer to this question is that they are victims of "false consciousness" or mystification, i.e., in this context "young athletes allow themselves to be exploited [because] they have often been conditioned from childhood to value athletic accomplishment above all else."[83] This view argues that student-athletes are exploited without their knowing it, that they are unalterably programmed to reproduce the system within which they are found.

A problem arises when student-athletes claim, or imply, that they do *not* feel that they are being exploited by the system. This finding is common in several studies of American student-athletes. As Jay Coakley puts it, "few athletes perceive themselves as . . . victims of exploitation."[84] There are at least two possible reactions to this view. First, the student-athlete may be making an accurate assessment of the situation and had not, in fact, suffered any exploitation at the hands of the university athletic department. Second, the degree of exploitation may be hegemonic rather than coercive, i.e., the exploitation has been so successful that the athlete does not *feel* that he or she is actually being exploited. This interpretation would imply that social structures such as sport are impossible to transform.

A third possible reaction is to consider the degree to which human beings are free agents and the extent to which they are "controlled" by the structures within which they operate. To argue that *all* human beings are passive and that none is able to work the structures to his or her own advantage may be too simplistic. Likewise, it may be too simple to argue that college sport per se is exploitive. Some colleges may be; some sports may be; so may some sports at some levels. Sport is obviously not a homogeneous phenomenon, and Wilbert Leonard has shown how in NCAA Division I schools, athletes perceived themselves to be more "exploited" than in schools in Divisions II and III.[85] In other words, the more sports-oriented the institution, the greater degree of perceived exploitation, defined broadly as the amount of pressure put on students to divert them from their academic studies. Even within Division I schools it is likely that the extent of perceived exploitation will vary among students and among sports. It might also be expected that it is in the big revenue-generating sports of football and basketball that exploitation, cheating, and the most serious abuses take place.

There are those observers of the American collegiate sports scene who would deny that the system is alienating or exploitive. For example, Hans Lenk doubts whether ideas of alienation or manipulation can be applied to sports in general or to college sport in particular. This, he argues, is because the aims of sport in the university match those of the athlete and that athletic scholarships are much the same as any other kind of scholarship.[86]

Conclusion

American college sports emerged in the late nineteenth century and assumed a unique form. In no other country in the world is the college-sport nexus so clear and strong as in the United States. Sport boosted a college and the presence of a college boosted a place. The role of boosters has been seen to be highly significant to the present day. The favorable attitudes toward college sports in America derive from the broad social system, the universities themselves, alumni and community, and athletic conference regulations.[87] College sports are highly organized, bureaucratized, and relatively autonomous, and have specialized and committed personnel who enjoy considerable power and influence. Together, the system inputs and the organizational structures seek to achieve financial solvency and victory in sports. Some observers would argue that individual development is a secondary aim.

Much of what has been described in this chapter will be taken for granted by many Americans, but to foreigners the boosterism and the billboards, the excitement and the exploitation, and the passion or the puerilism of college sports are part of a world which is totally different from anything in their countries. The American way of collegiate sports is the milieu in which foreign student-athletes find themselves when they become part of the conduit making up a particular form of talent migration. It is that migration—the brawn drain—which forms the subject of the rest of this book.

II Patterns

The pattern of recruiting has been greatly influenced in recent years, particularly since 1950, by the strong desire of geographically remote universities to gain national prestige through the medium of athletics.

John Rooney

THREE

Dimensions of
Global Recruiting

This chapter sets out to identify the extent of global recruiting of both students and student-athletes by American universities. Although the overall number of foreign students in the United States is well-documented,[1] this chapter includes the first serious attempt to identify the numbers, proportions, and contributions of student-athletes who make up the "brawn drain." While the United States is far from being the only nation in the world to import sports talent (world trade being commonplace in professional sports), its unique system of higher education makes it the only one to import student-athletes.[2]

Part of American liberal ideology has been the accommodation within its academic walls of a large number of foreign students. Indeed, foreign students may more easily gain entry to higher education in the United States than elsewhere. The reason for this, it has been suggested, is that less severely enforced student-entry requirements exist in the United States, little attempt having been made "systematically to evaluate either the various leaving examinations of the different countries or the level of attainment of secondary schooling."[3] A more pragmatic approach has been traditionally used, based on the accumulated wisdom of admissions officers in the very large number of institutions of higher education across the length and breadth of the country.

With about 350,000 foreign students, the United States attracts more than any other country in the world, its nearest rival being France (table 4). Such migration has been taking place for many

Table 4. Principal national destinations of foreign students, 1986.

Country	Number of foreign students
USA	349,610
France	126,762
West Germany	81,724
United Kingdom	56,726
Canada	27,210

Source: UNESCO, Statistical Yearbook, 1989 (Paris: UNESCO, 1989), 408-10.

decades and, especially at the graduate and post-doctoral levels, this "brain drain" has achieved a certain notoriety since the 1960s. The athletic equivalent, the "brawn drain," is the main focus of this chapter, in which the contribution made by foreigners to the intercollegiate sports scene is discussed. More detailed coverage of one sport, track and field, is given in chapter 4.

Before looking at the contribution of foreign student-athletes, however, it will be germane to consider some dimensions of the overall patterns of foreign student migration to, and within, the United States, i.e., the foreign-student population, of which student-athletes are but part. It is important to take note initially of the significance of foreign students per se because the pattern of foreign student-athlete migration could be a reduced mirror image of that of all foreign students. In other words, the proportion of the total number of student-athletes coming to the United States from a given country could be the same as the proportion of all students from that country. Likewise, the proportion of a university's students which was foreign could be the same as the proportion of its student-athletes who were foreign. The early part of this chapter will therefore identify general patterns within which the numbers of foreign student-athletes can be contextualized.

Foreign Students in the United States

In 1986-87 nearly 350,000 foreign students were enrolled at universities and colleges in the United States. Of these, 51.8 percent have been estimated to be undergraduates.[4] The total foreign student population has risen steadily over the years, from a figure of 29,813 in 1950.[5] The homes of these students span the globe but nearly half the 1987 total came from Asia. Africa and North America together contributed less than a quarter while Europe sent less than all the nations of Latin America. Table 5 shows clearly that the origins of foreign students in the United States are mainly in the so-called "Third World."

Table 5. Regional origins of foreign students in the United States, 1986-87.

Region	Number	Percent of total
South and East Asia	170,000	48.6
Middle East	47,000	13.4
Latin America	43,480	12.4
Europe	36,140	10.3
Africa	31,580	9.1
North America	16,300	4.7
Oceania	4,230	1.2

Source: Open Doors, 1986-87, 15.

Table 6. Countries with more than 11,000 students in the United States, 1986-87.

Country	Number of foreign students	Percent of total
Taiwan	25,660	7.3
Malaysia	21,640	6.2
China	20,030	5.7
Rep. of Korea	19,940	5.7
India	18,350	5.3
Canada	15,700	4.5
Japan	15,070	4.3
Iran	12,230	3.3
Nigeria	11,700	3.3
Hong Kong	11,010	3.2

Source: Open Doors, 1986-87.

At the level of individual states, the main suppliers of foreign students tend to shift with the changing tides of US foreign policy. In the 1970s the major national group were Iranians whereas in the late 1980s there were growing contingents from China. In 1987 nearly 26,000 students came from Taiwan, substantially more than from Malaysia, China, Korea, India, and Canada, the other major suppliers. Together, the ten countries shown in table 6 accounted for 48.8 percent of all foreign students in the United States.

Although only 2.8 percent of all students enrolled at US institutions of higher education are foreign,[6] some colleges and universities have substantially higher proportions than the national average. Of the eighty-five institutions with over one thousand foreign students, 7.1 percent of the two million total enrollment were foreign. Colleges with the largest number of foreigners in absolute terms are shown in

Table 7. Institutions with the most foreign students.

Institution	Number of Foreign Students	
	1985-86	1986-87
Miami-Dade Community College	4,730	5,010
University of Southern California	3,714	3,746
University of Texas, Austin	3,132	3,000
Columbia Univ., Barnard & Teachers Col.	2,679	2,807
University of Wisconsin-Madison	2,873	2,789
Ohio State University, Main Campus	2,690	2,739
University of Minnesota, Twin Cities	2,473	2,624
University of California, Los Angeles	2,488	2,506
University of Michigan, Ann Arbor	2,413	2,449
Boston University	2,493	2,422

Source: Open Doors, 1986-87.

Table 8. American universities with more than 10 percent of student numbers consisting of foreign students, 1979-80.

US International University	41.5
Texas Southern University	30.3
University of San Francisco	22.6
Massachusetts Institute of Technology	18.6
Los Angeles City College	16.3
Howard University	15.6
University of Southern California	12.3
American University	12.2
Columbia University	11.9
University of Southwestern Louisiana	11.1

Source: American Council on Education, *American Universities and Colleges* (New York: de Gruyter, 1983), 29.

table 7. Miami Dade Community College has over five thousand foreign students and this accounts for 12.5 percent of its enrollment; several other institutions have a larger relative share of foreigners, however, as shown in table 8. It is in institutions such as these that foreign student-athletes would appear least likely to suffer culture shock.

The extent to which student-migrants return home after their period of study is a subject which has attracted considerable attention. For example, one survey recorded that of a sample of 1,561 foreign students in the United States, 49 percent "definitely" planned to return home and remain there, while a further 26 percent felt that return migration was "probably" their most likely course of action.[7]

Again, these kinds of figures are worth bearing in mind when considering the experiences of foreign student-athletes.

Brain Drain and Brawn Drain

Despite certain similarities, brawn drain differs from brain drain in a number of fundamental respects. Some differences relating to age, academic qualifications, and experience will be explored in later chapters, but at this stage four important distinctions between the two need to be made.

First, scholarships are usually provided for "academic" students by agencies in the donor country, 77 percent of foreign students receiving most of their aid from home-country sources.[8] While some governments may provide loans of varying amounts to student-athletes while in the United States, for a percentage similar to that quoted above grants are obtained from the athletic departments of the sojourn universities (see page 52).

A second distinction, related to the first, is that academic students from overseas attend United States universities to develop skills which will aid the development of institutions (e.g., farming, industry) in their own countries. However, foreign student-athletes are recruited to the United States in order to further the needs (i.e., success and visibility) of institutions (i.e., universities) in the host country.

A third difference is that the academic level of study differs between United States-based foreign students and student-athletes. In 1987 half the foreign students were undergraduates,[9] whereas the respective figure for student-athletes would be 100 percent. Post-graduate students who happen to be athletes would compete for clubs rather than colleges.

A fourth point is that the number of foreign athletic recruits is tiny in comparison with the overall number of foreign students. By the end of this chapter the numbers involved will have been clarified but it should be stressed here that the numerical impact is insignificant compared with other impacts which foreign athletes might make. While possessing low numerical visibility, foreign student-athletes may make major contributions to sports events at local, regional, and national levels. The resulting media coverage will often be significant. Student-athletes are the most well known of all students and it is not unusual for foreign athletes to be among the most well known. Few would deny the newsworthiness and international high profile of someone of the stature of, say, Henry Rono, a Kenyan running genius who represented Washington State University and broke many world records during the 1970s. Having stressed these distinctions, we can now consider the contribution of foreign student-athletes to American college sports.

Foreign Athletic Recruiting:
Some Historical Considerations

Although foreign students who were also top-class athletes have attended US colleges since the early years of this century, the extent to which they were recruited or the extent to which they resemble present-day student-athletes is unclear. It is only since the 1950s, with the "legalization" of athletic scholarships, that overseas recruiting and the associated influx of foreign student-athletes have been significant. Foreign student-athletes have been increasing in number, concurrently with the overall increase in students in the USA. However, their numbers have stabilized or even declined in recent years.

This stabilization or decline may simply be part of the national trends shown in figure 4. The number of all student-athletes in NCAA Division I schools peaked in 1984, reaching a figure of 90,360; by 1986 it had fallen to 84,618. This decline has been mirrored in all sports in which a foreign presence has been traditionally felt.

The number of foreign student-athletes in American academe during the early 1950s was not large enough to cause any serious concern among coaches and administrators. The impact of foreign recruits on NCAA championships was present but not viewed as problematic. However, eyebrows were raised in the late 1950s and early 1960s with the recruitment of foreign athletes in their late twenties—or even thirties—who had several years' experience of big-time sport in their own countries. Initial reactions to the mature foreigner were uncertain and varied. Some conferences treated foreign student-athletes as they would treat any other foreign students, but others seemed more concerned about the methods of recruitment than the recruits themselves. In 1955, for example, Idaho cross-country coach Joe Glander advertised for runners in a British magazine and ended up with a team of Pacific Coast Conference champions, each member of the team a British import. Idaho was fined $1,000 for what was viewed as "illegal recruiting"[10] (see page 108) but the fine didn't stop the runners from running or winning conference titles; nor did it deter the further recruiting of foreigners in track, soccer, tennis, swimming, and other sports.

The Idaho cross-country runners were experienced athletes, and "against inexperienced Americans fresh out of high school, the age

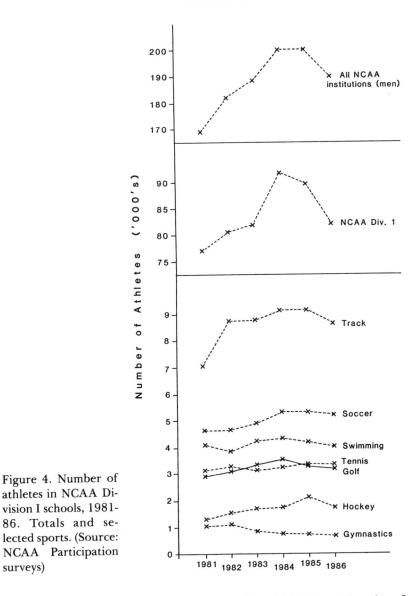

Figure 4. Number of athletes in NCAA Division I schools, 1981-86. Totals and selected sports. (Source: NCAA Participation surveys)

difference provided a critical advantage."[11] In 1960 the University of Houston cross-country team won the NCAA title with a team made up of foreigners, all over the age of twenty-six, and such perceived abuses were also taking place in tennis, soccer and, most notoriously, in ice hockey. The response of the NCAA was for the first time to formally define the status of the foreign student-athlete.[12] This was done in 1961 when an "overage foreigner" rule was imposed which stated that for every year foreign athletes competed after their twentieth birthday (later changed to nineteenth), they would lose a year of varsity eligibility for NCAA championship competition. The rule was quickly adopted by most of the major conferences.

The NAIA, however, imposed no such age restrictions in its member institutions, which were able to recruit overage foreigners with little difficulty. In the early 1970s it was often the NAIA schools with no age restraints that were quicker to go for African student-athletes. For example, Eastern New Mexico University rapidly developed a Kenyan network of contacts by first recruiting an "overage" athlete who subsequently contacted younger Kenyans who might have otherwise gone to NCAA schools. In 1972 the same university recruited a Kenyan hurdler who had originally been recruited by an NCAA school but was subsequently dropped because of overage ineligibility.[13] It was also often the smaller colleges which recruited foreigners,[14] since those schools were unable to compete with the major sports schools in the domestic recruiting race (see page 99).

Some NCAA institutions flouted the overage rule. In 1971, Howard University in Washington, D.C., a traditionally strong soccer school, won the NCAA title with several mature foreigners on their team. Two years later the NCAA stripped the university of its title because of its infringement of the over-age requirement. But Howard took the NCAA to court, challenging the constitutionality of the rule. The federal court ordered the rule suspended because it failed to comply with the equal protection clause of the Fourteenth Amendment. This decision contributed to the rapid increase in overseas recruiting during the 1970s, an increase illustrated in figure 5 which shows the growth and decline of overseas recruiting in two sports, track and soccer, at Clemson University. The seventies boom in importing foreigners at

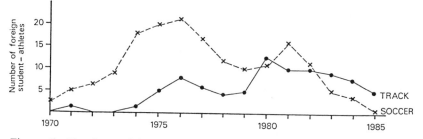

Figure 5. Numbers of foreign recruits on Clemson University track-and-field and soccer squads, 1970-86. (Source: Clemson University rosters)

Clemson, however, should not be regarded as altogether typical since some colleges have never recruited overseas while others are recruiting more foreigners now than ever before. The precise time and place of international athletic recruiting will depend on a number of factors, not least the recruiting philosophy of particular coaches and the nature of the contacts such coaches possess (see chapter 5).

The general increase in foreign recruiting in the 1970s led to more controversy in college sports and induced further objections to overage recruiting, so much so that the overage rule was more or less exhumed in 1980 when the NCAA applied to Division I schools the rule that every year of competition that athletes had after their twentieth birthday would count as one year's eligibility, whether such athletes were on college teams or not. Hence, a foreign athlete of twenty-five who had been competing since the age of twenty would be ineligible for collegiate competition.

Because this rule included Americans as well as foreigners it was regarded as non-discriminatory. Few Americans, however, enter the world of intercollegiate sports after their twentieth birthday and for this reason the rule does, *de facto*, discriminate against the mature overseas athlete. The imposition of the rule may have contributed to the apparent decline of foreign recruits during the 1980s (see figs. 4 and 14).

The problems of actually implementing the rule can be illustrated by a brief case study. A New Zealand middle-distance import at the University of Oregon informed the university that he had not competed between 1973 and 1977. Being twenty-five years of age, he therefore had one year of eligibility. It was alleged by a rival institution, however, that he had been seen competing in Fiji in 1975. If this were true he would have been ineligible, and to iron out the problem the university had to obtain written notification from New Zealand of the athlete's whereabouts in 1975.[15] Clearly, there is the distinct possibility of such cases never really being resolved, requiring, as they do, detailed knowledge of an individual's prior movements in a different place than where the enquiries are being made.

Other factors have contributed to the brake on the brawn drain. As early as 1974 the NCAA imposed on Division I schools a reduction (from eighty to seventy) in the number of scholarships for all sports except football and basketball. Several sports in which foreign recruiting was significant had upper limits placed on the number of scholarships. For example, fourteen was the upper limit for both soccer and track while the respective figure for tennis and golf was five. The implication for foreign recruiting was spelled out by Eastern Michigan

University track coach Robert Parks: "The rule will stop the recruiting of the marginal foreigner who may develop. You can get American kids like that for free. But it may increase the recruiting of the big foreign star; the overall number of foreigners may be cut, but quality will go up."[16] Ball State's Jerry Rushton stated that "the fourteen-grant limit definitely has stimulated large schools, except in 'track populated' areas, to go for the polished foreign athlete," adding that such developments would hurt US track and that coaches who recruited foreigners were "just business managers anyway, not coaches."[17]

It should be stressed, however, that these constraints did not apply to NCAA Division II (and III) schools, nor to NAIA affiliates or junior colleges. These institutions continued to provide opportunities for foreigners who wished to benefit from subsidized training and coaching in the United States. Furthermore, foreign student-athletes at NCAA Division II and III schools could compete in Division I championships if they had qualified in lower divisional meets.[18]

But further legislation to restrict foreign movement to NCAA schools was passed in 1983 when the military service exemption (which allowed overage foreigners athletic eligibility if they had been in the armed services) was only provided to athletes from the US armed services, thus eliminating many foreign athletes. This especially applied to Africans who were often nominal members of their nations' armies. Other exemptions, such as official church missions and foreign service, were eliminated in legislation enacted by the NCAA in 1984.

Additional factors contributed to the stabilization or decline in overseas athletic recruiting. These include the increase in tuition charges in many universities, which has meant that (in Texas, for example) the cost of a foreign student is twice that of an American. Budget cuts in many universities' athletic departments have also had the effect of limiting the overall number of athletes on scholarships. In addition, in 1986 the NCAA implemented a rule pertaining to the eligibility of incoming freshman student-athletes. Often called Proposition 48, this rule imposed higher academic standards for freshmen in Division I institutions. The rule was extended to Division II in 1988. Essentially, only high school graduates who achieved a cumulative minimum grade-point average of 2.00 in a core curriculum could now qualify for athletic scholarships. Furthermore, students entering college under the international standards described for each country by the NCAA (see page 24), had, under 1986 rulings, to achieve a combined score of 700 on the SAT test or a composite score of 15 on the ACT test. These tests are normally given only a few times a year and involve the payment of a fee. These requirements further reduced the incentive to recruit internationally.

The flattening out of the growth curve of foreign student-athletes might also be partly attributed to the fact that at the level of the individual institution a sport which had traditionally recruited foreigners may have been discontinued. For example, Oregon State, Northwestern, San Jose State, and Richmond have all dropped track in recent years. In the case of Richmond, the track coach, Fred Hardy, had been a major recruiter of Kenyan talent. With the elimination of the track program and Hardy's subsequent move, the university's Kenyan connection was severed.[19] The size of track squads has been trimmed, too, the average size of an NCAA squad being thirty-nine in 1985-86 but only thirty-two in 1987-88.[20]

Events contributing to a potential reduction in the number of foreign student-athletes in the United States have so far been discussed from an American perspective only. Events in donor countries, however, can also affect the number of foreign recruits going to the United States. In Canada, traditionally the major source of foreign talent for US campuses, attempts have been made in the last decade to keep skilled athletic talent at home. The Athletic Assistance Program, initiated in the 1970s and riding on a wave of Canadian nationalism, provides an income security program to help top Canadian athletes with living expenses. In other words, the program provides the "necessities" for contemporary high-performance sport. The Athletic Assistance program provides an alternative to sojourn in the United States and may have therefore contributed to the reduction in the number of student-athletes moving south from Canada in the 1980s. The number of recipients of these awards has grown steadily (see table 9) but, as Jean Harvey has noted, under the Athletic Assistance Program athletes have to sign contracts which make them virtually state employees.[21]

Table 9. Number of Canadian athletes gaining aid under the Athletic Assistance Program.

Year	Number of athletes
1981-82	645
1982-83	697
1983-84	732
1984-85	738
1985-86	745

Source: Government of Canada, *Fitness and Amateur Sport*, Annual Reports.

Likewise, in Australia the greater state provision for athletes and the establishment of a national sports policy may have reduced the attraction of going to America. At a global scale, one of the major sports involved, track and field, has in the 1980s adopted a more "open" approach to professionalism by means of subventions and trust funds. Given such financial rewards, athletes who might otherwise have migrated to an American college have remained at home.

Finally, a changing national political regime can stem the potential flow of foreign recruits. A prime example is Ethiopia which, like its African neighbor Kenya, has been a fertile source of distance running talent since the 1960s. American universities would have proved attractive destinations for Ethiopian athletes, but the establishment of a socialist government there has led to home-based development of talent instead. More recently Kenya has also adopted this model, to some extent (see page 80). In many cases, of course, the state's prevention of the citizens' freedom of movement has excluded them from the system of which the US athletic departments are a part. But with the dramatic developments that occurred in Eastern Europe in 1989, the recruitment of student-athletes from beyond what was once the "Iron Curtain" has already begun. The first Hungarian to take part in an NCAA track and field championship did so in 1989, having been recruited during the recent thaw in that country's political climate, and other Hungarian athletes were recruited to a small number of colleges ready for the 1989-90 sporting year.

The Extent of Overseas Athletic Recruiting

It has been shown that the number of foreign students in the United States is well documented. Given the precisely documented nature of American sports it seems paradoxical, however, that virtually no published data exist to inform us about the extent of foreign athletic recruiting, or the total number of what Gregory Sojka has called a "new breed" of student-athletes.[22] The NCAA and the NAIA, despite their general policing of the college sports scene, do not publish records of foreign student-athletes at their member institutions. The only way in which the total number of foreign student-athletes could be established would be to scrutinize carefully every roster of every sport of every athletic department of every university and college in the entire USA. Such an exercise would be fraught with numerous logistical problems and inevitably, therefore, one must rely on partial evidence derived from surveys and "guesstimates."

In reviewing the number of foreign student-athletes it is important to distinguish first between the *proportion* of athletes who are foreign and the *absolute* number who are foreign. High levels of visibility resulting from large numbers may be misleading since in some sports squad sizes are large (in track and field, teams average thirty-seven members in NCAA schools) while in other sports (e.g., tennis or golf) squad sizes are small, averaging about twelve student-athletes.[23] Five foreign recruits in a track squad of thirty amounts to only one-sixth of the squad, but five in a tennis squad could constitute over half the team. The most widespread and populous sports in NCAA colleges are shown in table 10. In order to evaluate the foreign presence, one should keep in mind the percentage contribution of foreigners to the total number of participants.

There are some minor problems in designating just who is or is not a foreign student-athlete. Someone born overseas but educated in America from the age of, say, seven has hardly been recruited from overseas. A student-athlete who was born overseas but attended a US high school from the age of seventeen with a view to subsequent enrollment in college is a different case. The college could have actually colluded in placing such an athlete in high school in order

Table 10. The major intercollegiate sports, 1986-87.

Sport	Number of NCAA institutions	Number of participants
(A) MEN		
Basketball	760	12,725
Tennis	686	7,589
Cross-country	681	9,762
Baseball	662	21,055
Golf	577	6,804
Track and field	569	19,055
Soccer	548	14,375
Football	510	51,087
Swimming	375	8,071
Wrestling	300	8,205
(B) WOMEN		
Basketball	757	10,526
Volleyball	701	9,688
Tennis	690	7,470
Cross-country	633	7,164
Track and field	526	11,430
Swimming	392	7,760

Source: NCAA, *Participation Surveys* (Mission, Kans.: NCAA, 1988).

to provide the chance for acculturation and familiarization with the American lifestyle. On the other hand, student-athletes who were born in, say, Germany as part of a US service family are clearly not foreign student-athletes in the sense intended in this book. Although in some cases the question of who is a foreign student-athlete is a grey area (for example, a person holding a Jamaican passport but who lived in New York for much of her life), the numbers involved are few and in general there is little ambiguity. Where ambiguous cases do exist, it has been decided to err on the side of caution; all estimates in what follows should therefore be regarded as conservative.

A final point of caution worth making at this stage is that when we talk about foreign student-athletes, we cannot be certain that they have necessarily received athletic scholarships. It is possible that they could be receiving academic scholarships or were financing themselves, representing the university as "walk-ons." A study undertaken in 1980, however, showed that 88.8 percent of foreign student-athletes responding to a questionnaire were athletic-scholarship holders,[24] while a similar survey of European student-athletes in the mid-eighties revealed a respective figure of 98 percent.[25] Of course, not all these grants-in-aid necessarily assume the form of a full scholarship, but most foreign recruits do seem to be on full grants (see page 177).

The remainder of this chapter is concerned with describing quantitatively and qualitatively the extent of foreign involvement in intercollegiate sports. For some sports, such as football, it might be expected that foreign involvement was minimal; after all, the gridiron game barely exists outside the USA. For other sports substantial foreign involvement might be expected, but this involvement might be dominated by recruits from a very small number of countries. For example, in the case of ice hockey a substantial Canadian involvement might be expected, given that Canada is the home of the sport and the nearest northern neighbor of the United States. But what of tennis, golf, and swimming? These sports are practiced in many countries but they tend to be associated with the "developed" world. And how about soccer, and track and field? These are truly global sports involving virtually every country in the world. The following sections try to answer these and other related questions.

Football

Although Americans regard football as one of their principal sporting passions, it is far from being an international sport. Despite an embryonic, low-key invasion of Europe, gridiron football is essentially a US preserve. It can safely be said that high school football—the seedbed from which recruits are plucked—is virtually unique to North America. For this reason foreign recruiting in football is hardly prominent.

At the same time foreign recruitment is not totally absent from the sport. Some college coaches have noted how foreigners have place-kicking talent, derived perhaps from their background in soccer or rugby. But the numbers are small and geographer Harold McConnell has noted that the football rosters of eighty-one major college football programs in the South in the early 1980s contained only eighteen foreign players, half of whom were from Canada.[26] The number of foreign football players accounted for only 0.2 percent of the total, a figure which if applied to all schools (not just Division I) would amount to less than one hundred foreign football players nationwide. Nevertheless, Gregory Sojka has gone so far as to suggest that "the only comparable example [to track and field] of foreign legionnaires in intercollegiate sports would be the increasing number of Samoan football players appearing on West Coast Pac-10 conference teams."[27] This is undoubtedly an exaggerated claim and it is as well to recall that the best-known foreign football player, Jan Stenerud, the former Montana State place kicker, was originally lured from Norway on a skiing scholarship, while the athlete selected in 1989 as the most valuable player in the NFL was a Nigerian, Christian Okoye, who arrived in the United States in 1982 on a track scholarship to Azusa Pacific University in California.[28]

It is just possible, however, that the number of European recruits coming to US campuses in the near future will increase as the result of the aforementioned expansion of the gridiron game in Europe. In order to develop the raw talent there, team or national federation bosses are fixing up scholarships for some of the best European football players so that they may improve their skills in the American intercollegiate game. At present a trickle, the trend could intensify into something more should the game really take off in Europe.

Ice Hockey

Restricted by physical geography and tradition to the northern periphery of the United States, college hockey differs dramatically from football by its great emphasis on foreign recruits—from the sport's birthplace in Canada. In the mid-1970s the Cornell hockey team was 100 percent Canadian,[29] and for universities in several northeastern states the Canadian boundary is a recruiting irrelevance (figure 6). An analysis of the origins of US college hockey players in 1973-74 showed that the province of Ontario "produced" 6.49 times as many

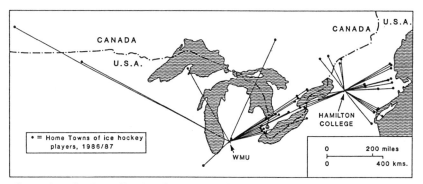

Figure 6. The Canadian border acts as a permeable barrier to the movement from hometown to college by ice hockey players at Western Michigan University and Hamilton College. (Source: 1986-87 rosters)

players as the North American per capita average, only Massachusetts and Minnesota being higher in per capita terms.[30] Alberta, Manitoba, Saskatchewan, and Newfoundland all had indices above the continental norm. Of the hockey players in the eight NCAA Division I finalists in 1983, 40 percent were Canadian.[31] If the less sport-oriented schools recruit over more localized areas, it is reasonable to suggest that 25 percent of all NCAA Division I hockey players are Canadian, which would mean that in 1986-87 there were about 430 Canadians on Division I campus rinks.

Football and hockey are two sports for which quite different patterns exist. The former is widespread in the United States but has few foreign recruits; the latter is geographically localized but has many. The rest of this chapter looks at sports that lie between these extremes.

Basketball

Although basketball is an American "invention" it is now global in scope and is popular in both "developed" and "underdeveloped" parts of the world. Despite this, however, it is one of *the* American sports, and because of its widespread presence in high schools across the nation the United States might be expected to be relatively self-sufficient in supplying its collegiate needs. In fact, only 3.5 percent of the players identified in a survey of NCAA college rosters in 1987 were foreigners—a substantially larger porportion than that found in football but much less than that in sports considered in later pages.

There will always be exceptions to a general pattern and the number of foreign recruits in college basketball is no exception. For example, in 1986, Houston Baptist University's thirteen-man squad contained six foreigners from four countries, the result of contacts set up by Baptist missionaries in Africa and Latin America.

Despite the relatively small percentage of involvement of foreigners in college basketball, there is said to be a substantial demand for basketball scholarships from overseas. In 1983, for example, the University of Houston basketball coach stated that he had about 250 foreign players wanting to try out for basketball each year.[32] This is almost certainly not typical but it does illustrate the overseas demand for athletic assistance in a sport which is growing in popularity throughout the world.

A small number of women basketball players are also found on US college courts. Of NCAA Division I players, 3 percent are foreign, two-thirds coming from Canada and the British Isles.[33]

Soccer

Given the somewhat recent growth in the popularity of soccer in the United States and the relative scarcity of superior domestic talent, it might be expected that soccer rosters in the most sport-oriented soccer schools would show a sizeable foreign presence, and there has been something of a tradition of importing foreign recruits for the round-ball game. In the early 1970s, for example, Howard University, a school that still attracts foreign soccer players, won the NCAA championship with a team made up of one Ghanaian, three Jamaicans, three Trinidadians, and four Nigerians.[34] In 1974 Clemson University had twenty foreign recruits on its twenty-two-man squad, eight each from Guyana and Nigeria and four from Jamaica. Indeed, it was foreign talent that led to the development of Clemson as a soccer power (see page 100). Most foreign soccer imports come from the British Isles—as many as 24 percent according to a 1986 survey.[35] Canada supplied 14 percent and no other country sent more than 5 percent (see table 11).

At the present time soccer appears to have a more significant foreign presence than most of the sports previously discussed. Soccer has been growing at the grass-roots level in the United States and it is likely that there is enough high school talent to support college soccer at a level thought impossible a few years ago. Yet estimates suggest that more than one in ten players (somewhere between 10 percent and 12 percent, according to two surveys) on NCAA Division I soccer teams come from overseas.[36] Among schools favoring a strong foreign presence in 1987 were Long Island University (11 out of 18),

Table 11. Major source areas of foreign soccer players in NCAA
Division I universities, 1986.

Country	Percent
United Kingdom*	18.5
Canada	13.6
Eire*	5.5
Norway	4.4
Trinidad	3.4
Colombia	3.1
German Federal Republic	3.1

* In this table the UK and Eire (the British Isles) are separated.

Source: Andy Smyth, Oklahoma State University, unpublished statistics.

Coastal Carolina (16/26), and Cleveland State (13/22), whose "international" team is shown in figure 7.

There appears to be a considerable overseas demand for soccer scholarships. In some ways this is surprising since standards tend to be higher elsewhere, but it is *the* world sport. An anecdote from Texas illustrates this surprising foreign demand. No men's varsity soccer team exists at Texas A & M University, and although the athletic department does sponsor a women's team, no scholarships are given. Coach Laura Johnson of the women's team is said to receive several enquiries a month from foreign players about joining the nonexistent men's team.[37] How typical this situation might be is unclear.

The growth of college soccer may well lead to the establishment of US professional soccer on the world stage. But it is rare for top foreign professionals to have been nurtured on, or even to have experienced, US college soccer. An unusual example of such a rarity, however, is Roy Wegerle, who in 1989-90 played in the First Division of the English Football League. South African Wegerle attended college in Florida at the age of seventeen on a soccer scholarship. While there he attracted the attention of cult English player Rodney Marsh of the Tampa Bay Rowdies. Marsh told an English club manager of Wegerle's potential and the former South African college import ended up playing in the oldest football league in the world.[38]

Virtually no foreign recruits are found in women's college soccer. It is possible, however, that this situation could change. Compared with the game in Western Europe, where it is rather poorly developed and to some extent ridiculed, women's soccer in America is well organized with a good standard of performance. The quality of women's soccer in the United States compares very favorably with that in

Figure 7. Soccer power Cleveland State has utilized foreign recruits to its advantage. Of the members of the 1986 Vikings' soccer squad, twelve (or 59 percent) were foreign, with recruits from the British Isles, West Indies, and Canada. (Source: Cleveland State University)

any country in the world, and a greater awareness of soccer scholarship opportunities in America among European women players could lead to an influx of foreign soccer talent.

Tennis

A long tradition exists in the recruitment of foreign tennis players to American universities. In the 1940s Ecuadoran Pancho Segura won NCAA titles for the University of Miami, while the University of Southern California utilized the talents of Alex Olmedo from Peru and Mexican Rafael Osuna.[39] In the 1983 World University Games, the entire "British" team was made up of students from American universities,[40] and each year the media reveal that players from, say, Scandinavia or Africa, who are in the public eye at tournaments such as Wimbledon, at some time benefitted from competition on the US college circuit.

In 1987 it was estimated that as many as 16 percent of NCAA Division I players were foreign.[41] In some institutions foreign players actually dominated the tennis teams; at South Alabama six out of eight players came from overseas and at Arkansas–Little Rock seven out of eight were foreign. Wichita State and Northeast Louisiana each had 70 percent of its team made up of foreign recruits; foreigners composed more than half the tennis team at other colleges, such as Texas A & M, Wake Forest, Alabama, Austin Peay, and Arkansas.

Foreign recruits are not restricted to big Division I schools, however. For example, four out of ten players at Division II school Ferris State came from overseas.

Tennis appears to be rather diversified in terms of the countries from which it draws talent. According to two surveys, the leading donor country, supplying around 15 percent of foreign student-athletes to Division I squads, is South Africa,[42] a country that supplies a far more modest number of athletes to other sports. The import of South African student-athletes is not without controversy, a subject addressed in chapters 5 and 8.

Women's tennis recruiting is similar to that of men's, though as with almost all sports the foreign women's presence is not as evident. A noteworthy exception in 1988 was the team at US International University, with nine foreigners, while Mississippi had six.[43] A 1987 estimate suggested that 10.9 percent of NCAA Division I women tennis players were foreign. Canada was the major donor nation (21 percent), with South Africa the other major source (see table 12). Campuses with a concentration of foreign women tennis players included Mississippi State, Alabama, Houston, and Idaho State.

Table 12. Major source areas of foreign tennis players in NCAA Division I universities.

Country	Percent of foreign total
(A) MEN	
South Africa	13.7
Canada	11.7
Australia	7.6
Sweden	7.6
Mexico	5.6
United Kingdom	4.1
Venezuela	4.1
(B) WOMEN	
Canada	21.5
South Africa	10.3
United Kingdom	9.5
Sweden	7.7
New Zealand	5.2
German Federal Republic	4.3
Netherlands	4.3

Source: Theodore Goudge and Peter Meserve, "Intercollegiate Tennis," unpublished paper, 1988.

Swimming

Global recruiting is commonplace in swimming. Half the Canadian Olympic team has traditionally attended US universities,[44] while in 1980 the University of Houston swim squad included seven Britons, two Australians, and one swimmer each from New Zealand, Singapore, and Zimbabwe. Not surprisingly the team became known as the "Cougar Commonwealth."[45] Noteworthy foreign recruits have included British Olympic gold medalist David Wilkie, who was a student at the University of Miami, and champion Australian swimmers Murray Rose and John Konrads, both of whom attended the University of Southern California. Many more foreign swimming stars have studied and swum in America.

It has been estimated that 6.2 percent of all NCAA Division I swimmers are from overseas though in some institutions the percentage is much higher.[46] An extreme case in 1987 was the University of Arkansas at Little Rock where ten of the eleven men on the swim squad were foreign. One-quarter of the UCLA thirty-two-man squad came from overseas while foreigners were also prominent at Louisiana State. Principal national donors appear to be Canada, Sweden, Spain, Norway, and the United Kingdom.

Women's swimming also has a visible foreign presence. In 1987, it was estimated that 4.2 percent of division I swimmers were foreign, 29 percent coming from Canada. LSU, Alabama, and Houston exemplify schools with a strong overseas contingent on women's swim teams.

Golf

With a smaller overall number of participants than the other sports considered here, golf has a relatively small number of foreigners (table 13). However, it has been shown for NCAA Division I that 6.7 percent of campus golfers are foreign, although for some universities the proportion is much higher. In 1987, for example, more than one-third of the golf teams at Miami (Ohio) and San Jose State were made up of foreign recruits. As with most other sports, Canada is the main donor nation—over 50 percent coming from Canada, according to one estimate[47] (fig. 8).

Women's golf, though a relatively minor sport, does have quite a strong foreign presence, 6.4 percent of campus golfers in NCAA Division I schools being foreign. Half of such recruits come from Canada.

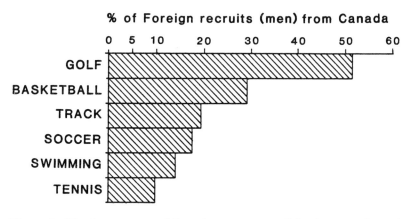

Figure 8. The importance of Canada as a source of foreign recruits varies considerably between sports.

Track and Field

The little-published (and unpublished) research into international athletic recruiting has tended to focus on track and field, giving the impression that it is the major sport involved in the brawn drain. In the late 1970s it was suggested that 40 percent of all foreign student-athletes in the United States were in track.[48] This is clearly an overestimate of the present situation and it is clear that a figure of 10 percent is more realistic. While track is among the more visible of the non-revenue college sports (as a result, perhaps, of its centrality in Olympic and other international games), it has been suggested that in absolute terms there are fewer foreign track and field athletes than soccer or tennis players in NCAA Division I schools (see table 13). In 1987 it was estimated that about 5.3 percent of Division I track-and-field male athletes were foreign—a smaller percentage than in golf, tennis, swimming, or soccer. As shown in table 14, however, foreign track imports make a substantially greater contribution to NCAA, NAIA, and JC championship events than to college sports per se, a contribution explored in greater detail in the next chapter. The case of track illustrates the danger of assuming that only big schools recruit foreigners. In 1987 NAIA track power Wayland Baptist University had thirteen foreigners on its twenty-eight-man track roster while Commonwealth 400-meter champion Innocent Egbunike from Nigeria attended another small NAIA school, Azusa Pacific University.

Foreigners have been estimated to account for 4.5 percent of all women track and field athletes in Division I schools. Canada is the

Table 13. Estimated involvement of foreign student-athletes in six inter-collegiate sports, 1987, based on 46 percent of NCAA Division I institutions.

Sport	Men		Women	
	Percent	Number	Percent	Number
Tennis	16.0	535	10.9	312
Golf	6.7	216	6.4	67
Swimming	6.2	249	4.2	152
Track and field	5.3	460	4.5	241
Basketball	3.5	157	3.0	116
Soccer	10.6	556	—	—
Estimates for six sports		2,173		878

Source: Author's research.

major national donor, accounting for 21 percent. Universities with a strong foreign presence on their women's track teams include LSU, UTEP, Alabama, Clemson, and Iowa State. The importance of non-NCAA schools is again illustrated by the case of Wayland Baptist with ten foreigners on its twenty-one-strong women's squad (fig. 9).

Although track and field has probably attracted more attention than many other sports regarding the foreign student-athlete situation, it does, in fact, accommodate fewer foreign recruits than other sports. Of the six sports shown in table 13, less than 25 percent are in track and field, and as noted earlier, if all sports were included the percentage in track would likely be about 10 percent.

It is evident that a number of sports not even mentioned here have a strong foreign involvement. For example, ten members of the Northern Illinois gymnastic squad in 1987 were from four foreign countries. British Olympic gymnast Terry Bartlett attended Penn State where in 1987 one-third of its nine-man squad was from overseas. An Olympic wrestling medalist from Britain, Noel Loban, was at Clemson. Skiing, softball, baseball, and crew also recruit some foreigners.

Foreign Recruits in High School

The international scramble to achieve athletic success in college sports may be currently paralleled by the same phenomenon at the high school level. While junior colleges have frequently served as temporary "acculturation centers" for foreign student-athletes prior to their enrolling at a university, it seems that the same function may be

Table 14. The foreign contribution to college track-and-field national championships, 1986-89.

Championship	Number of events won by foreigners			
	1986	1987	1988	1989
NCAA Div. I (men)	6	7	6	7
NCAA Div. I (women)	5	2	2	4
NCAA Div. II (men)	9	6	4	3
NCAA Div. II (women)	4	6	8	5
NAIA (men and women)	9	7	11	8
National JC (men and women)	9	10	11	9
Totals	42	38	42	36

Source: Track and Field News, various issues.

provided by certain high schools. In other cases high schools may actually be recruiting foreigners to boost their own local or regional images. In late 1987, for example, it was reported that a Kentucky county school board, concerned about the possibility of overseas recruiting by high schools, banned exchange students from competing on their varsity basketball teams.[49] The same situation may exist in high schools in southern California where substantial numbers of Mexican and Central American soccer players are enrolled prior to taking scholarships at local universities.

An Estimate of Foreign Involvement

On the basis of data collected in 1987, it can be inferred that most NCAA Division I universities have at least one foreign recruit in the major men's sports of soccer and tennis while about half have foreign student-athletes in swimming and track (table 15). Only about one-third have such recruits in basketball and golf. It is clear, therefore, that foreign recruiting was a widespread phenomenon of sports on the US campus in the late 1980s. It has been seen in this chapter that in percentage terms, over 16 percent of Division I men tennis players were foreign student-athletes, while only 0.2 percent of football players were foreign. The figures for selected women's sports do not show a markedly different range.

In 1977 Neil Amdur estimated that there were about a thousand foreign student-athletes in the United States.[50] This figure probably was, and certainly is today, a gross underestimate. On the basis of the figures presented in the previous pages, it can be inferred that for six men's sports—basketball, golf, swimming, track and field, soccer,

Figure 9. It's not just the big NCAA schools that recruit foreigners. Wayland Baptist University, an NAIA school of less than 2,000 students in Plainview, Texas, had 23 (47 percent) foreigners on its 49-strong track team in 1987. Among these were (left) Nzael Kyomo from Tanzania and Vicky Aoko from Nigeria. (Source: Wayland Baptist University)

Table 15. Percentage of universities with foreign recruits in six intercollegiate sports (men) in 1987, based on 46 percent of NCAA Division I institutions.

Sport	Percent
Basketball	33.1
Golf	37.1
Swimming	50.0
Track and field	52.2
Tennis	62.5
Soccer	68.3

Source: Bale, "Foreign Student-Athletes," 29.

and tennis—the foreign contribution to NCAA squads amounted to 7.1 percent of the total. Of course, the percentages varied among sports, but if those summarized in table 13 are applied to the total number of athletes in the six aforementioned sports in *all Division I* institutions, a total of 2,200 is arrived at—over twice Amdur's estimate for *all sports* in US colleges. If the percentages for women's sports in table 13 were applied to the same six sports, the total number of foreign women involved would be 878.

It should be stressed that only six NCAA Division I sports have been considered here and no estimates of numbers involved in other NCAA sports or divisions have been made. When analysis is restricted to Division I men's sports alone and the percentage involvement in the six men's sports in table 13 (i.e., 7.1 percent) is applied to the 62,905 student-athletes in all sports except football (in which some foreign recruits are found), the number of foreign recruits totals 4,500. Add women's sports and NAIA and JC institutions and a figure of around 6,000 foreign student-athletes in the United States does not seem unreasonable.

At the continental level this does not seem to be a large number but it is possible for foreign student-athletes to make up a substantial percentage of all foreign students in particular universities. *Open Doors* recorded that at Wayland Baptist—an extreme example, perhaps—forty-one foreign students were enrolled in 1986-87, yet the university's track and field roster revealed that twenty-three (or 56.1 percent) were on the track team alone. In other cases the sporting reputations of institutions can be founded on foreign athletes. Clemson soccer and UTEP track are the most well known, further examples being found in later chapters. In sports with small squads, one foreign recruit can make all the difference. For example, the basketball success of

Marist College in Poughkeepsie, New York, has been attributed almost entirely to seven-foot Dutch center Rik Smits.[51]

For the country as a whole a figure of 6,000 foreign student-athletes represents about 3.3 percent of the total foreign undergraduate population of 181,000. This is a slightly larger percentage share than that of the total US student population which is foreign (page 41). Put differently, there are more foreign college athletes in the United States than there are students from Pakistan, Mexico, or Brazil, and only fourteen individual countries send more students to the US than the estimated total number of foreign student-athletes.

Conclusion

It should be stressed that there would be more student-athletes in the United States if knowledge of the availability of athletic scholarships were evenly spread across the world, especially in the Third World. Systematic variations obviously exist in the knowledge available to particular people in particular places at a particular time.[52] Imperfect or nonexistent knowledge about the American college system means that potential recruits lack the basis upon which to begin the locational decision-making process. As knowledge of sports scholarships spreads beyond the existing knowledge frontier, so the numbers of foreign student-athletes might be expected to increase.

This chapter has described the extent of foreign recruiting in the United States. It has been shown that the numbers involved have grown over time and that in some sports, such as tennis and men's soccer, the foreign involvement extends beyond 10 percent of the total number of athletes in the most sport-oriented universities. In some other sports the foreign contribution is tiny. In whatever sports foreign recruits are found, however, their importance is out of proportion to their numbers. The information in this chapter will provide those involved in debates about foreign recruiting with harder facts than have hitherto existed.

These debates and arguments about foreign recruiting are examined in a later chapter, but before we look at these we should consider a more detailed case study. The next chapter looks at track and field, and highlights the fascinating patterns of national origins and campus destinations of foreign student-athletes in one sport.

FOUR

Track and Field:
The International Recruiting Game

The multi-event sport of track and field commends itself as a case study of international recruiting for a number of reasons. It is an international sport par excellence with over 180 nations affiliated with the International Amateur [sic] Athletic Federation; it is the center-piece of the Olympic Games; it is a sport that attracts a very wide range of physiological types to the diverse events which make up its repertoire. Countries often described as "underdeveloped" are frequently able to achieve high levels of success in events where extreme levels of technical expertise are not required. The cases of Ethiopia and Kenya are exemplary in this respect. The former nation hit the headlines as one of the poorest in the world yet in 1983 provided teams which won both the World Junior and Senior Cross Country championships. In the 1988 championships, Kenya did the same, placing eight runners in the first nine in the senior race, and six in the first seven in the junior. Both countries have also won several Olympic track medals.

Track and field, therefore, typifies a world sports system, one in which the rules and regulations are the same from San Diego to Santiago, from London to Leningrad. Track athletes in South Carolina are driven by the same motives as those in South Australia — and they increasingly find that the conditions under which they compete are the same, irrespective of global location. The synthetic running track and the measurement of performance to one-hundredth of a second has standardized the athletic environment to a degree the nineteenth-century founders of the sport would have believed impossible. Wherever they live, athletes have the same motives: to improve their personal records and to achieve victory in athletic competition. These fundamental ideologies (or deep structures) are inculcated in different ways in the majority of the world's countries. The sport, therefore, constitutes a global arena in which the international recruiting game can be readily played.

Track and field is a relatively popular sport in US colleges, consistently ranking fifth or sixth in terms of the number of institutions sponsoring competition; and third, after football and baseball, when based on the number of participants (see table 10). It is not a major revenue-generating sport, however, and most intercollegiate track meets are low-key affairs compared with football and basketball. A major reason for selecting track for detailed treatment in this chapter is that, because of its truly global distribution, it is the most visible sport to have been involved in international recruiting in recent years. This chapter describes the historical and geographical growth of such recruiting drawing attention to the national donors and to the state and college hosts.

Historical Trends

The numbers of foreign track-and-field athletes recruited to American universities and colleges grew slowly until the 1970s, peaked in the early eighties, and by the late eighties seemed to be static or even declining. This general pattern obscures a good deal of variation among and within individual conferences, and some colleges will never have recruited any foreign student-athletes.

Some foreign athletes competed for US colleges in the early years of the present century. In 1900, for example, Canadian George Orton attended the University of Pennsylvania and won a gold medal in the Olympic steeplechase.[1] A small number of Canadians also competed on the US track scene from the 1920s through the 1940s, though the extent to which they were recruited is uncertain. Former 400-meter world record holder Herb McKenley, from Jamaica, attended the University of Illinois in the mid-1940s, while Lloyd La Beach, a Panamanian sprinter who obtained a bronze medal at the 1948 London Olympics, attended UCLA, although he was ineligible to compete for the track team.

An indication of the number of superior foreign student-athletes in the United States in the 1950s (and subsequently) can be obtained by consulting the ranking lists published annually in *Track and Field*

News.[2] In the mid-fifties the number of foreign athletes totaled around twenty each year. Among the foreign athletes in US track at that time were George Rhoden of Morgan State and Les Laing of Fresno State, both from Jamaica, who competed successfully at the 1952 Olympics at Helsinki. In 1955 a Villanova University freshman named Ron Delaney was included in the rankings (see fig. 10). A year later he was to win a gold medal for Eire at the Melbourne Olympics. University of Iowa miler Rich Ferguson was in the rankings in that same year, having finished third in the previous year's "miracle mile" at the Vancouver Empire Games. In the late 1950s George Kerr of the University of Illinois and Jamaica was prominent on the collegiate circuit and was to become a medalist in the 800 meters at the 1960 Rome Olympics.

In 1955 only 4.4 percent of US ranked collegians in the *Track and Field News* rankings were foreigners. A decade later the respective figure was 6.8 percent and foreigners were starting to be noticed. Among them was Harry Jerome of Canada and Oregon, who won a bronze medal at the 1964 Olympics, and David Hemery of Britain and Boston University, who was to win gold and break the world 400-meter hurdles record at the Mexico City Olympics. Also in evidence were elite sprinters from the West Indies such as Lennox Miller of Jamaica and USC, and Edwin Roberts from Trinidad and North Carolina Central. Less well known was the fact that the Finnish winner of the European 10,000-meter championship in 1970, Juha Vaatänen, had briefly attended Adams State College in Colorado during the 1960s to benefit from altitude training.

Whereas in the fifties and sixties the overall impact of foreign student-athletes on NCAA championships was negligible, between 1971 and 1978 the number of appearances by foreign recruits in the annual NCAA championships increased by over 200 percent. By the mid-1970s it was widely felt that "the foreign influx [was] new enough and heavy enough to provide a major controversy."[3] From 1971 through 1978, foreign appearances in NCAA track championships totaled 959 out of 6,393, 15 percent of all appearances being by overseas recruits.[4] The growth of their influence is revealed by the fact that in 1971 their appearances represented 11.1 percent of the total while by 1978 the respective figure was 18.1 percent.[5] Whereas in 1970 there were two foreign winners of NCAA championships, by 1976 the figure had jumped to eight.

The feature of 1970s recruiting was the substantial number of African athletes who appeared on the US track scene. Among them were Henry Rono and Samson Kimobwa of Washington State and

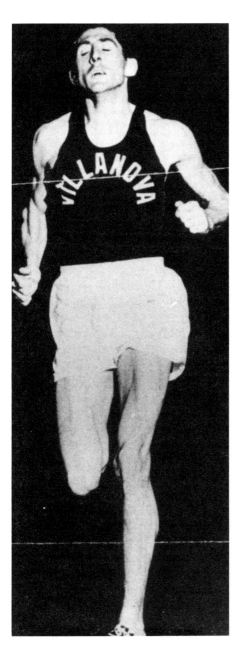

Figure 10. Among 1950s track recruits were Ron Delaney (left), Olympic 1,500-meter champion in 1956 and an early part of the trans-Atlantic talent pipeline between Eire and Villanova University. The 1960s were characterized by a growing migration of British athletes and the arrival of the first of the Kenyan recruits, such as Steve Machooka (right), who won IC4A and Heptagonal cross-country titles while at Cornell. (Source: *Track and Field News*)

Kenya, both of whom were to become world record holders. By the end of the 1970s and into the early eighties, the number of foreign recruits in the ranking lists was consistently around one hundred, and in 1985 13 percent of the collegians in the US rankings were from overseas.

Despite attempts to restrict the importation of alien student-athletes from the start of the 1980s, the foreign contribution does not seem to have been significantly affected. The overall number of foreigners in the ranking lists dipped to between sixty and seventy in the mid-1980s, but by 1986 it had risen to ninety-two, the sort of figure found a decade earlier. More significant, the impact of foreign athletes in the major championships was increasing. Such an impact can be dramatically illustrated by considering the effects of foreign student-athletes on the 1981 NCAA track and field championships. In the team competition the University of Texas at El Paso won with sixty-four points. If foreigners had been excluded and all else remained the same, their team score would have been twelve. The removal of foreign athletes from all teams would have resulted in significant differences in the results (table 16), UCLA rising from fourth to first and Arizona State moving from sixth to second. Whereas in the five-year period 1977-81 the average total number of points contributed by foreigners to the NCAA championships was 29.3 percent, the respective figure for the period 1982-86 was 33.3 percent, peaking in 1986 to an all-time high of 38.7 percent (table 17). It should be noted, also, that the peaking of the foreign contribution coincided with a downturn in the number of all track and field athletes in NCAA Division I institutions (fig. 11). In addition, foreigners were making a significant impact on track and field championships for NAIA institutions and for junior colleges (table 14).

Table 16. NCAA track-and-field championships, 1981. Team scores with and without foreign student-athletes; the top six teams.

Team results and points with foreign recruits		Team results and points without foreign recruits	
UTEP	64	UCLA	77
Brigham Young	43	Arizona State	42
Oregon	43	Oregon	41
UCLA	41	Tennessee	35
Southern Methodist	38	Kansas	28
Arizona State	34	Houston	26

Source: Track and Field News 34, no. 2, (1981): 66.

Table 17. Contribution of foreign student-athletes (men) to total points in NCAA track-and-field championships, 1977-86.

Year	Percent of total points
1977	29.9
1978	26.3
1979	29.3
1980	27.9
1981	33.3
1982	34.6
1983	36.0
1984	27.5
1985	29.7
1986	38.7

Source: Track and Field News 39, no. 8 (1986): 58.

In 1984, the year of the Los Angeles Olympics, student-athletes from overseas won many track-and-field medals for their countries. Among the gold medalists were Nawal El Moutawakel of Iowa State and Morocco who, in the absence of East European competition, won the women's 400-meter hurdles; Joaquim Cruz of Oregon and Brazil who won the 800; Julius Korir of Washington State and Kenya who took the steeplechase; and Ria Stalman of Arizona and the Netherlands who won the discus throw. At the World Championships in 1987 one of the outstanding winners was Abdi Bile (fig. 12) from Somalia, a student at George Mason University. The 1988 Seoul Olympics saw Paul Ereng of Virginia and Kenya winning the 800 while his countrymen Peter Rono of Mount St. Mary's College in Maryland took the 1,500 and Julius Kariuki, who studied at different times at Blinn Community College in Texas and Riverside Community College in California (see page 30), won the steeplechase. The foreign student-athletes' contribution to international track events should by now be obvious.

It is quite possible, of course, that the growth in the number of foreigners in the annual US ranking lists could be a reflection of falling standards in US track and field. This interpretation is rejected, however, since the increase in numbers up to the early 1980s would have been expected of a "free market" in the international movement of athletes which existed at that time. The slight decline in numbers in the eighties is also what would be expected given the overall decline in the number of student-athletes (page 45) and the developments in NCAA policy described in chapter 3.

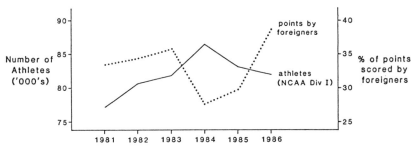

Figure 11. The number of track-and-field athletes in NCAA Division I schools was falling at the very time that the foreign contribution in NCAA championships started to peak. (Source of original data: NCAA and *Track and Field News*)

Geographical Patterns

The growth in the number of foreign track-and-field athletes in US colleges has been paralleled by a changing geographical distribution of the origins of such migrants. One tentative generalization that can be made about the changing geography of sports everywhere is that the spatial margins from which recruits are drawn have been widening over time (figs. 12-14). This widening might be viewed as illustrating the "internal dynamic" of achievement sports in which the spatial expression of their activities brings more and more of the world's population into a single global sports system.

This generalization applies classically to the collegiate recruiting scene. In the case of track and field, Canada was the major source of foreign recruits until the 1970s. As with swimming, half the Canadian track squad in the sixties attended US colleges and universities. Hence, the pattern for the 1950s and 1960s showed a modest flow of male student-athletes from Canada and Europe, with a smaller number from the Caribbean—regions geographically and/or culturally close to the United States. In 1955, for example, apart from four recruits from Sweden, all of the nineteen foreigners in the *Track and Field News* rankings had English as their native language. By the mid-1960s the flow of athletes had doubled but their geographic origins remained dominated by the traditional sources, although the West Indian contribution was growing. In 1965 Britain's contribution was still quite modest, but the presence of a small number of Africans—first from West Africa—hinted at things to come.

A more detailed breakdown of the changing geographical pattern of origins is shown in figures 13 and 14. It was the 1970s that witnessed

Figure 12. One of the truly world-class foreigners on the US college track scene in the late 1980s was Abdi Bile (left), shown here with decathlete Bob Muzzio. Running for Somalia, Bile won the 1987 world 1,500-meter championship. (Source: George Mason University Office of Sports Information)

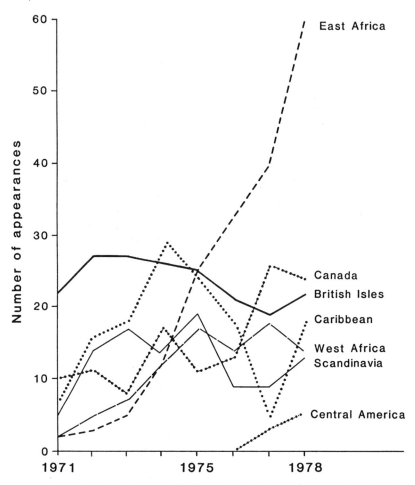

Figure 13. The athletic scramble for Africa in the 1970s: Graphs show the number of appearances by student-athletes from each region or country in NCAA championships, 1971-78. (Source of original data: Hollander, "A Geographical Analysis of Foreign Athletes")

the most fundamental change in recruiting patterns. Traditionally *terra incognita* as far as American college recruiting was concerned, Africa in 1960 accounted for only 7.9 percent of the total number of all superior college track-and-field athletes. In 1980 the respective figure was 32.6 percent. In 1971 Great Britain and Eire accounted for 32 percent of appearances by foreigners in NCAA (men's) championships, and the nations of East Africa accounted for 3 percent;

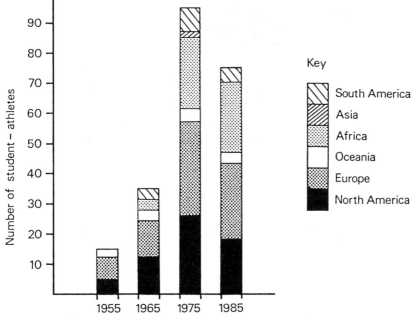

Figure 14. Numbers and continental origins of superior foreign track-and-field student-athletes. "Superior" athletes are those included in the annual *Track and Field News* ranking lists. (Source of data: *Track and Field News*)

the respective figures for 1978 were 13.5 percent and 35 percent (fig. 13). The West African contribution changed rather less dramatically during this period but nevertheless more than doubled in percentage terms, increasing from 3 percent in 1971 to 8 percent in 1978. Appearances by athletes from South America, southern Africa, and mainland Europe stayed stable in absolute terms but declined relatively, those by Europeans falling from 45 percent to 21 percent during this period.

The world geography of men student-athletes in track and field in the US college milieu for the thirteen-year period 1973-85 provides a more detailed case study. Using data from the annual *Track and Field News* rankings, the geographical variation in the pattern of origins of superior foreign recruits can be established. It is stressed that reference here is only to such superior athletes, i.e., those having achieved a sufficiently high standard to have been ranked in the US "top fifty" in any one year.

The global pattern of superior migrants is shown in figure 15. Over

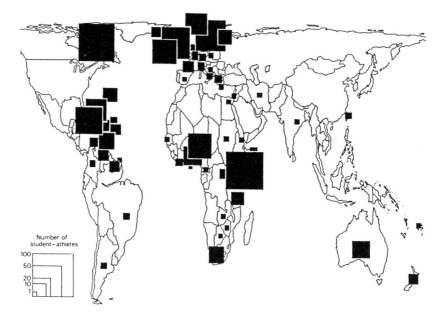

Figure 15. National origins of superior foreign student-athletes, 1973-85. (Source of data: *Track and Field News,* various issues)

a thirteen-year period the major flows of elite track-and-field talent came from Kenya (12.6 percent), Canada (12.2 percent), the United Kingdom (8.9 percent), and Sweden (8.4 percent).[6] Of such elite recruits, 60 percent came from seven countries (table 18). It will be obvious that colleges only recruit student-athletes who will be useful to them, and the absence of Kenyan discus throwers or Nigerian long-distance runners, for example, is clearly shown in the event-group specialties of particular nations (table 18). Of the Irish recruits, over 87 percent were middle- or long-distance runners; 86 percent of Jamaican and Kenyan recruits were sprinters and distance runners respectively; 78 percent of those from Sweden were throwers. The emphasis is placed on proven, not potential, talent, and the recruitment of athletes yet to prove their worth may be viewed as an unnecessary risk.

Using a somewhat different measure of long-term trends (i.e., NCAA championship appearances), we can see that a similar list of countries is dominant (table 19). Of the top ten nations, eight appear in both table 18 and table 19.

Seen here is a system of exploitation of geographically specific skills

Table 18. Major national donors of superior foreign track-and-field student-athletes (men), 1973-85 (n = 609).

Country	n	Percent	Event Groups*			
			S	D	J	T
Kenya	77	12.6	7	66	4	0
Canada	74	12.2	17	24	10	23
United Kingdom	54	8.9	3	41	2	8
Sweden	51	8.4	3	1	7	40
Jamaica	43	7.1	37	3	3	0
Nigeria	34	5.6	20	0	12	2
Eire	32	5.3	0	28	1	3
Norway	25	4.1	0	9	3	13
Ghana	18	3.0	9	0	9	0

* S-Sprints; D-Distances; J-Jumps; T-Throws

Source: Bale, "The International Recruiting Game," 190.

or a kind of international division of labor with different nations
"producing" different types of raw materials for the US collegiate
sports factories. Once upon a time the United States could satisfy its
college athletic requirements from within the confines of its national
boundaries; today the fragmentation of the source areas of recruits
is based on the variable nature of the available "raw material."

The above discussion described the long-term pattern, and it should
be remembered that at any particular time different countries may
assume different positions in the ranking of donors to the US college
track-and-field market. In 1987, for example, Canada was the major
donor, if the rosters of 109 NCAA Division I institutions are used as
a data base. Of 203 foreign track and field recruits in these institutions,
19.2 percent were Canadian—somewhat more than the long-term
percentage of elite recruits—and Eire was the second major supplier,
accounting for 13 percent (cf. table 19). The fact that only about 3.5
percent were from Kenya, however, reflects the declining number of
Kenyan athletes going to the United States since the mid-eighties.

The pattern of foreign student-athletes in track and field far from
mirrors the overall pattern of migration of all foreign students (i.e.,
including non-athletes) to the United States (see page 41). Most obviously, the contribution of Asia to the overall pattern is insignificant
in the geographical pattern of student-athletes in one sport.

The Kenyan Impact

Given its geographic proximity and cultural affinity, Canada might
logically be expected to be the major source of track talent for US

Table 19. NCAA foreign track-and-field athletes; championship appearances by countries, 1978 (n = 959).

Country	D	S	J	T	P	De	Total	Percent
Kenya	132	19	14	0	0	0	165	17.2
Canada	44	19	19	34	3	1	120	12.5
Eire	100	0	1	1	0	0	102	10.6
UK	81	2	0	5	0	0	88	9.2
Sweden	2	3	1	36	4	12	58	6.0
Jamaica	0	45	7	1	0	0	53	5.5
Nigeria	0	23	28	1	0	0	52	5.4
Australia	19	6	10	7	5	0	47	4.9
Trinidad	5	23	0	0	0	0	28	2.9

D-Distances; S-Sprints; J-Jumps; T-Throws; P-Pole Vault; De-Decathlon.

After Hollander, "Geographical Analysis of Foreign Athletes."

colleges and universities. As seen above and in chapter 3, this is indeed the case for many sports at the present time. In track and field for the period 1973-85, however, it was Kenya which was the principal source of elite foreign track talent for the campuses of America. Yet the recruiting of Kenyans did not really start until the mid-1970s (see table 20).

Kenya is widely regarded as one of the world's major track (though not field) powers and it is tempting to link this success with the training received by many of Kenya's brightest track talents in American colleges and universities. It is important to stress, however, that the recruiting of Kenyans *followed*, rather than initiated, Kenya's emergence as a world track power.

Track in Kenya had developed successfully long before the start of the American college recruiting boom. Figure 16 graphs the trends in the number of elite Kenyans going to US colleges and universities and the per capita output of world class Kenyan track athletes. The emergence of Kenyan track dates from the early 1950s and the inspired and uninhibited running of Kisii tribesman Nyandika Maiyoro at British championship events in London, at the 1954 Empire Games, and at the 1956 and 1960 Olympics. Maiyoro provided a role model for many of the great Kenyan runners of the mid- and late-1960s, athletes such as Kip Keino, Naftali Temu, Amos Biwott, and Ben Jipcho whose success was based on the foundations laid by British and Kenyan coaches in Kenya. Such progress continued into the seventies by which time Kenya was "producing" world-class athletes at more than six times the global per capita average. It was then that the US

Table 20. NCAA championship appearances by the ten principal foreign countries, 1971-78.

	Championship Appearances									
Country	1971	1972	1973	1974	1975	1976	1977	1978	Total	% of Total
Kenya	2	2	3	12	24	31	37	54	165	17.2
Canada	10	11	8	17	11	13	26	24	120	12.5
Eire	7	17	17	14	9	13	10	15	102	10.6
Great Britain	15	10	10	12	16	8	9	8	88	9.2
Sweden	2	8	10	11	9	7	4	7	58	6.0
Jamaica	6	12	11	11	5	4	0	4	53	5.5
Nigeria	1	2	4	6	10	7	12	10	52	5.4
Australia	5	5	4	5	6	3	11	8	47	4.9
Ghana	3	3	3	6	7	5	5	0	32	3.3
Trinidad	0	1	3	6	9	5	2	2	28	2.9

Twenty-eight other countries contributed at least one athlete.

Source: Hollander, "Geographical Analysis of Foreign Athletes," 22.

colleges responded with a latter-day scramble for Africa. A massive influx of Kenyan runners to American campuses followed. Some would argue that they were recruited in an almost ruthless manner. The assistant secretary of the Kenyan Amateur Athletics Association has been quoted as saying that "the American coaches want to take anyone who can run. Agents come over here and try to take schoolboys away from their homes before they are ready."[7] It is hardly surprising, therefore, that one cynical American observer has suggested that "recruiters go abroad on safaris, not recruiting trips."[8]

It is clear from figure 16 that Kenya's impact on the world track scene was in relative decline at the very time that the US colleges were recruiting Kenyan talent most vigorously, i.e., in the late 1970s. Subsequent decline in the relative standards of Kenyan track may have resulted, in part, from the exploitive and point-maximizing collegiate schedules to which athletes were sometimes exposed (see page 127), plus the seductive elements of the US money-oriented lifestyle with lucrative prizes from road races being more attractive than participating for one's country in the once-prestigious East African Games. Ben Jipcho, one of Kenya's greatest "home-produced" athletes, accused US-based Kenyans of putting money before patriotism,[9] and by the late 1970s there was talk of Kenya closing down its American connections. Kenyans were sensing the possibility of a diminishing number of home-based role models, and administrators responded by refusing to select foreign-based athletes for national squads.[10] This

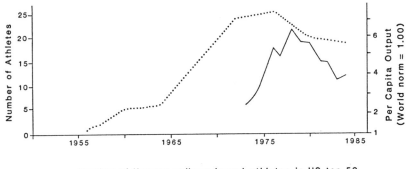

Number of Kenyan college-based athletes in US top 50

Per capita output of world class Kenyans. World norm = 1.00

Figure 16. The per capita production of world-class Kenyan track-and-field athletes (top graph) was declining just at the time the recruitment of elite Kenyans by US colleges was increasing most dramatically (lower graph). Whereas in 1976 Kenya was producing world-class athletes at over 6 times the global average level of production, by 1988 the respective index was 4.7.

tactic was subsequently dropped, the maximization of national prestige being impossible without the foreign-based stars.

Though it is dangerous to infer a causal relationship between the late-1970s decline in Kenya's position as a world track power and the increase in US importation of Kenyan talent, it is nevertheless clear that the so-called "Third World" countries do not necessarily improve their positions in the world sports pecking order if they rely solely on the United States to develop their athletes for them.

The relative decline in Kenya's world standing continued into the mid-eighties to the extent that the country again tried to impose some sort of control on US recruiting. The national track-and-field coach stated that efforts had been made to prepare athletes in Kenya and not to rely on results achieved in the United States.[11] New facilities were provided at home and Kenyan initiatives are now contributing to the emergence of women's track (see page 91). It remains to be seen whether the pattern of Kenyan migration of the past few decades is duplicated in the case of the nation's women athletes in the 1990s.

State and College Hosts

The spatial distribution of colleges that house foreign track recruits is neither regular nor random. Interstate variations in the numbers of foreigners recruited over a thirteen-year period (1973-85) are shown in figure 17. The pattern of states in which large numbers of overseas recruits attended school assumes the form of a broken arc extending from Texas to Washington, and four states—Texas, California, Washington, and Utah—together accounted for nearly 42 percent of the total number of elite recruits during this period. In the East, New Jersey (3 percent) and Tennessee and Kentucky (together accounting for 7.5 percent) were the main focuses.

Of course, the pattern described in figure 17 could simply be a reflection of the distribution of all student-athletes (or of all students) in the United States. After all, Texas and California are national leaders in the recruitment of foreign students per se. These two states are also hotbeds of enthusiasm for track and field, each producing over twice the national per capita average number of top-class high school track-and-field athletes.[12] But it is probably the location of particular campuses which provides the best clue to the overall pattern shown in figure 17. Many of the campuses (and states, in some cases) with an apparently disproportionate number of foreign track recruits happen to be places that most Americans find residentially undesirable.

Places like El Paso, Ames, Provo, or Pullman (towns in which major foreign-recruiting universities are found) have low levels of "imageability"[13] in the mind's eye of the homegrown student; they

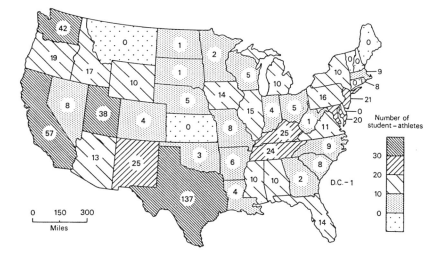

Figure 17. Destinations by state of superior foreign track-and-field recruits, 1973-85. (Source of data: *Track and Field News*, various issues)

are places that are perceived as having nothing to offer as residential environments. For example, John Chaplin, coach at Washington State University, who has been a major recruiter of foreign talent, has claimed that "it is difficult to recruit in places like Pullman, Washington."[14] Likewise, the coach at UTEP stated that "the competition for the American athlete is intense and we're way off in the desert where we can't impress the student with our facilities or campus. We can't compete [i.e., for homegrown talent] with UCLA or USC."[15]

It has been noted that "many colleges located in remote or sparsely populated regions have little to offer domestic athletes aesthetically,"[16] and the desert and mountain states clearly attract more track-and-field athletes than would be expected given their share of foreign students per se. Only when a foreign recruit arrives at places like El Paso or Provo does the nature of the locale become apparent and problems of adjustment begin (see chapter 6). Ted Banks, former coach at UTEP, summed up the situation in these words: "I can't get the top Americans here. . . . I couldn't believe there wasn't much greenery. You try and get a kid from anyplace but a desert area and they're not going to like it."[17] Foreign athletes, on the other hand, are less familiar with the regional geography of North America and might be more easily persuaded. Likewise, prominent US high school athletes prefer to go to schools that are well known nationwide. Coach Bob Teel of Missouri had a limited recruiting budget and a cinder track which he felt greatly hindered domestic recruiting; he therefore looked overseas for the less discriminating or less well informed foreigner.[18] Irish track star Ray Flynn, when asked why East Tennessee had so many foreign runners (see table 21), said that "American

Table 21. Foreign track-and-field athletes appearing in NCAA championships, 1971-78; leading college markets (n = 959).

College	1971	1972	1973	1974	1975	1976	1977	1978	Total	% of Total
Texas–El Paso	4	5	7	15	25	21	20	25	122	12.6
Washington St.	7	4	8	10	12	14	19	19	93	9.6
Brigham Young	9	7	11	10	12	4	11	5	69	7.1
W. Kentucky	1	4	3	5	13	5	7	1	39	4.1
East Tennessee	1	4	8	6	3	3	4	6	35	3.6
Villanova	8	7	2	5	3	2	1	4	32	3.3
New Mexico	1	3	2	1	2	4	7	12	32	3.3
So. California	4	7	4	2	3	3	4	3	30	3.1
So. Illinois	1	1	1	3	2	4	6	5	23	2.4

Source: Hollander, "A Geographical Analysis of Foreign Athletes," 43.

runners want to go . . . where the school is well known in the polls. The schools like East Tennessee get the second class of local athletes so they look elsewhere."[19]

From 1971 through 1978 over 26 percent of the foreign track-and-field athletes appearing in NCAA championships were enrolled in schools in the Western Athletic Conference, with another 18 percent found among the universities of the Pacific 8 Conference. Four universities, UTEP, BYU, Washington State, and Texas, accounted for 20 percent of the superior foreign recruits over a thirteen-year period (table 22) and three of these schools (UTEP, WSU, and BYU) accounted for over 29 percent of the appearances in NCAA championships for the afore-mentioned period. The campuses shown in table 22 frequently dom-inate state totals of elite foreigners and hence contribute to an expla-nation of the national pattern. Using the alternative measure of NCAA championship appearances during the 1970s, a similar pattern of cam-pus concentrations is revealed (table 21).

It must be stressed again, however, that for any single year the picture may be quite different from the long-term patterns shown in tables 21 and 22. For example, of 120 track and field rosters examined in 1987, the institution with the largest number of foreign recruits was Wayland Baptist University, an NAIA school in Texas, which had thirteen foreigners on its twenty-eight-man roster. This example il-lustrates not only the way in which a single year may fail to reflect long-term trends, but also the need to recognize the impact of schools outside the NCAA on the overall number of foreign recruits nation-wide.

But the recruitment of foreign athletes is far from inevitable and some coaches prefer a more literal interpretation of the term "All-

Table 22. Principal college destinations of superior foreign track-and-field athletes (men), 1973-85 (n = 656).

Institution	Number	Percent
University of Texas–El Paso	47	7.2
Brigham Young University	36	5.5
Washington State University	30	4.6
University of Texas, Austin	21	3.2
Iowa State University	14	2.1
University of Southern California	13	2.0
University of Western Kentucky	13	2.0
University of Oregon	13	2.0
Villanova University	12	1.8

Source: Bale, "The International Recruiting Game," 199.

American." The likelihood of winning at the highest level without foreign aid may, of course, be greater in universities located in hotbeds of high-school track production. UCLA may therefore possess a locational advantage over UTEP in this respect, though in the case of non-foreign track powers like Arizona State, Kansas, or Wisconsin (see page 70), coaches may adopt a more explicitly nationalistic ethic in avoiding overseas recruits.

International recruiting has had the effect of transforming the image of institutions, which might otherwise have been obscure, into nationally known contenders for sporting honors. In track the classic example is the University of Texas at El Paso. "Small and remote, without any great claim to academic distinction, except in geology, the school has found a source of pride and joy in the track team since it rose to prominence in the 1970s"[20] under former track coach Ted Banks. The success of UTEP hardly continued into the late 1980s following the slush-fund scandal associated with Banks's successor, Larry Heidebrecht, but the point to be made here is that the golden years of the late seventies and early eighties were founded on foreign talent. While UTEP may be the paradigm of foreign-built success turning an obscure school into a high-profile institution, other examples come readily to mind—New Mexico, Washington State, and Providence, for example. Even universities that can readily recruit Americans have, in certain cases, obviously enhanced their reputations with the help of foreign recruits.

Talent Pipelines

The range of countries from which particular institutions draw their foreign track talent is quite broad. Consider, for example, the situation in 1987 at four colleges. Figure 18 shows that two of these, Iona and Iowa State, each have a strong concentration from a single national source, Eire and the United Kingdom, respectively. Two other colleges, UTEP and Southern Methodist (SMU), have much more diversified sources of talent. In the cases of Iona and Iowa State the migratory flows can be termed "talent pipelines"—strong links between national sources and college destinations resulting in distinct lines of recruitment. Such pipelines can exist over prolonged periods of time, and this might be more typical since pipelines take time to develop (see chapter 5). For a thirteen-year period (1973-85), three major track universities typify different patterns of recruiting overseas talent. A wide variety of countries have been represented on the track and field teams of UTEP and Washington State (WSU). In the case

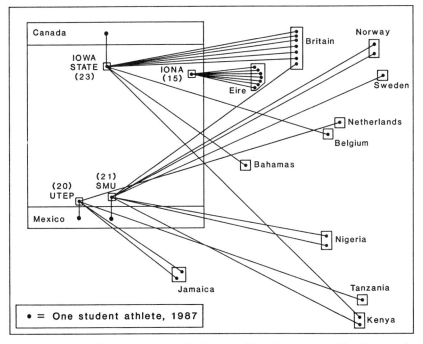

Figure 18. Pipelines and networks. Four colleges' sources of foreign track talent, 1987. Numbers in parentheses refer to the number of recruits from the United States. (Source: College rosters)

of Brigham Young, however, a very strong connection exists with Scandinavia (see table 23). Other universities with smaller numbers of elite student-athletes from overseas also seem to show clear national preferences. Seton Hall received 80 percent of its superior recruits from the Caribbean; nine of Oregon's thirteen foreigners were from Canada or Scandinavia, while seven of Western Kentucky's thirteen came from Britain. On the other hand, Fairleigh Dickinson had eight nations represented among ten foreign recruits, while USC had ten in its thirteen. The linkages making up talent pipelines may go back many years. Seton Hall's Caribbean connection goes back to the 1950s; Villanova's liking for Irish recruits dates back even longer. This theme is amplified in chapter 5, which gives specific examples of the ways in which such contacts were initiated.

Superior athletic talent from some particular nations seems to be concentrated in a small number of institutions. While Canadian talent is relatively well dispersed across America, elite Kenyan athletes have

Table 23. National elite contributions to track-and-field squads; four major recruiters of foreigners, 1973-85.

| | Superior foreigners | |
Country	n	Percent
Brigham Young		
Sweden	19	53
Finland	7	19
Norway	3	8
Mexico	2	5
Brazil	2	5

Argentina, Fiji, and Yugoslavia each provided one athlete.

University of Texas–El Paso		
Kenya	16	34
Sweden	5	11
Norway	5	11
Jamaica	3	6
Tanzania	3	6
United Kingdom	2	4
South Africa	2	4
Canada	2	4

Australia, The Bahamas, Botswana, France, Ghana, India, The Netherlands, New Zealand, and Trinidad each provided one athlete.

Washington State		
Kenya	9	30
Canada	4	13
Greece	3	10
Ivory Coast	2	7
German Federal Republic	2	7

Argentina, Cyprus, Eire, Ghana, New Zealand, Nigeria, Spain, Sweden, Surinam, and the United Kingdom each provided one athlete.

University of Texas, Austin		
Jamaica	7	33
Canada	4	19
Kenya	4	19
Iceland	2	9

Barbados, Guyana, Sweden, and Nigeria each provided one athlete.

tended to cluster on four campuses (fig. 19a). A similar pattern exists for athletes from Nigeria (fig. 19b) and from Eire (fig. 19d). Finnish talent is extremely concentrated at Brigham Young, while UK athletes seem to have focused on Kentucky-Tennessee (fig. 19c). These patterns of localization are the outcome of the long-term linkages which have already been touched on and will be explored further later.

Transfer Trends

The possibility of transferring between colleges is greater in the United States than in other countries, and foreign student-athletes share the opportunity of moving between colleges to enhance their athletic careers. Transfers of elite athletes seem to have taken place most frequently among African recruits. For a thirteen-year period, Kenyans alone accounted for 23 percent of transfers of elite foreigners, a figure which is over 10 percent more than would be expected given that country's share of the overall number of athletes recruited. Many such transfers were from junior colleges to four-year institutions.

Foreign athletes are sometimes enrolled first at two-year colleges to acquire basic language skills that will allow them to cope more easily with entry to four-year institutions. At a rather more sinister level, Ewald Nyquist has likened the "juco"-university nexus to an "incestuous" relationship whereby "sweetheart arrangements" are made to permit coaches to season athletes in easy courses so that they may transfer with acceptable grades.[21] Coaches may also be able to exceed the limit of their scholarships by placing extra athletes temporarily in junior colleges.

Transfer between colleges is not without further controversy. Julius Kariuki, a Kenyan who was to win the 1988 Olympic steeplechase, had always wanted to run in the United States, but in 1987, at the age of twenty-six, he was not eligible for an NCAA school. While attending the World Indoor Championships in Indianapolis that year, he started making enquiries about track scholarships and came to the attention of the coach at Blinn Community College in Texas. Kariuki subsequently joined the growing track program there. When he later went to Riverside Community College in California, there were accusations that he had been "stolen" by Ted Banks (formerly of UTEP fame), the track coach at Riverside, who had been tipped off about Kariuki's availability by a former Kenyan student-athlete of Banks from his days in El Paso. Investigations followed but Kariuki stayed on the West Coast.[22]

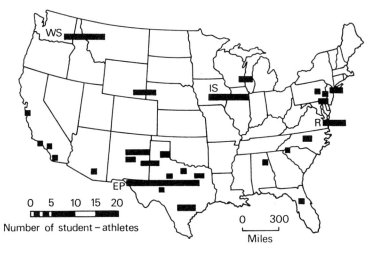

a. Superior track and field student-athletes from Kenya are found in Universities throughout the U.S.A. but "talent pipelines" have developed between Kenya and the University of Texas, El Paso (E.P.), Washington State University (W.S.), Iowa State University (I.S.) and the University of Richmond (R.).

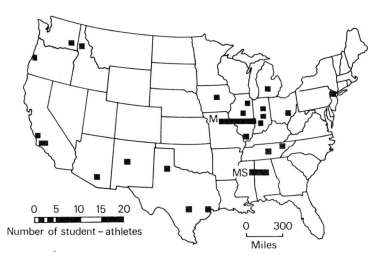

b. Track and field talent from Nigeria is concentrated at the University of Missouri (M.) and at Mississippi State University (M.S.).

Figure 19. Campus destinations of superior male track-and-field athletes from (a) Kenya, (b) Nigeria, (c) United Kingdom, and (d) Eire. The development of "talent pipelines" for the period 1973-85 is clear.

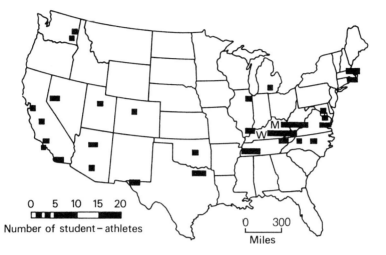

c. Destinations of superior male track and field student-athletes from the U.K. are widely distributed over the U.S.A. but "pipelines" have clearly developed at Western Kentucky University (W.) and at Murray State University (M.).

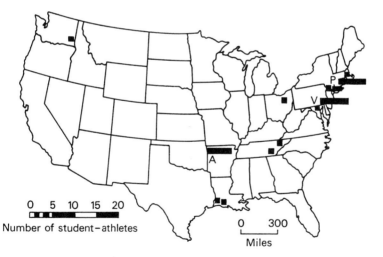

d. Superior track and field athletes from Eire are concentrated at Villanova University (V.), Providence University (P.) and at the University of Arkansas (A.).

Women Student-Athletes

This chapter has mainly focused so far on male student-athletes and, in fact, until relatively recently the recruitment of foreign sportswomen to American universities was almost nonexistent. This lack of visibility of foreign women recruits resulted from the traditionally inferior status of women's intercollegiate sports and the cheerleader role to which most women in college sports were relegated. Following the passage of Title IX of the Education Amendment Act of 1972, which provided for equality of funding irrespective of gender, funding for women's competitive sports increased.[23] In 1966-67 women accounted for 9 percent of all participants in NCAA intercollegiate sports; in 1985-86 the figure was 32 percent.[24] Track and field has grown in popularity as a women's sport. In 1981, 427 NCAA schools sponsored track and field, accounting for 9,217 athletes, whereas the respective figures for 1988 were 537 and 11,520.[25] With the increased participation and seriousness of women's track, the sport has gone along the same road as that of the men, and a steady flow of foreign recruits has accompanied the sport's expansion.

The foreign impact on the women's NCAA championships has been significant and is beginning to match the importance of foreigners at men's meets. In the 1988 NCAA women's cross-country championship, foreigners occupied the first five places (though the parents of the winner, Michelle Dekkers from South Africa, were US residents at the time).[26] The contribution of foreign recruits to women's track events has also been evident, though not yet as significant as the foreign contribution to men's championships. In 1986 five winners of the NCAA women's track championships were foreign and overseas recruits accounted for 28.5 percent of the total number of points (table 24). Among the most well known of the foreign women in college track in recent years have been Merlene Ottey of Jamaica and

Table 24. Contribution of foreign student-athletes (women) to total points in NCAA track-and-field championships, 1982-86.

Year	Percent of total points
1982	28.4
1983	25.8
1984	22.8
1985	21.9
1986	28.5

Source: Track and Field News 39, no. 8 (1986): 58.

Nebraska, and Liz McColgan from Scotland; McColgan attended the University of Alabama and gained a silver medal in the 1988 Olympics.

The geographical origins of 182 superior foreign women in college track and field for the period 1977-85 are strongly skewed toward Canada and the Caribbean, with Western Europe being the other major area of supply. Compared with the equivalent pattern for men (fig. 15), there are few recruits from Africa. Kenya, for example, supplied only 1.6 percent of the total for the nine-year period (fig. 20).

Such under-representation of Latin America and Africa can be explained in large part by the inferior status of women in those regions of the world.[27] In patriarchal societies women tend to be excluded from competitive sport; they are regarded as childbearers and house-wives, and teenage pregnancies are common. In addition, an attitude of overprotectiveness exists toward women, inhibiting their traveling abroad. Figure 20 is, therefore, virtually a surrogate for a map of women's status in the noncommunist world. But there are signs which suggest that the situation is changing. In the 1989 World Junior Cross

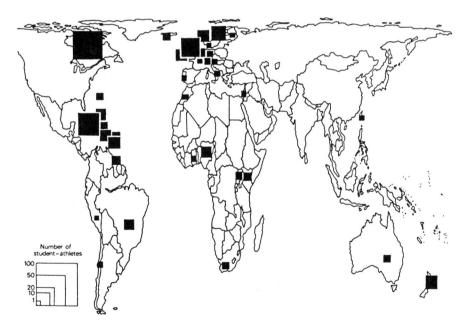

Figure 20. Global origins of superior women track-and-field athletes, 1977-85. Note the limited contribution of Africa, Latin America, and Asia. (Source of original data: *Track and Field News*)

Country Championship, Kenya won the women's title and three Kenyan runners were in the first five places. American college recruiters will find such "development" hard to resist.

The three main states of sojourn for elite foreign women recruits are Texas, California, and Tennessee, together accounting for 31.8 percent of destinations (fig. 21). Unlike the case of men's track the pattern of destinations for superior women foreigners is more geographically diversified. Tennessee State University and the University of Texas–El Paso each recruited 4.9 percent, Nebraska 4.4 percent, and San Diego State accounted for 3.3 percent. Whether the pattern shown in figure 21 will intensify and come to mirror that of the men remains to be seen.

A Note on Race

According to Harry Edwards, black athletes obtain less than 6 percent of the ten to twelve thousand athletic scholarships distributed annually in the USA.[28] Allowing for the fact that this is an average figure for all sports and that hardly any blacks take part in sports like gymnastics or swimming, the percentage of scholarships going to blacks in track and field could be between 10 percent and 20 percent. Although it is impossible to establish with accuracy the racial mix of athletic immigrants to US colleges, it can be inferred, given the national origins of foreign recruits discussed above, that about 45 percent of superior

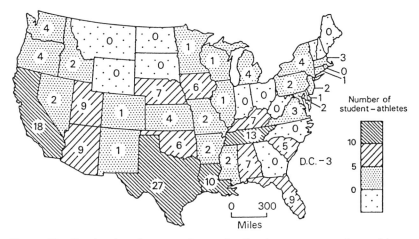

Figure 21. Destinations by state of superior foreign women student-athletes in track and field, 1977-85. (Source: *Track and Field News*)

foreign student-athletes in track and field for the period 1973-85 were black. This figure included a number of black athletes among Canadian and British recruits.

A figure of 45 percent is substantially *less* than that for blacks (including Asians) as a proportion of all foreign students in the United States (see table 5). It is substantially *more*, however, than would be expected if the proportion of sports scholarships going to American blacks were duplicated for foreign black recruits. Black athletes are over-represented among foreign student-athletes in track and field. Attention has been drawn to this subject because of the influence it might have on the experience of being a student-athlete from overseas, a subject considered in the next two chapters.

Conclusion

Several generalizations can be made about the recruitment of foreign track-and-field athletes to American universities. First, numbers of such recruits have increased steadily since the 1950s but at the present time seem to be stabilizing; second, foreign recruits make an impact on NCAA and other championship events that is substantially greater than their numbers alone would suggest; third, the spatial margins of overseas recruiting have expanded over time and whereas Canada was the traditional source, the world has now become the stage on which the recruiting game is played; fourth, colleges in somewhat inhospitable parts of the United States are the sojourn locations of a disproportionate number of foreign student-athletes, a response of these colleges to their inability to attract homegrown talent; and fifth, the patterns shown to exist for men are gradually being adopted by women recruits.

From the quantitative data in the last two chapters, we have obtained a broad perspective on the extent of overseas athletic recruiting. Whereas 90 percent of all foreign students in the USA come from the so-called "underdeveloped world,"[29] it is evident that the respective figure for student-athletes is far less. The major national donors of foreign students (table 5) are quite different from the donor nations supplying student-athletes, with the obvious exception of Canada. Such information is necessary to inform debate and discussion of the various issues surrounding international athletic recruiting.

III Experiences

There is a general consensus that life was not meant to be easy for persons in contact with members of other cultures.

Adrian Furnham and Stephen Bochner

FIVE

Recruiting Tactics
and the Migration Decision

College coaches and their representatives have engaged in nationwide searches for elite high school sports talent for well over half a century (page 16), and the previous chapters have described patterns resulting from the fact that increasingly, college athletic departments are making global searches for such talent. The coaches themselves are unable to scour the world, but they do manage to recruit from a large number of nations. This chapter considers the principal actors on the international recruiting stage, namely the coaches and the athletes. It explores coaches' attitudes and the ways they go about global recruiting; further, it makes an initial assessment of the athletes' backgrounds and the motives which lead them to make a decision to migrate.

The Coach's View

So far it has been suggested that the overseas recruiting game derives from the ideological bases of US college sports on the one hand, and from the achievement-sport ideology of potential recruits on the other. In part, the ideology is formed by the pressures placed upon members of university athletic departments to produce a winning team. Coaches do not deny that this is a major factor influencing the places from which they seek recruits. A Florida track-and-field coach, Roy Benson, said that "those who want desperately to win at all costs will go for foreigners."[1] Tom McLaughlin, track coach at Southern Methodist

University in Dallas, has reinforced this view in no uncertain terms. He said, "We emphasize going for quality athletes who can compete on a national level. So why should I restrict myself to the United States? My job is to win for our school, not develop US Olympic athletes."[2] Ted Banks, former track coach at UTEP, said that "a lot of people here want us to win naturally, and if we win with black Africans, or white, whatever, the bottom line is you win."[3] The track coach at Eastern Michigan University recruited foreign athletes for what he called "instant help," i.e., older, more experienced athletes who will immediately contribute to the team, hence reducing the risk of "investing" in eighteen-year-old high school graduates. It has been noted that "the main reason for instant help is often associated with personal prestige in having a winning program, although administrative pressure is another factor, especially at major universities."[4] A coach at Brigham Young University said that "the coach will try to get the best mileage possible out of his scholarships. So the foreign athlete will be in demand. . . ."[5]

The "instant help" model of foreign recruitment is graphically illustrated by the strategy used by the Clemson University soccer coach who built a NCAA soccer championship team out of foreign talent. Unable to recruit an American squad through both lack of money and playing credibility, he stated that "in essence we used our recruiting and scholarships to build a program American players would recognize and find attractive enough to play for."[6]

Vern Wolfe, head track coach at USC, has said that "in general, when you recruit in the United States you're looking for an athlete you can develop. If you're bringing in a foreign runner you look for someone who can help you right away."[7]

Not only is there pressure to win. There is also pressure to reduce costs. Although some coaches, such as Don McClimon of the University of Wisconsin, feel that the energy and cost expended in trying abortively to recruit foreigners could be better used on coaching native Americans,[8] paradoxically it is often the case that foreign recruits are actually cheaper than domestic talent. For example, the Brigham Young track coach has commented that the American recruiting system is simply too complicated and that he could get a quality athlete from abroad for the price of a few telephone calls and a postage stamp.[9] The head track coach at Western Kentucky University in Bowling Green felt that his small school simply could not compete with larger institutions in the domestic recruiting race. He noted: "I have a barely adequate recruiting budget. I can get a foreign athlete for maybe a $28 phone call. With a top American prospect I have to bring him in for a visit and write and phone repeatedly. I can wind up spending $300 or more on a guy and he might not come anyway."[10] Precisely the same point was made by the gymnastics coach at Northern Illinois University who remarked that "it's gonna cost $400 to $500 to recruit someone in this country whereas it only costs the mailing fees for outside the country. Foreigners know exactly what they want to do in school. They don't have six schools interested in them."[11] Although the latter comment is far from true in many cases, the relative ease and cheapness with which foreigners can be recruited should be obvious from such comments, especially as the cost of getting to the United States is invariably borne by the student-athlete, though it is not unknown for some to have their air fares paid for them.

It has also been suggested that for small schools some foreign student-athletes (notably those whose knowledge about the US higher education and sports system is somewhat limited) are cheaper to recruit because they are more appreciative of what is provided for them in situations which might be quite modest by American standards. They do not bid for the many commonly demanded "extras" (under-the-counter benefits such as cars or apartments) which the big schools could afford.[12] The early 1970s therefore saw many African students going to schools such as Howard Payne, Angelo State, North Carolina Central, and Eastern New Mexico.

Part of an athletic scholarship is made up of university tuition fees, which may be greater for out-of-state students. However, out-of-state tuition fees are waived in the case of foreign students in some states, making it less expensive to recruit foreigners than out-of-state student-athletes. For this reason some universities might adopt a recruiting strategy that initially favors in-state students, second, foreigners, and only third, Americans from a state other than that in which the university is located. Small colleges may recruit overseas because local talent may already be monopolized by institutions in major conferences. For example, unable to recruit the better basketball talent in the northeast because the Big East Conference colleges (such as Georgetown, Seton Hall, Pittsburgh and Syracuse) had achieved a monopoly on the best high school talent, Dave Magarity, coach at Marist College in Poughkeepsie, New York, chose the Netherlands as an alternate source. Having recruited Rik Smits (who made the NBA's all-rookie team as a player with the Indiana Pacers), he visited Holland in 1989 to successfully recruit another Dutch player and to establish contacts there.[13]

The greater expense needed to "Americanize" college sports squads is described by Clemson soccer coach I. M. Ibrahim:

In 1979, when we went to the national finals against Southern Il-
linois-Edwardsville, we had predominantly a foreign team. . . . For the
entire season only 2.3 percent of our goals were scored by American
players. At that time [Clemson] President Bill Atchley and I sat down
to discuss the situation. He asked me what it would take to Americanize
our program. I told him it would take money, because we would have
to travel and recruit. There weren't any soccer players in the vicinity
of our university, so we would have to make trips to St. Louis, Miami
and so on. President Atchley, with the help of [Athletic Director] Bill
McLellan and [Assistant AD] Bobby Robinson, decided towards that
move."[14]

The concern with cost minimization could be interpreted as a further
example of the "corporate athleticism" of college sports referred to
in chapter 2. With a world system of sporting activity, college athletic
departments are able to seek cheap "athletic labor" in favored political
regimes in order to ensure their continued viability.

Recruiting Tactics

The recruitment of foreign athletes by American universities assumes
a variety of forms. Although the scouring of the United States for
talent is a relatively systematized affair (see page 30) the recruitment
of foreigners is sometimes almost serendipitous. Recruiting systems
range from the well-planned network of contacts in a particular country to almost random events which cost the university nothing. Nevertheless, the number of students who eventually migrate to an American university is a small proportion of those approached. Don
McClimon suggests that for every foreign student-athlete who has
been to the United States there were probably fifteen who were sought
but for one reason or another couldn't make it.[15]

Essentially, recruiting involves persuasion and the familiarization
of potential recruits with their eventual destinations. Such information
tends to be transmitted to foreign student-athletes as a part of a
locational decision-making process. This can be conceived of as a
modified form (fig. 22) of the locational decision-making models developed by geographers researching the decision to migrate and the
subsequent adjustment to migration. Knowledge of opportunities in
the United States are preceded in the model by the necessary presence
of certain stress factors which lead athletes to evaluate the satisfaction
gained from continuing to live in their existing location. Internal
stressors (e.g., young peoples' expectations about their athletic futures)
or external ones (e.g., the characteristics of the academic or sporting

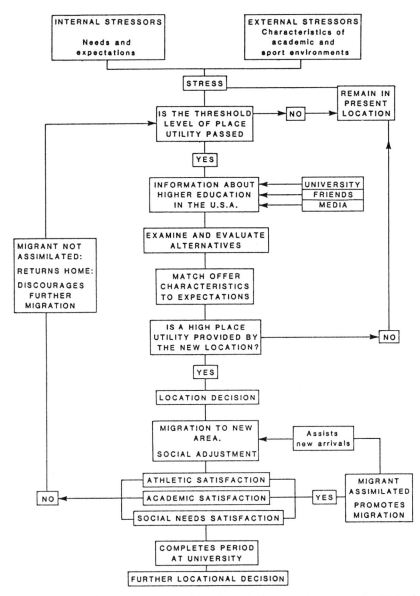

Figure 22. A foreign student-athlete's decision to migrate to the United States can be viewed as a locational decision-making model. The model involves students' responses to stressors which may push them beyond the level of place utility. An acceptable image of a new location leads to the decision to attend an American university. All this operates within the structures of achievement-sport and the US education system.

environment in which athletes find themselves) may work upon young people with high levels of achievement-orientation, as part of the sport ideology alluded to in chapter 1. An appreciation of the sport-achievement ideology therefore aids an understanding of why stresses may exist among foreign athletes and induce them to migrate to the United States. This ideological structure also acts as a reminder that such migration is not totally voluntary.

It is clear that stress factors are important in pushing athletes to decide to go to the United States. Some examples of the kind of stresses involved include lack of facilities, lack of time for training, or lack of coaching in their home countries. For example, although 18 percent of respondents to a survey of European swimmers and track-and-field athletes who had attended US colleges and universities claimed that the training facilities at home were "poor," only 13.9 percent perceived that they were "good"; however, as many thought domestic facilities were unsatisfactory as those who thought they were satisfactory.[16] Foreign student-athletes often complain about the ways in which the training facilities at home inhibit their sporting development. Consider, for example, the comments of Andrew Castle, Britain's best men's tennis player in the late eighties, who found that facilities for playing and training in his hometown were virtually nonexistent. In bemoaning the fate of British tennis players, one newspaper reported that "Castle had no indoor courts in Taunton to hone his skills during bad weather. The non-stop tennis offered by the Seminole Junior College in Florida and then by Wichita State University in Kansas was then the only way forward."[17]

Keith Connor, a European and Commonwealth triple jump champion while at SMU said: "When I'm here [in England] in the summer I can't get into a routine. I live twenty-five miles from Crystal Palace [national sports center in London]; if I want good weights facilities I have to go from Slough to Uxbridge and use them when everyone else is using them, and as I haven't got a car it means taking two buses. It takes me an hour and fifteen minutes to get there, work out, and another hour and fifteen minutes to get home."[18]

Prior to taking up a track scholarship at Northern Arizona University, British distance runner Richard Sliney "was working in London, commuting daily the twenty-five miles or so from Tonbridge, and trying to train for track, road and cross country."[19] In other words, it is not so much the lack of facilities but the lack of immediate access to them, often combined with the need to work full time, that creates the stress. Adrian Leek, a Welsh runner who enrolled at the University of East Tennessee, said that "in South Wales I have to make a forty-mile journey to get the sort of training I need."[20] The Dutch Olympic discus champion Ria Stalman, who attended the University of Arizona, perceived the need for better coaching. She said, "I was fed up with track in Holland. There are a few coaches who are somewhere between reasonable and good."[21] Lack of domestic competition may be another stress factor inducing athletes to look for athletic scholarships in the United States. Canadian high jumper Milt Ottey, a student-athlete at UTEP, commented, "There is a definite advantage in competing in the States. In Canada the competition isn't that stiff because there isn't enough depth."[22] Lack of status for a particular sport in a donor country may also induce migration. In Third World countries, gymnastics is a low-status sport with very limited opportunities for training and competition. Such stress factors place athletes at the threshhold level of place-utility. Beyond this level the place is not providing sufficient satisfaction (utility) to keep them there (see fig. 22). If this level is passed they may seek, or consider, information about life as a student-athlete in the United States from a number of possible sources.

Before considering these sources of information, we should note an additional factor which almost certainly attracts young people to the United States. The United States has a highly favorable image among young foreigners. Certain images are communicated globally by television, film, and print media and are received by millions of people, creating favorable attitudes. The United States, the source of McDonald's, Walt Disney, "Miami Vice," gridiron football, thousands of top-ten hits, electronic gadgetry, skyscrapers, Flo-Jo, Coca-Cola, and many more components of popular culture, is today the most significant cultural influence on the lives of many millions of people. "American English" is the most rapidly growing (developing?) form of the English language, Americanisms in large numbers being added annually to the Oxford dictionary. The pervasiveness of American culture leads many young people to see it as a goal, or at least something to be imitated at home. A holiday in Disney World is the prize coveted by thousands of people across the world. Indeed, the "American way of life" is one which we are sometimes led to believe should be the goal of all societies.

Ask average European teenagers which country in the world they would most like to visit and there is a good chance that they will give the United States as their number one choice. It has been shown that by the age of fourteen, students from a wide variety of countries would, if given the choice, "most like to be" American.[23] Likewise, people from different countries tend to feel friendly toward Americans as well as frequently viewing them as "progressive" and "practical."[24] "Go West, young man" is far from obsolete as advice provided to upwardly aspiring youth in almost any walk of life. America is viewed, correctly or incorrectly, as the land of opportunity, where hard work rather than pedigree and status is the source of success. The opportunity to succeed in sports is not excepted and for this reason a coveted lifestyle (perhaps only temporarily as a student-athlete) is worth grasping for many foreign recruits. If athletic scholarships were available in the Soviet Union or China, it would be interesting to see how acceptable they would be, compared with those in America. In other words, the positive, seductive image of America should not be underestimated as a factor influencing the decision of the foreign student-athlete to migrate to the perceived land of promise and adventure.

Generally speaking, students involved in choosing a university can gain information about potential locations from an information field made up of *direct* contact space,[25] i.e., that geographic area they can visit. It is possible for an American high school athlete to have an expenses-paid visit to any number of campuses of universities wishing to recruit them. For potential foreign student-athletes, however, their locational decision-making invariably involves an *indirect* contact field, information about which is obtained from secondary sources. In the context of international recruiting such contact with possible future sojourn environments is obtained from three possible principal sources, i.e., (1) direct contacts by representatives of universities or by friends who have been (or are) student-athletes in America; (2) advertising media; or (3) as a result of personal application. Each of these can be considered in turn.

Direct Contact

Most foreign recipients of athletic scholarships are initially approached by the head coach, an athlete, an alumnus or someone somehow associated with the institution in question. Some coaches believe it is crucial to have a network of contacts. Ted Banks, ex-track coach at the University of Texas, El Paso (as noted earlier, the major destination of elite foreign track and field talent), commented that "everybody likes good foreigners. It's just that other schools don't have the contacts . . . so there is bound to be some bitterness."[26] A mid-1980s survey found that 78.6 percent of those responding to a questionnaire distributed to foreign student-athletes in the United States had been contacted by the college they eventually attended.[27] In a survey of European track-and-field and swimming recruits, it was revealed that

51.6 percent had been approached by a representative of the university where they ultimately enrolled[28] (table 25).

The nature of these contacts varies from the carefully planned to almost chance events. Seen initially by a high-school basketball coach on a US-sponsored coaching clinic in Zaire, Dikembe Mutombo was recruited by Georgetown on the advice of the cultural affairs officer of the US embassy in Kinshasa following a tip-off from the coach.[29] The track coach at Eastern Michigan University explained that a "Caribbean connection" existed as a result of "one of his former athletes who, while serving with the Peace Corps in Trinidad, suggested to an athlete that he attend Eastern Michigan. After the first foreigner arrived, he talked another countryman into attending Eastern Michigan. Gradually the number of contacts grew to several Caribbean countries, and for several years [there was] a consistent flow of West Indians to the school."[30]

Contacts are built up in a number of ways. Colorado University coach Don Meyers had the Ghanaian sprinter George Daniels as his first foreign recruit. Meyers commented, "Bill Toomey, the former Olympic decathlon champion, met him on a trip to Ghana and since Bill is a Colorado graduate, he told me."[31] Daniels passed the news about Colorado on to other Ghanaian athletes. Nigerian basketball player Akeem Abdul Olajuwan, the University of Houston center who dominated much of the 1983 NCAA tournament, arrived in Texas as a result of contacts with the State Department in Africa.[32] British swimmer Debbie Rudd, on the other hand, was recruited by USC on the advice of her English coach, who had US contacts.[33]

Washington State University has housed many foreign track-and-field athletes over the years and illustrates how the recruitment of foreign sports talent is no exception to the fact that "the role of

Table 25. Nature of recruitment of European student-athletes (n = 93).

Nature of recruitment	Number	Percent
Approached by a representative of the university	48	51.6
Found out from friends or contacts who had been there	37	39.7
Answered an advertisement	6	6.4
Other	8	8.6

Note: Totals do not add up to 100% because some respondents included two answers.

Source: Bale, "Alien Student-Athletes," 83.

friends and relatives as suppliers of information about places is important for migration at all scales."[34] The "friends-of-friends" syndrome plus a somewhat random element is shown by the way John Chaplin, the WSU track coach, recruited Kenyan distance runner John Ngeno and, subsequently, the great Henry Rono: "Professor Ngeno (no relation), an instructor at the University of Puget Sound, went to the coach at the University of Washington and told the coach he had a brother, Kip, who had run 14 flat for the high hurdles. He also said Kip had a friend who was a 13:16 three miler. Apparently the coach didn't believe the story. When Professor Ngeno contacted me, I didn't believe it either, but I figured it was worth the price of a stamp. So I wrote a letter and they both came. Can you believe it? A great hurdler and an NCAA champion for 10¢."[35] The Ngenos subsequently told Henry Rono, one of the world's greatest long-distance runners, about WSU and he was enrolled there for a number of years.

Less-well-known schools have recruited in the same way. Take the case of Kankakee Community College in Illinois. Basketball coach Denny Lehnus heard about Nigerian Andy Kpedi from another coach. He sent a letter to Nigeria, forgot about it, and was later astonished to receive a phone call from Kpedi to say he was coming. The fact that his recruiting budget was less than $500 (with most of that coming out of his own pocket) also made Kpedi his cheapest-ever recruit.[36]

Various international games and sports gatherings provide contact between US coaches and potential recruits. The system is typified by the case of two Israeli basketball players who were spotted by the George Washington University associate coach while he was assistant US coach at the Maccabiah Games. He recommended them to the GW coach who then offered them scholarships. The Olympic Games are a fertile seedbed for the cultivation of contacts with foreign athletes by US college coaches. Among the earliest Kenyans to come to US athletic departments were Robert Ouko and Julius Sang, both of whom enrolled at North Carolina Central. They first met Leroy Walker of NCCU at the Mexico Games of 1968. Walker "iced the deal on a visit to Kenya in 1971 while he was busy organizing the first US-Africa track meet."[37] He visited both runners at home and aided them in getting leave of absence from their duties in the Kenya Prisons Service.

An Irish connection with Villanova University began as long ago as 1948 when two Villanova students met Irish athlete James Reardon at the London Olympic Games.[38] As a result Reardon was persuaded to become a Villanova student; the Irish connection with the Villanova running tradition was subsequently enhanced to the extent that today there is what amounts to a transatlantic talent pipeline between Ireland and suburban Philadelphia (fig. 19d). It can be virtually guaranteed that at least one Irish athlete will be on the Villanova track team each year. As former world 5,000-meter champion Eamon Coghlan commented, "I didn't hesitate a moment to go. It's the dream of every Irish runner to follow in the footsteps of all the great Irish runners from Villanova."[39] Famed Villanova track coach Jumbo Elliott stated that "we have a recruiting policy developed over a period of more than forty years. By now most of the kinks have been worked out of the system"[40] The Irish element would have to be included as an integral part of that system.

The friends-of-friends network extends well into the so-called Third World. Abdi Bile Abdi (world 1500-meter champion in 1987) from Somalia was recruited to George Mason University by coach John Cook "unseen on the advice of a Somalian runner at Fairleigh Dickinson University" in nearby New Jersey.[41] Bile later recruited two other Somalian athletes to the university. Brigham Young University, the second most significant importer of elite foreign track talent after UTEP, not only admits to benefitting from the friends-of-friends syndrome (with many BYU alumni being coaches abroad) but also to the fact that the university track team tours every three years and has the university missionary program which brings student-athletes into contact with potential future colleagues.[42] Baptist missions overseas can act in exactly the same way.

Despite the friends-of-friends networks, it is still possible that foreign student-athletes' resulting knowledge of the system they are entering is extremely limited. In the case of Nigerian 400-meter runner Innocent Egbunike, for example, his parents insisted that if he went to the United States he would have to go to a Christian college. He got the address of a small Californian NAIA school, Azusa Pacific University, from a friend's minister father and wrote to the university without even knowing if it had a track coach or not. He decided to go there even though it offered less than a full scholarship.[43]

Contact may not be direct—an athletic intermediary may inform the athlete of the nature of sport in an American university. Friends who have attended the institution pass on information to others. Table 25 shows that nearly 40 percent of European student-athletes found out about the institution they finally attended from friends or contacts who had been there. Nick Rose, an English long-distance runner who attended Western Kentucky University, said that he acted "as a sort of agent for juniors going to the States on scholarships."[44]

Advertising Abroad

The most publicly visible form of overseas recruiting is in the placing of advertisements in foreign sports magazines. These stress greatly the availability of scholarships for quality athletes and, at the same time, often try to "sell" the academic quality of the institution and its environment. Advertising for foreign student-athletes in this way, however, would appear to constitute a flagrant breach of NCAA rules. The NCAA *Manual* unambiguously states that "the publication of advertising or promotional material . . . designed to solicit the enrollment of prospective student-athletes is a form of recruiting not permitted by the Association." While the purchase of advertising space is prohibited, it has clearly not stopped many institutions placing ads in foreign sports magazines. Those shown in figure 23 are typical of the genre that has appeared in the British track magazine *Athletics Weekly* regularly over the years. Some athletes are undoubtedly recruited in this way, although as table 25 shows, the number so recruited may not be very large compared with that contacted personally. Superior athletes will not need to respond to an advertisement; they will invariably have been approached directly by the institutions.

The idea of the agent or intermediary in the recruiting process has been taken a stage further in Britain by the establishment of the so-called Sports Scholarship Foundation (SSF), which by advertising in the press aims to set potential student-athletes up with US coaches face to face, offer advice and information, and negotiate scholarship arrangements when one is offered. Although the SSF claims to be a nonprofit organization, it provides a costly service; moreover, its claims are on the one hand spurious and on the other simply incorrect. Preliminary information about the nature of athletic scholarships and the US higher education system costs (in 1989) £2.99 (about $5.00). If a potential student-athlete then decides to "apply to register" with the SSF it will cost £75 (about $127) plus a further £125 (about $212) payable prior to a two-day residential event in London where skills can be displayed to visiting coaches and seminars are held with prospective applicants. For sports other than those covered by the SSF, it will cost up to £500 (about $850) for personal telephone contact to be made with, and information about prospective student-athletes to be sent to, between five and fifteen American universities and colleges.

The SSF claims only a 30 percent "success rate" in placing students. In its documentation SSF prints only students' comments which praise the US system and states that four-year colleges and universities "are equivalent to a British university or polytechnic," despite the well-

Figure 23. Advertising for athletes. These kinds of advertisements appeared in the British track magazine *Athletics Weekly* in the 1980s.

known evidence to the contrary in terms of the value of an undergraduate degree. In explaining why US universities want to recruit
abroad, the SSF's brochure claims that the "sports coach is interested
in building a strong team at his/her school, while at the same time
ensuring that the athlete receives a good education. . . ." No mention
is made of the "payment by results" syndrome which pervades much
of US college sports. It hardly needs adding that information provided
by agencies such as the SSF could be obtained for a minute fraction
of its costs if prospective student-athletes contacted a range of US
universities themselves and discussed the prospects and problems with
a well-informed coach.

Student Applications

In a relatively small number of cases (fewer than 10 percent; see table
25), students apply direct to a university without having been approached or having seen scholarships advertised. David Hemery, then
track coach at Boston University, commented that he did not actively
pursue recruiting. "Most of the British athletes that went to Boston
University (people like Bob and Sharon Danville) arrived as a result
of word-of-mouth contact. If an athlete chooses to write a letter to
me that expresses an interest, it's not pulling them out of a country."[45]
Applications could result from students having traveled in the United
States. However, one survey revealed that only 2 percent of those
European athletes questioned had ever visited the States prior to
taking up a scholarship.[46] A lower figure would likely result if African
and Asian student-athletes had been included.

A problem with direct applications from overseas is that, given the
geographic distance between home and host institution, cheating during the application process is more likely to be successful than with
American applicants or those who have been directly approached by
an institution on the basis of known athletic ability. The problem of
cheating by student applicants is addressed later in this chapter.

While few student-athletes are awarded scholarships by their own
countries to attend US universities, such a practice was not unknown
in some African countries—until they realized that they were paying
out grants to athletes (instead of students) who were often attending
institutions that, the home country subsequently discovered, did not
award "acceptable" degrees. In other cases a small number of foreign
students who successfully apply to universities in America in order to
benefit from the athletic facilities may pay (at least part of) their own
way or borrow funds from family, friends, and neighbors.

Motives for Migration and the Locational Choice

Although stresses related to sport are undeniably important, the attraction of America lies not only in the perceived facilities and better athletic competition. The motives influencing the migration of foreign track-and-field athletes do not entirely confirm the somewhat stereotypical view that foreign student-athletes are solely concerned with improving their athletics at the expense of their academic work. "Education" as a motive for visiting America was described by 74.5 percent of respondents to Tom Hollander's survey as being "very important," whereas the respective figure for "increased competition" was 49 percent (table 26). A typical comment was made by Paul Causey, who attended Oklahoma Baptist University as a freshman in 1987 at the age of twenty. He said: "I want to get my degree here and then get a coaching job in the United States. I came over here because I wanted to further my education and I also wanted to run. In England you can do one or the other but not both."[47] The educational motive may be greater for participants in some sports than in others. For example, in soccer, it is hardly likely that European or Latin American recruits would attend US colleges and universities to hone finely their soccer skills, given the many opportunities at club level, and the much higher standards in the game, in their home countries. However, while the quest for soccer of the highest quality would be undertaken at home, the search for education may be better satisfied in the United States. Hardly any Latin American or European soccer internationals have ever attended college in the United States. The same cannot be said in the case of track, swimming, golf, basketball, and other sports.

The education motive may also be significantly stronger among students from "Third World" countries than those from Europe or Canada. Higher education in the Caribbean and in Africa, for ex-

Table 26. Importance of migration variables for NCAA foreign track-and-field athletes.

Migration Variable	Very Important %	Some Importance %	Not Significant %	No Response %
Education	74.5	13.3	11.2	1.0
Athletic Scholarship	59.8	28.7	11.5	0.0
Increased Competition	49.0	30.6	12.2	8.2
Cultural Experience	17.3	41.8	24.5	16.3
Climatic Factors	17.3	23.5	40.8	18.4

Source: Hollander, "A Geographical Analysis of Foreign Athletes," 77.

ample, is restricted to a small number of institutions, and the chance of higher education in the United States may be very attractive for students who, in the normal course of events, would be denied such an opportunity. Such students perceive any degree as being better than no degree at all. But even in much of the Western world the opportunities for higher education are simply not available to the extent found in the United States. As Phil Banning, a British recruit to Villanova in the 1970s, put it, "the scholarships give us less brainy chaps a chance to have a go at further study and a fair amount of time for training."[48]

The availability of the athletic scholarship—something virtually unknown outside the US—is therefore crucial. The extent to which it is *more* important to foreigners than to Americans seems problematic, however. In response to a question asking how important an athletic scholarship was to the chance of gaining an education, 90 percent of a sample of US student-athletes claimed that it was of importance, whereas for a sample of foreign recruits the respective figure was 100 percent. Responses to a question concerning the importance of the athletic scholarship to gaining athletic training and experience were 85.7 percent and 92.1 percent respectively (table 27).[49] Although differences between US and foreign student-athletes were not found to be statistically significant, the figures may at least suggest that an athletic scholarship is of greater importance to foreigners. And the fact that 88.5 percent (table 26) of respondents to Hollander's research claimed the athletic scholarship to be of importance underscores the unquestionable significance of sport per se.[50] Indeed, a number of student-athletes attend American universities

Table 27. Importance of an athletic scholarship to (A) chance of gaining an education and (B) gaining athletic training and experience for American and foreign track-and-field athletes in US universities.

| | A Respondents | | | | B Respondents | | | |
| | American | | Foreign | | American | | Foreign | |
	n	Percent	n	Percent	n	Percent	n	Percent
Very important	16	76.2	28	73.7	13	61.9	28	73.7
Somewhat important	3	14.3	10	26.3	5	23.8	7	18.4
Not too important	2	9.5	0	0	3	14.3	2	5.3
Of no importance	0	0	0	0	0	0	1	2.6
Total	21	100.0	38	100.0	21	100.0	38	100.0

After Stidwill, *Motives for Track-and-Field Competition.*

with no intention of earning a degree and simply use the period of sojourn as a means of using the athletic facilities and competition found there. A recent graphic example is that of Andrew Glaze, an outstanding Australian member of Seton Hall's 1989 NCAA basketball championship final squad who admitted that, as a twenty-four-year-old, he had come to America for one year just to play basketball.[51]

For foreign recruits who can subsequently cash in on their sports success, an economic motive for coming to the United States will clearly exist. Such motives seem to be rarely expressed explicitly. One student-athlete who has commented to this effect is Kenyan long-distance runner Geoffrey Koech, who claimed that the reason so many Kenyan athletes have gone to the States is basically economic. He added, "Running gives us prestige and a lifestyle that we wouldn't otherwise have."[52]

The amount of information about alternate possible locations in the United States will, in large part, derive from the number of overtures and offers made to the potential recruit. The number of scholarship offers varies considerably in accordance with student-athletes' abilities. A young Olympic gold medalist with some years of athletic eligibility could attract the interest of thirty or more institutions, but generally the figure is much lower, between one and six being the most common number of offers. For European student-athletes the average number of scholarship offers appears to be 3.4 though the modal number is 1 (fig. 24). When more than one offer is made, the student-athlete is faced with selecting among alternate offers of scholarships.

Factors involved in the locational choice are shown in table 28. Two factors seem to dominate, though neither of these may be necessarily the most important for individual athletes. The most frequently cited factor appears to be climatic or similar locational characteristics, warm weather being the most desirable. A West Coast or Southern location is frequently mentioned, and the advantages of Mediterranean or subtropical climates for most sports barely need laboring. Though not particularly important at the point at which the decision to migrate is made, this factor assumes considerable importance when the actual selection of a particular university is involved. If a sufficiently positive image is projected by more than one institution, an evaluation of alternatives has to be made before a location decision is reached. This may have to be done by a substantial number of foreign recruits, i.e., those who receive more than one offer of a scholarship (fig. 24).

The second most frequently cited factor, mentioned by 47.1 per-

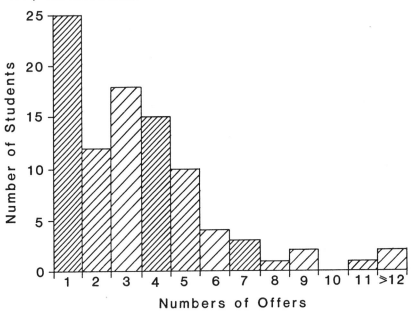

Figure 24. The number of athletic scholarship offers made to a sample of European student athletes (n = 93). (Source: Bale, "Alien Student-Athletes")

cent, reinforces the significance of the "friends-of-friends" syndrome discussed earlier. Nearly half the respondents said the fact that friends or compatriots were at the institution of their choice was important as a locational consideration. Having friends or compatriots at an institution reduces the risk of moving into a *totally* alien milieu and lowers the chance of loneliness and homesickness. From the perspective of the athletic department the presence of compatriots means the new student-athlete will be better adjusted and will more readily fit into a training regimen.

The nature of the scholarship, cited by 38 percent of the respondents, basically referred to the amount of money being offered. In most but not quite all cases, the best financial offer was crucial. Differing academic reputations as well as the perceived sporting facilities and the sporting reputation of the college were other frequently cited factors influencing final locational choice. The influence of the coach as a location factor was cited by about one-third of respondents. This is worthy of elaboration since it was not so much the coach's reputation which was thought to be important but his (or her) apparent ability to exert an element of persuasion; the coach is seen as the one human point of contact between the university and the prospective student.

Table 28. Factors influencing choice of university by European student-athletes receiving more than one scholarship offer (n = 68).

Location factor	Number citing factor	Percent
Climate and weather	38	55.9
Presence of compatriots or friends	32	47.1
Nature of scholarship	26	38.2
Academic reputation	25	36.8
Sporting facilities	23	33.8
Influence of coach	22	32.3
Sporting reputation	22	32.3
Competitive program	9	13.2
Others	17	25.0

Source: Author's research.

Consider, for example, the following student responses to my question why they selected the college of their choice (italics added):

"the coach was *constantly* phoning me and *seemed* nice";

"mainly because the coach came over from America to explain all about the university and the benefits to me";

"the coach at the college was very enthusiastic";

"coach telephoned two to three times a week";

"coach *appeared* a reasonable person";

"the track coach was obviously keen on me without being pushy";

"the coach *seemed* sound but as it turned out was a _____";

"although approached by other US colleges, _____ State was the *most persistent* and their senior coach convinced me."

The coach can also be instrumental in making promises that often transcend the bounds of legality. Gestures of generosity such as providing a flight to the States from Europe, housing for a student-athlete and spouse, and a car are not restricted to American-born football or basketball blue-chippers. These inducements are also used to influence foreign recruits—even those to JCs, in some cases.

By whatever means student-athletes are recruited from overseas, it is evident from a number of sources that dubious practices on the part of the athletic coach are not unknown. Students may only become aware of recruiting irregularities or broken promises when they actually get to the United States. All foreign students (including athletes) wanting visas to enter America must have a I-20A immigration form which they turn in when they arrive. The form includes a statement of what they will study, how their educational costs will be met, and, if there is more than one source of finance, what each source amounts to.

If a foreign recruit is informed that he or she will be on a full scholarship, it will be entered on the I-20A form. If upon arrival at the campus the athlete finds that the coach has reneged on the full-scholarship offer and instead states that only a partial scholarship is available, the athlete is placed in a difficult financial situation. The NCAA line on this possibly unpleasant start to the sojourn experience is that the athlete is entitled to full aid if his or her I-20A reflects full aid, but violations of agreements by the college are a matter for immigration, not the NCAA. Immigration officials rarely penalize offenders, however, because of the high level of bureaucracy involved. Examples of differing perceptions by athlete and coach on what has, in fact, been offered are considered further in chapter 6.

Whether the locational decisions which student-athletes make can be considered optimal or not is dependent in part on the amount of information available and their ability to use this information.[53] Operationalizing these terms in the present context is difficult. However, given the limited number of offers made to many student-athletes it could be argued that they possess an extremely limited amount of information about the system they are entering. Because student-athletes may be trying to achieve multiple goals (education, athletic performance, excitement, and travel, to name a few) it is difficult to arrive at any criteria which could define optimality. It may be more worthwhile to concentrate on the experience—athletic, educational, and social—which students obtain. This forms the bulk of chapters 6 and 7.

The Educational Background of Foreign Student-Athletes

The "dumb jock" image of the student-athlete dies hard. We have already seen in chapter 2 that for many American student-athletes, lower than normal academic achievement has been common at both the high school and college levels. But what of foreign student-athletes? A number of indicators suggest that foreign recruits are brighter than their US peers. Three main indicators can be used to establish academic competence; first, the quality of high school certification; second, the extent to which foreign recruits intended to enter university in their own countries; and third, whether or not they obtained their bachelor's degrees during their period of athletic eligibility. The first will be examined in this chapter and the others discussed later.

A distinction needs to be drawn immediately between student-athletes from, say, Canada and Europe and those from countries of the Third World. In the latter cases, levels of secondary and tertiary education are much lower than in Europe and comparisons between each group of countries would be meaningless. However, evidence collected from British student-athletes suggests that they are far from dumb. At the age of sixteen students in British high schools have traditionally taken examinations in a number of school subjects, usually about eight or nine. These examinations are called "Ordinary Level" and if students pass in five or six subjects they are considered fit to proceed to "Advanced Level" courses in three or four subjects, examinations in which are taken at eighteen years of age. It is the level of success in these examinations which determines students' chances of proceeding to higher education.

It should be recalled that the NCAA recognizes five "O"-level passes as minimal British academic qualifications which are commensurate with the GPA 2.0 rule (page 24). A sample of British athletes who had attended US universities showed that, on average, they possessed higher than this minimal standard (table 29), the average number of passes being 6.5. Indeed, over 80 percent had obtained five or more passes. What is more, as many as 61 percent of the British student-athletes had obtained at least one "A"-level pass, the average number of such passes being 1.5.[54]

The same research revealed that of ninety-three Europeans who had been student-athletes in the United States, about half had been sufficiently serious about undertaking study to apply to institutions of higher education in their own countries. In a small number of cases, students had rejected places at university in favor of an American offer while in others students had returned to universities in their own countries following sojourn in America. These kinds of findings suggest strongly that academically able students *are* found among foreign student-athletes. Indeed, there is a strong suggestion that many will be academically superior to their American peers.

Table 29. Academic background of British student-athletes (n = 81).

	Mean	Median	Mode
Number of "O"-level passes	6.5	7	7
Number of "A"-level passes	1.5	1	0

Source: Author's research.

For foreign student-athletes with modest educational qualifications, the problem of finding courses to follow in higher education in their own country could act as a further factor in their evaluation of existing place utility. In Kenya and Jamaica together there are only five universities. The American higher education system simply opens its doors to a larger percentage of the academic ability range than many others; it gives far more people the *chance* to work for a degree.

Although non-English-speaking students form a sizable minority of foreign student-athletes, those from, say, Scandinavia and Germany generally have a sufficiently high level of proficiency in the English language to enable them to satisfy university entry requirements, though it is not unknown for some Europeans to arrive unable to speak or understand English. For those with limited competence in English, pre-entry problems can result. For example, Brazilian Olympic 800-meter champion Joaquim Cruz found it necessary on transferring from Brigham Young to the University of Oregon to take the latter institution's English admission test four times before passing.[55] (This alone seems to say something about BYU's admission procedure.)

The average age of foreign student-athletes seems to be different from their US peers. The latter invariably enter college at the age of eighteen, direct from high school. One survey of European recruits, however, showed the average age of entry into American higher education was 19.23 (though for swimmers it was over a year younger than for track-and-field athletes — 18.25 and 19.85 respectively).[56] In relatively few cases were student-athletes over twenty-five at their time of enrollment, though in the late 1950s and early 1960s much older student-athletes were not uncommonly recruited from overseas. (Fred Norris, a British distance runner, enrolled at McNeese State University at the age of thirty-nine — some years older than his coach!) Older athletes have entered NCAA schools despite the traditional overage legislation mentioned in chapter 3. One example was that of former world mile record-holder Filbert Bayi of Tanzania. Because he had been in the Tanzanian army since the age of eighteen he was able to enter the University of Oklahoma in 1982 at the age of twenty-nine under the "military clause."[57] Foreign student-athletes entering university a little later, on average, than their US counterparts have often been fully employed between leaving secondary school and starting at a university. Over one-third of a sample of European student migrants had been employed prior to enrollment at a university in the States. The nature of such employment varied considerably, but the most frequently held jobs were clerical, office, and skilled manual work.[58] Another survey indicated a further characteristic of foreign recruits, i.e., that exposure to national or international athletic competition was more common among them than among US track-and-field athletes, in part a result of age differences.[59]

Exploitation by Athletes?

In chapter 2 it was suggested that the recruitment of foreign student-athletes could be considered a form of exploitation. It should be stressed, however, that athletes are not passive pawns at the total mercy of the structures in which they operate. The significance of human agency is seriously underestimated in such interpretations as those that present the university—or at least the athletic department—as exploitive. There is growing evidence that during the process of applying to universities in the United States, it is the foreign athletes that are doing the exploiting. Such exploitation basically involves one of four forms of deceit. In addition, other kinds of cheating involving the NCAA itself can also be identified. Each can be exemplified in turn.

Lying about Age

Two examples reveal the rationale behind students lying about their ages, but before examining them let us recall the NCAA eligibility requirements, namely that for each year of competition after the age of twenty, the period at athletic eligibility is reduced by one year. The Kenyan 800-meter runner Sammy Koskei was ruled ineligible in 1982, after evidence was obtained that his birth certificate had been tampered with in 1981.[60] Koskei had claimed that he was nineteen when applying to Southern Methodist University, although records at Iowa State and New Mexico Junior College, to which he had also applied, showed him to be twenty-four.

The case of Ugandan steeplechaser Lucus Oloo is instructive in a somewhat different way. He said: "I had been interested in coming to the United States and I talked to some American tourists about it. They gave me the names of some schools to write. A friend of mine told me, 'Lucus, they want older students over there. You don't have a chance if they know your real age. You should tell them you're twenty-three or twenty-four.'"[61] The twenty-year-old Oloo did, but because of the age limitation on foreign students NCAA schools showed little interest in him. As a result he ended up at Spokane Falls Community College as one of the nation's leading junior college athletes. In the case of non-NCAA institutions, of course, lying such as this is not necessary.

Lying about Qualifications

Students already having bachelors degrees do not meet NCAA eligibility requirements. Gareth Brown, a British middle-distance runner, was accepted at Iowa State University despite having graduated from a university in England. After he won the NCAA indoor 1,000-yards title, his "offense" was discovered and he was expelled and the university fined.[62] By contrast, his fellow Briton, steeplechaser Graeme Fell, claimed that he did not realize when applying for a place at San Diego State University that his years at Nottingham University in England would affect his eligibility to compete in intercollegiate sports. When his background was discovered, no sanctions were applied to the university and the whole affair was viewed as a genuine mistake.

Lying about Athletic Performance

Two Ghanaian young men lied to the University of Texas, Austin, track-and-field coach Cleburne Price about their athletic abilities, claiming that they had achieved highly respectable athletic performances in Ghana. After arriving at the university, however, they achieved performances inferior to those of members of the university's women's team. "The two Ghanaians perpetrated the hoax through a counterfeit newspaper story in which names were substituted and stripped over original headlines."[63] This is but one example of a form of deception which may well be commonplace.

Lying about Identity

A foreign student-athlete's distance from the United States makes it difficult to detect lies concerning identity. Some examples illustrate this form of cheating, which is similar to lying about athletic performance, in many respects. In the late 1970s the track coach at Toledo University received an application from a Kenyan calling himself David Kimaiyo. It was known that Kimaiyo was the Commonwealth 400-meter hurdles champion for the event, possessing an outstanding time of 49.2 seconds. In Ohio, "Kimaiyo" achieved no better than 56.5. A Kenyan coach was subsequently contacted and he stated that the real Kimaiyo was still in Kenya and that having second thoughts about going to America had, at the last minute, given his papers to a cousin. Needless to say, the athletically undistinguished cousin had his scholarship revoked and he disappeared from the scene.[64]

The NCAA is fully aware of the abuses which blemish the international recruiting game. In the *Guide to International Academic Standards for Athletic Eligibility,* two countries, Ghana and Nigeria, are highlighted as each having "a serious problem of falsification and alteration of records."[65] However, it would be naive to assume that it is from West Africa only that abuse of the system is practiced.

Precisely how much cheating is undertaken by student-athletes from overseas at the application stage is unknown. It is clear from these few examples, however, that it is relatively easy for students to manipulate the system for their own ends, albeit for a relatively short period of time in some cases. Given the NCAA's poor record of catching cheats elsewhere in the intercollegiate sports system,[66] it is reasonable to assume that more foreign athletes get away with cheating than is officially recognized. The readiness to cheat reflects not only the magnetism of life in an American university athletic department but also the deep-seated sport-achievement ideology possessed by athletes the world over. But in recruiting such athletes the coaches' professional reputations—which rest on the capacity to recruit effectively—must be brought into question. Cheating by foreign student-athletes at the recruitment stage is therefore one of the hazards of recruiting overseas.

Another Kind of Cheating

While on the subject of cheating we should note that being a foreign student-athlete in the United States confers certain advantages on those participants who have been caught by their national athletic federations in the act of using drugs. While athletes can, in track and field at least, be banned by their national federations for such forms of cheating, they can continue to take part in intercollegiate competition in the United States because the NCAA ignores suspensions imposed by all other governing bodies. The cases of Abilene Christian shot-putter Ahmed Shata, from Egypt, and Lars Sundin, Brigham Young discus thrower from Sweden,[67] exemplify this form of abuse—in collusion with the NCAA. According to NCAA regulations, athletes can only be suspended if they fail a drug test at a NCAA championship event. Foreign student-athletes can, of course, be introduced to drugs while in America. Canadian sprinter Tony Sharpe, who attended Clemson University, stated at a Canadian government enquiry into drugs in sport, following the Ben Johnson scandal, that he had started on steroids while at college in South Carolina.[68] The extent of such initiation is not known.

The South African Connection

Finally, it should be pointed out that the NCAA acts independently of global opinion in its willingness to accommodate South African athletes in its intercollegiate sports programs. In most countries and in most sports, South Africans are banned from competing, the result of international agreement deriving from South Africa's apartheid policy. Devious ways of obtaining competition outside South Africa include athletes' changing nationality (as in the famous Zola Budd example), or as in the case of the US college scene, accepting athletic scholarships in American universities and hence being able to compete, nominally as students, on the college circuit. In some sports the number of South African recruits is sizable. For example, in tennis, 16 percent of foreign players in Division I schools has been estimated to be South African; in swimming the figure is about 6 percent, and in golf, about 5.5 percent.[69] South African athletes often assume various forms of subterfuge while in the United States. A bizarre example is said to have occurred in 1977 when a total of forty South Africans took part in a masters' competition in the United States, posing as American college students.[70] At one major sport-oriented university, South African student-athletes were so embarrassed about their nationality that two of them told an instructor that they were Swedish and Austrian; a third, whose name was Botha, could hardly disguise his South African origin. In such cases the NCAA, a national bureaucracy, acts as a transnational political organization.

Conclusion

Coaches view recruiting foreign student-athletes as an expedient way of maintaining—or in some cases, creating—a winning team. International athletic recruiting can hence be viewed as an outgrowth of domestic recruiting. Such overseas "trade" in athletes may result in reduced recruiting costs and involve less of a risk than taking on eighteen-year-old American high school graduates. It has been shown in this chapter that foreign student-athletes tend to be well qualified academically and well motivated toward participation in both academics and athletics. Some are serious enough about academic work to have applied for places in universities and colleges in their own countries.

The decision to go to America can be interpreted as a form of locational decision-making. Locational choices derive from stresses that push student-athletes to consider moving to the United States. In some cases the stress may be sufficient to induce cheating. In general, however, overtures are made to potential students by the universities (or via their representatives) or through a friends-of-friends network. Limited choice is available for many students and in hardly any cases are campuses visited before enrollment.

This is not to say, of course, that the foreign recruits are pawns in the hands of alien athletic departments; the ability of the recruits to work the system to their own ends through cheating indicates this. But neither are such migrants operating in a totally voluntaristic way; their deep-seated sport-achievement ideology drives them to the point where opportunities for improvement are seen as most propitious, a migratory process encouraged by the favorable sport ideology of American academe.

Having enrolled, the foreign student-athlete encounters a new world. It is the experience of that new environment that forms the bulk of the next two chapters: chapter 6 considers general experiences, while chapter 7 presents more specific autobiographies.

SIX

The Student Experience

Having arrived at college in America, foreign student-athletes enter a world with which they are, in large part, unfamiliar. This chapter identifies their experiences at college — academic, athletic, and social. Initially the foreign student-athlete (like all foreign students) is likely to be faced with problems of adjustment or adaptation to life in a new environment. His or her failure to adjust or adapt may lead to the decision to return home with negative impressions of a brief period of sojourn. On the other hand, the student's ability to cope successfully, through successful social adjustment, and academic and athletic satisfaction, may lead to eventual graduation and even full assimilation into the culture of the host nation (fig. 25). In a few cases the student-athlete may decide to seek naturalization.

It should be stressed from the start that any comments made here about the experiences of foreign student-athletes in the US *are* generalizations. It must be recognized that such generalizations obscure a good deal of variety and that the sojourn experiences of foreign recruits varies tremendously. This is because foreign recruits come from a variety of backgrounds; they vary in origin, geographically, culturally, and socially; and they vary in the amount of change that they experience during the course of migration. It would be equally wrong to assume that the athletes from any single nation were an undifferentiated group.

Initial Adjustment and the Educational Experience

One of the most well-known generalizations relating to the adjustment of foreign students in an alien educational milieu is the "U-curve

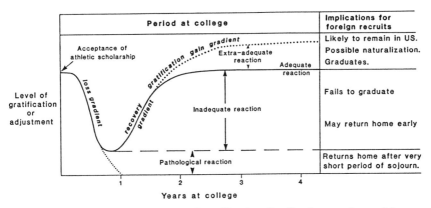

Figure 25. Levels of adjustment/gratification for foreign student-athletes. (Adapted from Furnham and Bochner, *Culture Shock*)

hypothesis."[1] This states that adjustment is related to time. Initially, adjustment seems easy and this is implicit in the decision to migrate; it is followed by a period in which the student feels less well adjusted, finally there is a period when he or she feels better adjusted and more at home in the foreign situation.

In coping with an unfamiliar environment, the foreign student-athlete may encounter four aspects of the adaptation process.[2] These are:

1) Cultural adjustment; e.g., feeling "at home," socially interacting with the host group, finding satisfaction with a new lifestyle;
2) Identification; e.g., a feeling of belonging, changes in reference groups, formal membership of a group;
3) Cultural competence; e.g., acquiring new cultural knowledge and skills;
4) Role acculturation; e.g., the active use of the host language, the desire to conform to culturally defined modes of behavior.

There are good, logical reasons to suppose that foreign student-athletes would adapt to the foreign sojourn situation better than other foreign students. This is because several of the aforementioned aspects can be readily satisfied in the athletic department. It has already been stressed that foreign student-athletes will share a common ideology with their American sports peers. To an extent this could serve to bridge any culture gap which might exist and hence make adjustment relatively easy. It has been shown that student-athletes form "extremely strong social bonds among themselves. . . . They are bonded together into a reference group and a peer sub-culture. Relations within this group [are] especially cohesive because they [have] lived, played and travelled together."[3] Such close bonding, which in some cases will include living together in an athletic dormitory in which student-athletes are segregated from other students, may create a more favorable environment in which foreign student-athletes can adjust to a new location than would be the case for other foreign students who have to find their friends for themselves.

Newly acquired friends in the athletic department will assist the foreign student-athlete in obtaining new cultural knowledge and skills and can quickly induct the visitor into the idiosyncracies of "American" English. A feeling of belonging and the formal membership of a group will be readily provided by the very fact that the foreign recruit is a member of a relatively prestigious group which represents the university (and, indirectly, the locality). A sense of belonging to a group is reinforced by the social segregation experienced by many student-athletes (see page 135) and the constant reinforcement of sport-place bonding in artifacts of various kinds, ranging from sport-oriented welcoming signs to T-shirts and other forms of personal display. A kind of loyalty develops to the university, more intense than loyalty to other forms of organizations. Because athletic departments recruit student-athletes on the basis of talent, failing to consider to any extent whether recruits will "fit in" or not, the students are subjected to intense socialization experiences.[4] This might be logically expected to apply even more to foreign than to domestic recruits.

Nevertheless, in spite of these remediating characteristics favoring foreign student-athletes over other foreign students, sojourn can be brief. In the late 1960s, British middle-distance runner John Davies briefly attended Washington State University but returned home after a few months "in protest against the widespread use of drugs by students there."[5] More dramatically, Scottish runner Nat Muir attended Providence College in Rhode Island for just eight days in the early 1980s. He attributed the brevity of his career as a student-athlete to homesickness on the one hand and an unappealing track coach on the other.[6] Within a few months of starting his freshman year at the University of New Mexico, Canadian steeplechaser Alain Boucher returned to Ontario. "To Boucher the weather provided neither romantic nor simplistic results. . . . When training sessions began the temperature was about 30° Celsius, but when the athletes headed down into the valley for the basic ten-mile workouts, it reached an unbearable 36° or 37°."[7]

The case of English swimmer Adrian Moorhouse is also instructive. He was recruited by the University of California, Berkeley, in January

1983 but was back home in England in April of the same year. Enjoying the West Coast life and getting good grades, he found that it was the swimming that caused the problem. His arrival in January did not help because the squad had completed its intensive autumn training. "As a star recruit to the Berkeley swimming program he found himself thrown in at the deep end of the intercollegiate circuit, jetting back and forth across the country from meet to meet, with no time for proper training or build-up to each event."[8]

The early months are crucial. David Wilkie, British Olympic swimming gold medalist, said: "My first year at Miami was one of adjustment. The social differences were quite vast, the people were different, and I had to gear myself up for the American way of life. The first year wasn't a bed of roses and I had some problems."[9] Another international swimmer commented: "I find that, especially speaking to other athletes attending universities in the States, the most crucial time is in the first month. Personally I hated it because I was so far away from home, no friends and quite lonely. If you make it through the first month everything after that picks up. . . ." English swimmer Debbie Rudd found various aspects difficult to adjust to: "I went through a lot of doubts those first couple of months but my team mates were very supportive and I got over my homesickness all right. The biggest adjustment was in training. I had never done weights before and here we would do lots of weight training and then go out and do calisthenics on the practice field before we ever hit the water."[10] World-class Kenyan runner Mike Boit said that initial problems came from over-racing, though few other foreign student-athletes seem to view too much competition as a problem (page 142). Boit said: "I went to the United States with a scholarship to Eastern New Mexico and for the first year I had a hard time getting adjusted to the USA. I ran in so many races, some of them relays, that by May 1973 I was completely tired."[11]

Coach Robert Parks of Eastern Michigan University feels that problems can arise in the early months of sojourn if foreign recruits have too many preconceived ideas. He said: "Some think that coming to a United States college will be an all-expenses-paid vacation, and the coach will take care of everything. When their preconceptions do not occur, they are disillusioned and often go home."[12] British javelin thrower Roald Bradstock, a student at Southern Methodist University in Dallas, put his initial reservations graphically in these words: "In my first year I was very sceptical, but after going back and sorting out problems of culture shock and leaving home, I was more relaxed. You could symbolically say that I had withdrawal symptoms of missing

English beer and had to get used to iced Texas beer and for some months a diet of McDonalds, Wendy's, Burger King and Colonel Sanders."[13] An older student-athlete said that because she had been out of full-time education for over ten years it took her almost a year to settle into studying again. Another mature athlete, ten years older than most other student-athletes, said that she had hardly any contact with other students or student-athletes; from her vantage point she felt that "eighteen- to twenty-year-old Americans are quite boring!" A very different kind of initial adjustment (to the climate rather than to the society or culture) is exemplified by the case of half-miler Wesley Maiyo, who arrived at the University of Wyoming in a bitter Laramie winter in 1974 having never seen snow before. He arrived dressed in clothing appropriate for his Kenyan homeland.[14]

These examples typify the problems of initial adjustment for foreign student-athletes. For some foreign recruits the period of sojourn is brief, but having overcome initial problems of adjustment the majority continue at university and, as will be seen, a good proportion end up earning a degree.

Other aspects of the educational experience are worthy of comment. Once at the university, student-athletes are involved in making a choice of a major area of study. In addition, they are exposed to new teachers and may also have some preconception of the value of an American degree, should they eventually obtain one. Studies of American student-athletes have shown that there has traditionally been a strong tendency to obtain degree credits in PE courses or in other areas cognate to their involvement in sports (see page 159). Such courses, it is thought, ease the route of student-athletes on their way through college. A limited amount of evidence exists to show that this may not be the case with foreign recruits. European student-athletes in US universities apparently do not dominantly major in PE or sport-related subjects. While broad divisions among academic disciplines are hard to draw, European recruits have been shown to opt for the social sciences.[15]

Foreign student-athletes seem to rate highly the teaching they receive in American universities. Over 82 percent of respondents to one survey rated the teaching quality as "satisfactory" or better (table 30), though one student was careful to point out that in American higher education "their exams are all multiple choice . . . hard to adapt to after 'A' level English, Geography and Economics" in which the essay-type examination is the norm. However, problems with teaching appear to be rare.

It has already been noted that foreign student-athletes, especially

Table 30. The quality of teaching in American universities as perceived by European student-athletes (n = 93).

	Number	Percent
Good	29	31.2
Satisfactory	48	51.6
Neutral	10	10.7
Unsatisfactory	3	3.2
Poor	2	2.1

Source: Author's research.

those from Europe, compare more than favorably with their US peers in terms of academic ability on entry to university. The generally high level of academic competence is supported by the (anticipated or actual) rate of graduation among foreign recruits. Of ninety-three European student-athletes from the sports of track-and-field and swimming, fifty-six—or 60.2 percent—had either obtained, or expected to obtain, a degree during their period of eligibility.[16] This is an impressively high figure, especially as the foreign recruits were most likely to be on substantial or full-grant scholarships and American athletic scholarship holders often tend to obtain lower graduation rates than athletes on partial scholarships (see page 23). Swimming coach Nort Thornton of the University of California has proudly claimed that the graduation rate of foreign athletes on the Cal swim team is 99 percent, with the only four NCAA post-graduate scholarships awarded to Cal student-athletes for excellence in classroom and pool in the last decade going to foreigners.[17] For African students, too, high graduation rates have been recorded. Coaches Bob Teel of Missouri and Larry Heidebrecht of UTEP claimed that African athletes are highly motivated in the classroom because it would be considered a disgrace to return home without a degree. Coach Teel claimed that while many of his Nigerian athletes had initial problems with reading English, they all graduated.[18]

There is a need to compare the high graduation rates recorded for foreign student-athletes with those for the US student population that graduates in five years. This figure will vary among institutions but a figure of 65 percent has been suggested by Mihailich.[19] If this is typical, foreign student-athletes may be achieving graduation rates only slightly different from the average US student. We have already observed that the graduation rates for US student-athletes are much lower (see chapter 2).

Given the provisos stated in chapter 2 concerning the lack of equivalence between American degrees and those from foreign countries, it is salutary to discover that over 66 percent of a sample of European student-athletes who obtained (or expected to obtain) a bachelor's degree perceived it to be of value in obtaining a job in their own country.[20] The majority of the respondents were from Britain, and it is noteworthy that many American undergraduate degrees are not regarded as conferring graduate status upon their holders in many sectors of the UK job market. A good example is the case of the teaching profession where US degree holders receive salaries commensurate with British non-graduates. While this may not be true of *all* countries from which foreign student-athletes are recruited, it certainly indicates that the British student-athletes concerned are not fully informed about the lack of equivalence between a US and a UK degree.

Precisely the same problem exists in the case of African students. For example, Kenya, like Britain, does not accept American university degrees indiscriminately, and many Kenyan athletes have returned home to find their American qualifications to be virtually worthless. An educational criticism of the international recruiting game was made by the then secretary of the Kenyan Amateur Athletic Association in 1977 when he said that "it is time we examined the conditions attached to these scholarships objectively to find out if these athletes will be a liability or an asset when they return home. The athletes' standard of education in most cases leaves a lot to be desired."[21]

It should be noted, however, that some foreign recruits do recognize the lack of comparability of degrees. My own research elicited this comment from one British student: "I must stress that the standard of education was not quite up to English university standards. I hardly ever did homework and still maintained a C average."

The Athletic Experience

Sport is central to the student-athlete's lifestyle on the American campus. The student-athlete's best friends tend to be other student-athletes, often of his or her own nationality. Student-athletes live and mix with others of their kind. It is therefore important to consider a number of aspects of the athletic experience of foreign athletes in American academia.

Perceptions of the Coach

A central figure in the life of a student-athlete is the coach. Generally regarded as a highly authoritarian figure,[22] the coach may be perceived as a god or a tyrant. Generally speaking, the quality of coaching in American universities seems to be seen as satisfactory or better by most foreign recruits, if the data in table 31 are representative.

My research has elicited positive views of the coach, exemplified in the following comments by athletes:

> The coach and his assistants are of the highest standard.
> The coaching staff is always high in numbers and of the best quality. The athletic department and athletics advisers are always available if any help is needed.
> . . . interested in the athlete as an individual more than the team and scoring points at a meet.
> American swim coaches are *thinking* (British coaches only rarely do) many years in advance of the level the British domestic scene is on. They care for their swimmers. . . . They realize that to swim fast the swimmer has to be comfortable in all aspects of life.

Richard Simonsen, a British sprinter who attended the University of Minnesota in the late 1960s, spoke highly of his track coach: ". . . although I and other athletes were expected to train with the team, the coach always insisted that studies came first. The coach was always willing to give me a break from training whenever I felt it necessary to concentrate on my studies. . . . not once did he suggest that I should try to leave classes earlier so that I could train with the team."[23]

However, it has already been pointed out that the coach can exert a great influence on foreign student-athletes at the initial stages of the location decision. What is more, the coach is able to convince foreigners of the need to change long-established codes of practice, even deeply held religious ones. A middle-distance runner from Somalia was successfully persuaded to modify the fasting required by his Moslem faith in order to run for his university,[24] a small but classic example of the Americanization of lifestyle of one foreign visitor.

Table 31. Quality of coaching as rated by European student-athletes (n = 93).

	Number	Percent	
Good	34	36.5	} 59.1
Satisfactory	21	22.6	
Neutral	16	17.2	
Unsatisfactory	12	12.9	} 22.6
Poor	9	9.7	
No response	1	1.1	

Source: Author's research.

Of course, some foreigners do recognize that the coaching can be unsatisfactory or poor. My research elicited negative impressions, captured in the following comments:

> Due to my persistence our old coach was forced to quit. He was bad!

> I had a coach barely two years older than myself who borrowed identical sessions, etc., from his old coach from a totally different climate, set-up, and group of athletes.

> I had no trust in the man at all; as a coach he was rubbish (straight from the book).

> My coach the last two years was rather incompetent; I had programs from my coach in Sweden to follow.

Some foreign recruits feel that promises made by the coach were broken. British runner Ian Whittle became disenchanted with life in the United States following what he perceived to be deception by the college track coach. Whittle said: "Recently I gave up classes . . . , which I believe the coach knows, solely to concentrate on running and earning money. The scheme under which I thought I was coming home isn't operating now so the fare is going to be over £100 [in 1973]. One of the reasons I am coming home is that promises made to me regarding pocket money and feeding arrangements have been well and truly broken."[25] Other athletes cite the absence of a *specialist* event coach as causing problems; it is not so much the coaching, but the lack of particular coaching. John Ridgeon, British silver medalist in the 1987 World track championships, summed up his experiences: "I went to America for seven months because most of the world's top hurdlers were there. I went to Southern Methodist University in Dallas. I thought if there is a secret about it, it must be there. I had all the facilities, the weather, everything except a hurdles coach. I was being coached by Keith Connor, who is very good but does not know much about hurdles technique. I was getting quicker over the flat but my technique fell apart. . . . I don't regret going to the States; in some ways it was a mistake, but it's best to do it when you're nineteen. When you're young, you've got to take these sort of risks."[26]

It clearly cannot be *guaranteed* that coaching standards will meet those expected by some foreign migrants. For this reason the decision to accept a scholarship may be a serious risk. But it is not simply the *standard* of coaching which may cause problems, and other difficulties involving the coach are dealt with below (page 141).

The Facilities

A top sport-oriented university in America will invariably possess athletic facilities superior to those found in many countries throughout the world. If potential student-athletes, who already have an achievement-sport ideology, are fully aware of such facilities, the temptation to accept them could be overwhelming. The effect of such provision on a foreign student-athlete can be grasped by comparing the comments of Keith Connor on his problems in the United Kingdom (page 102) with the facilities he encountered at Southern Methodist University: "I went where things were easy for me. . . . In America I go to classes for four hours a day, work out for two, go home and do my homework and go to bed. A routine. . . . At school [Southern Methodist] I run two miles and the weight room's there. Walk two blocks and the track's there. I just went where things would be in my favour."[27] Philip Parkin, British amateur golf champion and a student at Texas A & M University, could play eighteen holes a day, practice usually for one-and-a-half hours, and hit chips and putts until tired. For a European, this was remarkable. He commented that "it's unbelievable the kind of money they have in Texas. They have so many alumni who have made it big and they give thousands of dollars to the athletic programme."[28] Given these kinds of comments it is hardly surprising that European and other foreign recruits perceive the quality of the university athletic facilities to be excellent. It has been shown that whereas only 13.9 percent found facilities "good" at home, the respective figure for the American university was 80.6 percent. In less than 5 percent of the cases were the facilities said to be unsatisfactory or poor (table 32).

The provision of such excellent athletic facilities can further encourage the *routinization* of sports-training. The swimming pool, golf course, weight room, and running track within minutes of the dormitory permit regularized training which is often difficult to establish

Table 32. Quality of facilities for training in American universities as perceived by European student-athletes (n = 93).

	Number	Percent	
Good	75	80.6	} 94.6
Satisfactory	13	14.0	
Neutral	1	1.1	
Unsatisfactory	2	2.2	} 4.4
Poor	2	2.2	

Source: Author's research.

at home. For the neo-Marxist observer such as Bero Rigauer, this would identify the sport-university as being analogous to an assembly line, utilizing "Taylorized" methods of "production."[29]

Motivation

The ability to achieve the status of a student-athlete implies that the individual concerned is highly motivated, since even high-school sports success requires more than a modicum of effort in practice and training. There is some evidence to suggest, however, that differences in motivation may exist between American and foreign student-athletes. Howard Stidwill's research has shown that of coaches interviewed in a study of motivation among US and foreign track-and-field student-athletes, 86 percent felt that the foreign recruits were generally more motivated to perform both academically and athletically than their American peers. What is more, foreign student-athletes appeared to be more confident of success than Americans, such differences possibly being the result of their greater exposure to national or international competition.[30]

Performance

Given the generally positive attitude toward coaching and the presence of first-class facilities, it would be surprising if athletic performance did not improve for foreign student-athletes during their period of sojourn. For a European sample, 85 percent found that their sporting performances improved; in only 10 percent of the cases did their athletic performance worsen, while 5 percent reported no change.[31] Of course, improvement in athletic performance cannot be *causally* associated with the US college environment. Frequently athletes improve in spite of facilities at home and it is possible that had students not gone to America their athletic performances would have actually been better.

One problem relating to sporting performance is that athletes may be expected to "peak" twice during the course of one year, first for the intercollegiate sports season — say, in May for track and field, and again in September when the European and international seasons tend to reach their climax. It is not uncommon to find European athletes who have achieved excellent performances in the States returning home in a state of semi-exhaustion to achieve mediocre results. The same can apply to Canadian athletes. Distance runner Lynn Williams from Saskatchewan gained a PE degree from San Diego State in 1982 but her comments about her athletic experiences are somewhat contradictory. She said that she "had a good coach down there but my body couldn't handle all the races. I came home injured every summer. I never once had a summer of competition in Canada."[32]

The Social Experience

A number of studies of foreign students in the United States allude to the social benefits and problems of sojourn in an unfamiliar environment. Benefits are said to be the exposure to a new culture and the resulting international linkages which are forged. Problems may include homesickness, loneliness, and discrimination. Various aspects of the social experience of foreign student-athletes can be examined in turn.

Friendships and Discrimination

The peer-group subculture of the student-athlete has already been mentioned. While at the American university there is a definite tendency for the foreign student-athlete to develop friendships with other student-athletes rather than with non-athletes. Of eighty-one British student-athletes, no fewer than 72.8 percent selected other student-athletes as their best friends. Of best-friendships which had developed during sojourn in America, 32 percent were with other British student-athletes. That limited levels of non-sporting contacts had developed is reflected by the fact that only 24.6 percent of best friendships were with others than student-athletes (table 33).[33] Because foreign student-athletes *are* athletes, many (39.5 percent in table 33) can develop close friendship patterns with members of the host culture and "stick with their own kind" at the same time.

Although friendship with student-athletes from their own country

Table 33. Best friends of British student-athletes in American universities (n = 81).

	Number	Percent
American student-athlete	32	39.5
British student-athlete	26	32.1
Other foreign student-athlete	18	22.2
American student (non-athlete)	14	17.2
Other foreign student	3	3.7
Other	3	3.7

Note: Totals do not add up to 100% because in six cases respondents cited more than one person as their "best friend."

Source: Bale, "Alien Student-Athletes," 86.

can be highly advantageous to foreign student-athletes in overcoming problems associated with culture shock, it can nevertheless pose problems for the large number of students for whom English is a second language. Northern Illinois University tennis import Mats Persson soon found a Swedish teammate to whom he could relate when he arrived in DeKalb. Persson stated that "it's good in one way because we look at things more the same way," but added that "when we're together we always speak Swedish, and I need to improve my English."[34]

Three Brazilian student-athletes at Northern Illinois agreed that a "Brazilian-gymnastic subculture" helped overcome excessive culture shock. Colleagues from the same country in the same sport provided a ready-made social group which formed a cushion against the conflict which might exist between their own culture and that of the host nation.

The sport subculture is clearly present among foreign student-athletes, which again stresses the routinized nature of much of the college experience. A "locker-room" culture appears to dominate the milieux in which foreign student-athletes find themselves, serving to reinforce and strengthen their existing sport ideology.

We have already observed that the transition into a foreign culture can be initially traumatic. That over one-third of British student-athletes had other British student-athletes as their best friends could be argued to be a factor seriously reducing the potential level of culture shock; indeed, the fact that over 70 percent selected other student-athletes as their best friends suggests that membership of a sport subculture replaces membership of a cross-cultural group as the dominant form of social network during sojourn as a foreign student-athlete.

Discrimination

Satisfaction with the period of residence in America would be expected to be reduced if discrimination against foreign students were common. Of an overwhelmingly white European sample, 12.9 percent had personally experienced discrimination while in the United States. This is a much lower figure than that quoted in studies of samples of non-athletic migrants, which would have consisted of a much more ethnically diverse group. For example, figures for foreign non-athletes in the United States cited by Klineberg and Hull suggest that 30.6 percent perceived that they had experienced discrimination in the United States.[35]

Racial discrimination against black student-athletes from overseas has been alluded to by several observers of the US college sports scene. Ballinger has argued that while Swedish hammer-throwers, for example, were welcome in US colleges, Kenyan steeplechasers were not, beyond point-scoring for the university. He alleges that African athletes "have been threatened on many occasions with deportation if they don't do as they are told, if they don't race in every meet that comes along," and that the basic view of some US coaches can be summed up as "send them back to Africa."[36] One foreign recruit commented that many of the "redneck" coaching staff at the college he attended would frequently use words like "nigger" to refer to West Indian recruits when in the company of colleagues—though not to the black student-athletes themselves.

A correspondent to *Track and Field News* rhetorically asked whether "an overage foreign distance runner attending an American university using a free-ride scholarship honestly expects to endear himself to the crowd while beating a younger native American?"[37] Racial discrimination against foreign black student-athletes is well documented. In the 1978 NCAA indoor championships it was noted that while the field in the three-mile was heavily manned by foreign recruits, the cheers were reserved for a white-skinned Irish runner rather than the blacks from UTEP or Washington State.[38] An interpretation of such discrimination has been provided by Washington State track coach John Chaplin, who, in the mid-1970s, noted that "not until you have seen black men beating Americans in the long distances— where black men aren't supposed to be able to beat white men—not until then has there been a controversy. . . . Blacks are supposed to be sprinters. The foreign athletes, especially African distancemen, are upsetting the prejudices some of these guys who have complained about the presence of foreign athletes at US colleges have been carrying around. They didn't look up when a foreign black won the 100. But when he wins the 10,000 they notice—and they holler."[39]

In the early 1970s it was questioned whether racism and discrimination would prevent a Third World athlete from finding work in the university's athletic department once his eligibility was used up.[40] It is difficult to establish the validity of such a claim. Certainly some Third World athletes have achieved the status of members of the coaching staff. For example, Jama Aden, a former Olympian from Somalia and an outstanding athlete at Fairleigh Dickinson, was [in 1987] on the coaching staff at George Mason University. William Wuyke, a Venezuelan 800-meter runner, acted as a graduate assistant at his alma mater at Alabama; George Mehale from South Africa was a star distance runner at UTEP and subsequently became a graduate assistant and then a full-time assistant coach at Oklahoma State while teaching in the PE department. In soccer a number of Third World athletes have achieved the status of chief coach. Perhaps the best known is Ibrahim H. Ibrahim at Clemson, while Berhane Andeberhan at Cal State LA is another example. It is impossible to say, however, the exact extent to which discrimination exists against Third World foreigners wishing to take up such work. The evidence cited above suggests that where such "workers" appear useful to the athletic department they can be employed in much the same way as they were as student-athletes, i.e., to enhance the status of the institution.

Although personal experience of discrimination seems limited for student-athletes from Europe, 23.6 percent had friends who had experienced discrimination while in America (compared with 41.6 percent in Klineberg and Hull's data for foreign non-athletic students), while 19.3 percent found more discrimination in the United States than they had expected (little different from that reported for the foreign non-athletes in Klineberg and Hull's study—20.2 percent).[41] For some, on the other hand, "positive" discrimination seems to exist. A British athlete noted that "there was a certain amount of jealousy from some American students but this was outweighed by the warmth of the majority." Another Briton said that "the English tend to be admired rather than ridiculed in this country," while still another noted that "when they found out I was English they made a point of coming up to speak to me." Likewise, another English athlete stated that "being a scholarship athlete, particularly from England, put me in an almost 'celebrity bracket.' By this I mean that people would wish to meet me and talk to me and there is always a big joke in the classroom the first day of a new course when the teacher discovers I am English. This usually leads to class discussions at which I am the centre of focus. And then on, throughout the term people will come up to me just to ask me questions. Therefore I never felt discriminated against, lonely, or unhappy about being there."

Loneliness and Homesickness

Despite the previous comment, sojourn in a foreign country would seem likely to produce loneliness and homesickness among some foreign student-athletes. Of foreign students in general it has been shown that "sometimes" and "rarely" are the most common responses they gave to questions about the extent of loneliness and homesickness,[42] and foreign student-athletes in the United States appear to be no exception. However, in only 5.4 percent of cases do student-athletes seem to be lonely "very often" or "often" (table 34). A higher figure

Table 34. Frequency of loneliness and homesickness experienced by European student-athletes at American universities (n = 93).

(A) Loneliness	Number	Percent
Very often	1	1.1
Often	4	4.3
Sometimes	35	37.6
Rarely	30	32.2
Never	23	24.7
(B) Homesickness		
Very often	5	5.4
Often	8	8.6
Sometimes	40	43.0
Rarely	26	27.9
Never	14	15.0

Source: Bale, "Alien Student-Athletes," 90.

was more common in cross-cultural research on foreign students, Klineberg and Hull noting a respective figure of 16.4 percent.[43] Again, the group identity found among student-athletes can be argued to provide a remedy for loneliness that is not so readily available to other foreign students. Although loneliness and homesickness can mean almost the same thing, more student-athletes appear to be homesick than lonely; here they differ hardly at all from the foreign non-athletic students in Klineberg and Hull's study. Fourteen percent of a sample of (European) student-athletes reported feeling homesick,[44] with a respective figure for a larger intercontinental sample of non-athletes being 13.2 percent.[45] Loneliness can be overcome by the closeness of fellow student-athletes who have similar ideologies, interests, and aspirations; homesickness cannot. Nevertheless, the figures must be kept in perspective since 43 percent of the European student-athletes claimed that they rarely or never felt homesick while in America. Loneliness and homesickness can be felt by foreign student-athletes if they are the only foreigners on the athletic team or if they attend a "commuter university," i.e., where the overwhelming majority of students come from the immediate locality. In addition, boredom can be common during vacations when foreign students could find themselves relatively devoid of company.

Problems

A large number of difficulties can confront the foreign student in America. Most frequently these are likely to be of a financial nature or deal with the sports coach (table 35). Other problems revealed in a survey of European student-athletes in the United States included personal depression, adjustment to climate, lack of motivation in studies, and dealing with the university administration. Other problems, mentioned by a relatively small number of student-athletes, are shown also in table 35.

Financial problems are among the difficulties most commonly cited by foreign students all over the world, and the proportion of student-athletes with such problems seems little different from that for all foreign students.[46] One British student-athlete claimed that at one stage of his college career he was "down to £1," an extreme example but nevertheless one that is far from uncommon. Dependence on handouts from parents or revenue from clandestine jobs may overcome the worst of financial problems. The cash available to student-athletes in the revenue sports such as football and basketball (money obtained via alumni handouts and under-the-counter ticket sales, for example) may not be so forthcoming for foreign student-athletes in the less glamorous non-revenue sports to which they are predominantly recruited. Dealing with the sports coach is another frequently cited problem. The authoritarian nature of the coach has already been noted and for this reason problems with the coach should not be surprising. Yet as we have already seen, the student-athlete attitude toward the coach must be regarded as somewhat ambivalent, praise being more frequent than criticism.

Nyquist has alluded to "the frequent recruitment of foreign athletes who are given false promises of financial assistance by institutions intensely concerned with remaining competitive."[47] Evidence certainly exists for such a divergence between the anticipated and actual experiences. One British distance runner who attended an East Coast

Table 35. Problems encountered by more than 10 percent of European student-athletes at American universities (n = 93).

Problem	Number	Percent
Financial problems	30	32.2
Dealing with the sports coach	29	31.2
Personal depression	25	26.9
Adjusting to climate	23	24.7
Lack of motivation in studies	19	20.4
Dealing with college administration	19	20.4
Difficulties with courses	14	15.0
Relations with opposite sex	11	11.8

Source Bale, "Alien Student-Athletes," 90.

school commented: "I had a chance to go to six colleges on full scholarships but decided on _____ College. I had just got married but the coach said everything would be OK and he got us an off-campus apartment. But it turned out that I had to pay the rent. I told the coach that I would not come back the following year as I didn't have an income, my wife (who the coach had promised a job) had no employment and I couldn't afford the rent. The coach told me everything would be sorted out the following year." Several foreigners who were recruited to the UTEP track team of the late 1970s and early 1980s claimed that at the time of recruitment promises of full scholarships were made, only to find that when they arrived at El Paso they were given a half-scholarship (see page 178). George Mehale, a South African runner, arrived at UTEP with a I-20A form stating that he was on a full scholarship. Upon arrival at El Paso, former track coach Ted Banks told him that he would be on a partial scholarship and that only All-Americans had full scholarships. When Mehale confronted Banks on the discrepancy, Banks was reported to have said, "Do you want to go home or what?"[48] Another foreign recruit added: "Many other foreign athletes were admitted to UTEP on the basis of a full scholarship that for no reason was cut immediately after arrival in this country. I have valid reasons to believe that someone at UTEP is purposely cheating immigration, just to get the foreign athletes into the country easier."[49] Foreign recruits have also stated that they have been offered financial incentives for good performances. Dutch middle-distance import Jan Boogman stated that he took home about $500 above expenses from at least one track meet.[50]

The extent to which these ruses go on is not clear, but examples such as these show that cheating and exploitation are not restricted to the big-time sports such as football and basketball. Track and field, at least, seems to provide enough evidence to suggest that such abuse is deeper than might be at first thought and that at the center of such abuse is the college coach.

Depression associated with sojourn at an American college was cited by a quarter of respondents to one survey of foreign recruits (table 35), but as noted earlier this was most likely to occur in the early stages of the period at college. While severe stress would seem to be rare, it is not unknown. Having been ill for four months, one foreign athlete claimed that due to his coach's broken promises he returned home where he was told that he was halfway through a nervous breakdown.

Adjustment to climate is a problem to many foreign recruits. For Europeans from the British Isles and Scandinavia, the cool, temperate oceanic climate of their homeland contrasts markedly with the Mediterranean or more continental and subtropical zones into which they may be recruited. For Africans, North American winters can cause problems. Billy Konchellah, a Kenyan recruit to San Diego State, initially enrolled at a school in the Midwest but found it too cold.[51] The athletic *and* physical environment of southern California was much more to his liking.

Another problem for a number of recruits is the lack of motivation in studies. This again may not be surprising in view of the fact that many recruits are athletes first and students second. As one British recruit told me, "I never went with much idea of getting a degree. . . . It was to enjoy my running, improve my situation, and see a bit of the USA that I really decided to go." It must be stressed, however, that foreign student-athletes *generally* appear more motivated than their American peers with regard to their academic work (see page 134).

A relatively small number of foreign student-athletes encounter problems in training too hard and being asked to compete too often in sports. Few European student-athletes in fact appear to see "overtraining" as a problem, despite the comments made by some who obviously do (see page 145).

Some problems will be specific to particular institutions and particular individuals. For example, Swedish discus thrower Kjell Bystedt became disenchanted with the Mormon institution Brigham Young University, a major destination of foreigners, because of the rigidity of the campus rules (page 21). He commented, "I didn't like having to sneak a beer. . . ."[52] Likewise English distance runner Dave Hindley commented: "I often feel angry at the atmosphere at BYU, particularly the stringent rules which attempt to govern one's life (such as abstinence from tea, coffee, alcohol etc.) and the insistence that these be maintained everywhere."[53] On the other hand, Carey May, an Irish distance runner at the same institution, said: "I think you have to be open minded and accept the views of others. It's a really clean and healthy atmosphere in which to live and train."[54]

The Overall Experience

The scholastic, athletic, and social experiences combine to produce an overall experience of life as a student-athlete in the United States. This overall experience has been evaluated for European recruits by asking them to score their general feelings toward the experience on a "feeling thermometer"[55] on which values range from 0 to 100, 50 being a neutral response. (Scores of over 50 reveal a positive or "warm" feeling toward the experience; those of under 50 a negative or "cool.") For a sample of 93 Europeans who had been (or were) in US athletic departments, the modal value ascribed to the overall experience was 100, a very warm or favorable feeling. The average score was 87, and only 4 (4.3 percent) respondents indicated a value of 50 or less. None at all gave a value of less than 40. Such an overwhelmingly favorable response to the American experience was confirmed by another survey which found that 77.6 percent of respondent track-and-field athletes from overseas affirmed that they would encourage athletes from their home countries to attend US colleges on the basis of their own experiences.[56] These kinds of responses broadly confirm the feeling of most American student-athletes, i.e., that they certainly do not see themselves as victims of an exploitive system, despite the writings of the more radical sports sociologists mentioned in chapter 2. This is not to say, of course, that exploitation may not have existed (see page 34).

Many qualitative statements describe graphically the overall feelings held by current and former student-athletes of their years in the States. My research suggests that comments fall into three categories. First, there are those who portray unqualified enthusiasm for their years at college; second, there are those who present a more considered, but nevertheless enthusiastic, response; and third, there is a group who responded by including a critical element within their still generally favorable response. Each of these types can be illustrated with several examples in turn.

The "unqualified enthusiasm" group is typified by comments made to me, such as:

> I am now three years through a five-year course and it has been the happiest and most enlightening years of my life. I have never regretted going.

> I had the greatest time of my life in the USA! *Great* in every respect.

> I wouldn't trade my experience as a student-athlete in this country for anything. I have a younger brother . . . who dwells glumly in a city [in England] of 22 percent unemployment. America has given me the chance to escape that nightmare, and I count myself very lucky.

> I can honestly say that from my own experience the four years I spent at university in the USA were the best years of my life. It was a great experience and has made me a better-rounded and much more aware individual.

A slightly more cautious view of the overall experience was expressed in these terms:

I think for the right kind of person it is worth going to the US. It is a chance to further your education and see a different part of the world—an invaluable experience in itself. I went there with the attitude of a sixth-month trial period—if I didn't like it I could always go home, so I felt I had nothing to lose going out to the US.

I went to the States with an open mind but with the idea that whatever happened I was going to enjoy myself and I was going to be successful. I enjoyed myself immensely and learned a great deal more about myself and life in general. It was a thoroughly worthwhile experience.

A runner, who applied for but failed to get into a British university, said: "It's been a great experience for me and I wouldn't give it up voluntarily. Even though I understand US degrees are not equivalent to here, I still feel that it is worth completing a degree programme there. They gave me a chance which Britain did not." Another student-athlete, who had been accepted at one of Britain's most sports-oriented universities, said: "I feel that although I may not have had such a good academic education I have a better education in life."

A few student-athletes, while having a favorable attitude toward the sojourn experience, do hint at an awareness of some of the ideological—and even exploitive—demands of the American system of awarding athletic scholarships. One commented that "what has to be dealt with is the *feeling of obligation* to the athletic department for the grant/scholarship to be there. Performing well should not be the pressure point of being able to stay in the USA but often it is, for financial reasons." A runner who did not obtain a full scholarship said that he "had to work full-time, train and study. It was tough!" Another stated: "Although I did very well in my studies the motivation was not quite there, mainly because so much emphasis was put on sport and winning at all costs. This is a major problem with American universities. . . ." One foreign recruit summed up his feelings bluntly, saying, "In my opinion athletes on scholarships earn every cent of scholarships and I think most people appreciated this." Samantha Purvis, a British Olympic swimmer who enrolled at Louisiana State after reaching the butterfly final at the Los Angeles Olympics, gave up her scholarship and returned home after a year. She said: ". . . my studies were going well but when one is given a sports scholarship like mine, one feels under an obligation to swim well for the university, and this I was not doing to my satisfaction."[57]

The *obligation* to represent the university (in return for the athletic scholarship) can create problems for athletes (and their national federations and administrators) if representing the university clashes with representing their country. This is relatively rare since major championships and the Olympic Games tend to occur outside the collegiate season. Conflicts of interest can occur nevertheless. Tanzanian administrators were angered when their 10,000-meter runner, Sulemein Nyambui, was refused permission to represent his country by UTEP officials in the Commonwealth Games in Australia in 1982.[58] Other such bans have been applied to athletes from Nigeria and Jamaica.

A negative view, with an almost explicit recognition of exploitation, has been articulated by Jim McLatchie about his experience at Lamar Tech in the mid-1960s. He wrote: "I was working in Glasgow during 1962 leaving my digs at 7:30 A.M. for work, training, and returning at 8:30 P.M. when I received an offer to go to Lamar Tech, Beaumont, Texas, on an athletic scholarship. . . . I accepted what I thought was a golden opportunity to really make it big. I made it big all right; all I learned was how to race two or three times per day and make points for the school. . . . I was reduced to a hobbling wreck. . . . and finally after two and a half years I told the coach to take his scholarship and cram it."[59]

Perhaps the problem of *generalizing* about the sojourn experiences of foreign student-athletes can be illustrated by somewhat longer comments by two former British students. The first was written in 1985 by an athlete who, while never fulfilling the promise expected of him at the time of recruitment, nevertheless felt that he gained tremendously from exposure to life in the United States:

> It may be a cliché, but America is still the land of opportunity, with American colleges drawing some of the top athletes from around the world. I would probably have had the same injuries in England that I had in America, but with much less access to medical help, and motivation to continue, through all the problems. I attended Murray State University from 1976-1979. It is a small school in Kentucky that had a facility that compares to the top tracks in Britain. It provided England with an Olympic finalist in the 800 meters in Moscow, Dave Warren. As far as competition goes, of course athletes are encouraged to score points for the team, but a coach is also concerned about your welfare. An athlete can't score points if he's injured, can he?
>
> Obviously, Bill Cornell, who was my track coach at Murray, and myself, would like me to have shown some of the form I've had since leaving university. It was one of the most trying experiences of my life, but one which I can look back on and see how much I learnt, in terms of character and maturity.
>
> After meeting my wife, Amy, in the last semester at university, I moved to Louisville, at the beginning of 1980, and got married. Things could hardly be better. I work in a modern downtown hospital, we

have two cars and a nice apartment. Also, I live in a city with athletes the calibre of Dave Murphy and Dave Long. My running has gradually picked up again, and two years ago I joined Team Etonic. I'm due to get my US citizenship next month, and hope to compete in the '88 US Olympic Trials. Coming to America was the chance of a lifetime. If I had to give advice to a young athlete, I'd have to say "Go west, young man."[60]

The second remark is from an athlete who rejected the US system but did emerge as an international athlete:

I went out to Providence College on a scholarship about five years ago; and lasted eight days—I wasn't impressed. The collegiate system is rubbish, nothing like what it's made out to be. I don't base that on my short experience, but on what other athletes have told me as well. It suits some, but a lot of them find it a hostile and pressurized environment.

I suppose I was a bit homesick—that's not so surprising, but I wasn't over excited about the attitude of the athletics coach either. His idea of training was "Well boys, today you can go for a long run . . . or a short run." Not exactly scientific; I don't know how widespread that was, but I was having none of it; I made a spur of the moment decision, packed my bags, and disappeared. To be fair, I'd probably be a bit more tolerant now, though I'm still sure that it wouldn't suit me.[61]

Interpreting the Overall Experience

What are we to make of these responses in light of the fact that many previous studies of college sport have exposed it as being dehumanizing, exploitive, and alienating? Several interpretations are possible. A crude form of cultural Marxism avers that those who praise the system for the wonderful experiences it provided have been mystified by the achievement-sport ideology and have been the subjects of false consciousness.[62] As false consciousness is only recognized retrospectively, it is quite possible that "the inebriated college student *may* have to wait years while the opium runs its course before he or she can see the *negative* and positive features of the sport experience."[63]

It should also be stressed that while exploitation may be readily observable in NCAA Division I football, it may be less readily apparent in the non-revenue sports to which foreigners are mainly recruited. While pressures to win are great in track and, say, swimming, they are undoubtedly less great than in football and basketball.

Some former athletes *are* explicit in their accusations of exploitation. This may be especially true of Africans who not only tend to be discriminated against but also are at a disadvantage in being culturally distanced from the North American scene. Robert Ouko, a former student-athlete from Kenya, stated that "it wouldn't be going too far to say that in many cases African athletes are being exploited by American colleges and getting precious little in return."[64] Yet it is claimed that on balance African athletes on the college scene feel that, overall, the college experience has been a positive one.[65] But the temptation to aggregate both sports and institutions into homogeneous groups should be resisted since different sports and different universities have characteristics about which it is difficult, if not impossible, to generalize. Add to this the many personalities represented among coaches and student-athletes and generalization becomes extremely hazardous. Structures *are* important and international recruiting reflects both American education and achievement sport; but individuals within these structures are also important and they will react differently to the situations in which they find themselves.

The Brawn Drain and the Preference to Remain

A frequent problem associated with talent migration is that following education abroad, talent may be permanently lost to the donor countries. Athletic talent, like academic talent, can be interpreted in an economic sense. Many former foreign student-athletes provide their talent to the American public, providing role models for local potential athletes and psychic income for local residents or university affiliates. They may, on graduating or leaving the university, also provide non-athletic talent to the American business or economic system and are lost to their home country. In rare cases they may take out US citizenship during or following their student careers and even represent the United States internationally. The best example of this was the case of Sydney Maree, a black South African who was recruited by Villanova University. Unable to compete internationally because of the boycott of South African sports, he assumed US citizenship and was selected to represent the United States in the Olympic Games.

European evidence suggests that a quarter of foreign recruits are likely to reside in the United States after leaving college. Nearly 42 percent appear to be uncertain about returning home, and slightly less than one-third decided not to live in America upon the completion of their college careers (table 36). This latter figure contrasts with Hollander's finding that 59.2 percent of foreign student-athletes in track and field planned to return home after college.[66] However, the discrepancy is likely to be explained by the greater cultural heterogeneity of his sample, which contained African as well as European respondents. The greater the cultural distance between foreign stu-

Table 36. Intention of European student-athletes (track and swimming) to remain in USA after college (n = 93).

Response	Number	Percent
Yes	24	25.8
Perhaps	39	41.9
No	29	31.2

Source: Author's research.

dents and the United States, the greater the likelihood of their returning home on leaving college.[67]

Of course, it is impossible to be certain how long students would reside in America following completion of their time at college. The temptation to stay might be great; salaries on obtaining a bachelor's degree are substantially higher than in the UK, for example. The decision to stay in America may not be the preferred option but is often undertaken for solely financial reasons. One athlete told me: "I have chosen to remain in the USA since graduation in 1981 because generally the financial rewards and opportunities for outstanding athletes are higher than those in the UK. I do miss many aspects of British life, e.g., the humour, the landscape, the variety of daily newspapers, and perhaps in later years I will want to return on a permanent basis. *But* only if financially stable!" Another added: "When I returned to Britain my degree did not help me. That is why I returned to the States where I am currently pursuing an MA in English. I hope to teach in the States, not out of choice but out of necessity."

Conclusion

The outcome of culture-contact between foreign student-athletes and US residents is probably nearer to assimilation than to segregation, although given the heterogeneity of the student-athlete recruits, considerable variation will exist. By implication, a positive image of the United States will exist prior to sojourn and the high profile given to sports in US popular media and in American life in general will probably assist in overcoming, or at least helping to reduce, culture shock. Assimilation is far from total, however, since most student-athletes are temporary migrants and a very high level of return migration occurs, if not always immediately after a period at college. All the evidence suggests that most foreign student-athletes enjoy the period of sojourn in America. They are often academically bright; they improve their athletic performances while in the United States and, if not culturally distanced from America, display an inclination to remain in the United States after college. While in college they tend to be immersed in an athletic subculture which serves to reinforce their existing achievement-sport ideologies.

Despite the pleasure apparently gained by foreign student-athletes in the United States, the subject of foreign recruiting is not without controversy. Indeed, recruiting per se is probably one of the most controversial subjects in American sports and American higher education. For this reason chapter 8 will explore these controversies. However, foreign student-athletes are given the chance to relate their stories in more detail in the next chapter.

SEVEN

Being There

The previous chapter described the general experiences of a large number of foreign student-athletes. It should be stressed again, however, that such generalizations obscure a good deal of variation. Some student-athletes gain degrees while others only go to the United States to take part in sports; some attend high-powered NCAA schools while others go to junior colleges with small enrollments; some come from Europe, others from Africa; some are men, others women. Many other differences could be identified. The purpose of the present chapter is to explore the foreign student-athlete experience in more depth by allowing such students to speak for themselves.

What follows are transcriptions of oral statements by or conversations with a small number of foreign students who spent varying amounts of time in American universities, taking part in sports. I conducted interviews with the students in the United Kingdom and in the United States between 1986 and 1989.[1] These "career stories" are used to show "how necessary it is to maintain an open attitude toward both the unique [i.e., this chapter] and the general [i.e., previous chapters], and suggest what a loss it would be if a pluralism of styles could not be encouraged."[2] The names of persons and schools in this chapter have been changed to honor confidentiality.

Maria

(Maria talked about her experiences in the United States, having been at a major sport-oriented state university for a year and a half.)

I was introduced to golf by my father back in Sweden and by the time I was in my teens I was playing pretty seriously. At the age of sixteen, I left school and entered a technical college to study engineering. I did consider going to a university in Sweden and though my high school grades were okay, they were not quite good enough — and anyway, a Swedish university would not have been a good place for me to carry on my golf. You see, by my late teens I was among the best golfers in Sweden. Anyway, I qualified in engineering and then I felt I needed a break from the Swedish educational system.

While playing golf I met some Americans on a tour of Sweden. I had talked about the US college system with fellow golfers but I didn't really know too much about it so the discussions with the Americans helped me quite a lot. As a result I wrote to four universities in the United States. One replied quickly and asked me to do a test and write a short autobiography. This took me a little time to do and while the university was partially satisfied with my efforts they were not totally happy. Nevertheless, they offered me a place, but in the meantime I heard from another college in the southwest, offering me a scholarship but not requiring a SAT. With two offers I had to make a choice. The second offered me the best scholarship, including tuition fees but not accommodation. But I had got a loan from the Swedish government to supplement my athletic scholarship. People in Sweden told me that the second university was better than the alternative, which was in Florida and didn't have much of a reputation for golf.

So I decided to take "Wobegone State's" offer. I knew nothing at all about the climate of the area to which I had decided to go. The only areas Swedes know anything about are California and Florida and the only thing I knew about the town in which my university was located in was that it was small! It was really a surprise when I eventually arrived at the airport and found that it was very hot and humid, the temperature being over 100°F. The golf coach picked me up at the airport. I was so tired that when I arrived at the campus I went straight to bed and slept soundly. The early days at the university involved enrolling, walking around the campus, and meeting the golf coach, along with the rest of the golf team. I actually met the golf team before my roommate (a basketball player) and on my first weekend started to play my first rounds of golf since leaving Sweden.

At first I felt that the transition from Sweden to the US had been too great and my golf suffered. But after the initial problems had been sorted out I recovered my form and now, with one year over, I'm the third best golfer on the team. As I was twenty-two years old when I came here I have two more years' eligibility. I have managed to cope with the academic work even though when I came here I knew nothing at all about the American university system. I had no expectations about the US environment but the schedule I have set myself leaves me with little spare time. I attend class in the mornings, play golf in the afternoons, and study in the evenings. I don't know if I'll get a degree or not; I'd certainly like to but it depends how far I get during my period of eligibility. I'm close to my coach and see her every day but I don't find that she puts too much pressure on me; I put pressure on myself.

Eduardo

(Eduardo was interviewed during his second year at a large university [25,000 students], "Southern Lakes University," in the Midwest.)

When did you start gymnastics and when did you recognize that you had some talent?

I started gymnastics when I was eleven and by the time I was eighteen felt that I had got some potential.

Did you have offers of scholarships from universities other than SLU?

Yes I did. I had offers from Oklahoma State and Indiana State.

How did the people in the US get to know about you? What was the contact?

What happened was that there were a few Brazilian gymnasts in the USA, one of whom was doing his graduate work at SLU. Basically, he was the person who introduced me to everyone here.

How did they contact you—phone, letter, or what?

After the guy from Brazil talked to the coach here, the coach phoned me and tried to explain everything about the program and how it worked. When he phoned me the first time, he introduced me to the basic things about the university.

Did you feel that you were being pressured at all by the coach?

Not really, because it was a decision I had taken a long time before.

Did they tell you about any of the potential problems you might encounter in the US?

I don't think they told me about any problems, and I don't think I was worried about it at the time. I was more concerned about getting to America than anything else. That was June 1986.

What were your first impressions of SLU and the set-up there?

I liked it a lot. I got a real good impression when I first came here. The buildings, the campus, and everything looked so organized and clean.

Who met you at the airport when you first arrived?

The Brazilian guy I was talking about picked me up; he was my roommate for the first year or so and he introduced me to everything.

How about contact with the academic departments and the courses? Did the athletic department help you out with that or did you sort things out for yourself?

The athletic department didn't really help me but there is an office for international students and they do the whole thing—like introduce me to the university and the way it works and to advise me about what classes to take for the first semester.

Did you find that there was any conflict between your academic work and training for gymnastics?

I think that in my case they pretty well complemented each other. I find time to study and to do gymnastics. I've had no problem studying for tests or anything. I'm doing fine with my academics—so far!

Since you've been here do you find that you spend most of your time with athletes—particularly in the gymnastics team—or with non-athletes?

I spend most of my time with the athletes. Having fellow Brazilians here helped me overcome some of the problems when I first arrived. The gymnastics team has people from Norway and Germany as well, and I socialize with everybody.

Since you've been here have you had to make adjustments to "culture shock," or has anything like that posed a problem?

I think I've changed a lot in the way I act. Things here are real different from in Brazil; people react differently.

Have diet, climate, people been a problem?

The worst problem was the culture. Like going to a party and knowing how to act different was difficult for me. Women are real liberal here; they can say things to men that wouldn't be allowed in Brazil; they have stronger opinions here.

Any problems with the diet?

I don't think I had any problems; I cook the Brazilian way!

And the weather?

It is way colder here than in Brazil but it wasn't a real problem.

How about the other foreign athletes; have they had any problems as far as you know?

I don't think they experienced the same kind of difficulties I had. I think the fact that they were brought up in Germany or Norway means that they are closer to the US than the way I was brought up.

When you complete your degree in another two years, have you thought about staying in the US, continuing to grad school, or returning to Brazil?

I'm thinking about staying in America for a long time, like possibly going to graduate school or maybe getting a job here. I don't really feel like going back to Brazil, especially with all the problems we have down there. It would be real hard for me to readapt to things down there.

What problems are you talking about down there? The culture, the poverty, or what?

Both, but the economic problem would be the major one.

If you could get a job there and live a good life materially, would that be more of an inducement to go back?

Not really. With the degree I'm getting here I would probably make good money there but everything that is going on around you is really depressing.

Have you ever felt that you've been exploited at all as a student-athlete?

I don't think so. With gymnastics I'm getting my degree. I don't think I should be getting any more than that.

What advice would you give to a Brazilian thinking of coming to the US as a student-athlete?

I would say to be prepared to change and modify yourself, to accept different things and try to learn from them. On balance I think it is a good experience. Everybody ought to be able to go to some place which has a different culture. I think it makes you grow.

Brett

(Brett talked about life at college while at "Anastasia State," one of the major sport-oriented state universities.)

In Australia I had played tennis since the age of seven or eight and won some national titles. I never studied at all at high school and certainly never thought about going on to higher education in Australia; I would simply never have got near a university over there. I had never heard about athletic scholarships in the States until I was sixteen. Then I met a guy who had been at university in Tennessee and he suggested I went there on a scholarship. In addition, the tennis coach from Arkansas was in Australia and he talked to me about going there. What is more, the coach from Wichita telephoned me and sent information about the university there. So I was approached by a number of US universities in my late teens.

I left school at seventeen; tennis had been my life in high school and I totally ignored the academic side. In Australia I met a group of students from Anastasia State; the coach was with them and after talking, he offered me a full scholarship. Accepting his offer and coming to America was the most important decision of my life and, so far, I've not regretted it. Although some people at home said that tennis standards in American colleges were not very high there was nothing to keep me in Australia. More tennis circuits existed elsewhere. But it is quite hard to recruit Americans to Anastasia State because of its negative image—you know, in the middle of nowhere.

Before I enrolled at Anastasia I played in Europe in September and then returned to Australia to enjoy our summer. Having done so I set off for the US and arrived in January, dressed only in a T-shirt! It was really cold in that part of America and it came as a bit of a surprise. My first impressions were that the tennis facilities were excellent. I met the three other new recruits that semester, one of whom was from South Africa. We were accommodated in the athletic dorm and I liked that; we had a kind of fraternity house of our own.

We've had quite a few foreigners here on the tennis squad. I have noticed that foreign student-athletes often have a different, less competitive attitude than Americans: Europeans in particular seem to have some problems while they're here. We had a Swedish tennis player here who clashed with the coach and soon left. We also had two South Africans who left before their eligibility was finished.

My full scholarship ran to about $250 per month—$1,300 per semester [in 1985]. My eligibility has now finished so I'm helping out with the coaching before I graduate. I've been majoring in Recreation Administration and Development. The coach stresses that we are representing the school when we are playing tennis. But I've never felt that I've received preferential treatment because I'm an athlete. Most of my friends were initially on the tennis team but now they're in the fraternity. I enjoy being here but being in the US has changed my attitudes to certain things.

I go back to Australia at Christmas but I hope to get a job in the US when I graduate. I would like to be a tennis coach; in fact, I am going for an interview for this kind of job in Denver, Colorado. I could make $30,000 a year as an assistant coach so I will not be going back to Australia straight away. I'll make some money here and maybe return later.

(Brett did not get his degree but continued working as a tennis coach in the United States.)

Louise

(This interview with Louise was held about one year after she graduated from "Nokowa University," a major sport-oriented institution in one of the principal conferences.)

Can you tell me when you started sports in a serious way? How old were you when you started?

I was about twelve years old when I started running, although I had done other sports before then, like swimming and some others.

And by what age did you begin to realize that you had considerable potential as an athlete?

Not really until I was about fifteen or sixteen and I didn't really show through until I was about seventeen or eighteen internationally.

What sort of standard domestically were you achieving at that period?

I ran for the junior Great Britain squad when I was eighteen but I wasn't a regular international.

Did you find that during the period, shall we say between the ages of sixteen and eighteen, your participation in sports interfered very much with your school work?

No, not at all really. I think it fitted in just has it had done all along.

So you were able to achieve good school results while carrying on with your sport?

Oh yes, definitely, nothing changed—I just got better. I was able to do my "O" levels and my "A" levels without any problem at all. I didn't train that much though. Some people trained a lot more than I did; I only trained three times a week and raced on a Saturday.

With good academic results, did you have any expectation about going on to higher education in Britain?

Yes, I had applied to go to university before I did my "A" levels but I didn't receive any offers that year. I wanted to go to Loughborough especially and for some reasons (I am not really sure why) I didn't get offered a place, but when it came to my exam results I had done okay. When this offer of a scholarship came up to go to Nokowa University, I decided that I would take that and reapply to go to Loughborough. I came home the following Christmas after being in the USA for a few months and they offered me a place at Loughborough, which I then deferred for a year, as I liked it so much in Nokowa. When it came to the end of the second year there, I had to decide whether I was going to come back and go to Loughborough or not; I decided not to.

Can I go back to the time you had the offer from Nokowa. Had you had any other offers from other American universities at the same time?

When I was about sixteen or seventeen I had an offer from Iowa State and from Arizona State (I think). At that time it just seemed too out of this world. I didn't want to go to America; it just seemed like too far away and I couldn't handle that. But having done my "A" levels and then having nowhere to go, it seemed like it was a really good opportunity. Nokowa was really the only one that was there at the time. They contacted me in July and I said that there was no way I wanted to go. So I went away, did my "A" levels, went to France, came back, and I thought about what I could do. It was either taking a chance and going anywhere in the UK that would take me or going to Nokowa, so I contacted them again and they asked me if I could still come.

Now how do you think these people in America got to know about you?

Well, as far as I know they read through the rankings and they contact quite a few people. I was quite highly ranked that year so I was just one of the people that they contacted. They spend a lot of money recruiting people and some people get flown there for visits in the States. I know they had a girl there this year from Holland who they were bringing to the university to see if she liked it, but I never visited a university before I went.

Did you speak to anybody from the university on the telephone before you went?

Yes, I did, that's how they contact you.

They contacted you by telephone and therefore you would have had some time to make a decision. Did they counsel you at all or did you feel that they were pressuring you at all? Did they advise you on the benefits and possible problems that might occur, or did you feel a sort of hard sell to get you to go there?

I wouldn't say that they counsel you or set out the problems that you are going to experience. I think that you are very much left to find those out for yourself. I do think that they are selling the university to you in a way because they are trying to encourage you to go there, just as much as any university here publishes a brochure or a pamphlet and wants you to go there. Obviously, over the phone it's much harder. In Nokowa it was a bit different because I didn't have that much time from July until August, but with Iowa State before that they sent me a package of information, of statistics, of how their runners had done and what courses I could take, so it's a bit of a sales job really, but no more than you would have anywhere else.

So what time of the year was the decision finally made that you would go out to the USA in '83?

I didn't decide until the last week of August in '83 and then I went that week.

What were your initial impressions of the university and the set-up over there when you landed in the United States?

Well, I was met at the airport by the coaches, who took me back to my hall of residence. It was dark at the time and it took me a long time to get my bearings. It seems funny now but the university seemed so big and I was left alone with a roommate (you have roommates there). I didn't know American people and I think it's a totally different culture to ours and it took me quite a while before I got settled in. They put me in the charge of one of the other runners on the team who was very nice. For the first weekend, which was Labor Day weekend, I stayed at my roommate's home. I was a week late arriving and the university had already just begun, and so it was ever so quiet and I couldn't understand how this vast university had no students, but they had all gone home for the Labor Day weekend. For the first two months, I felt very lonely and I had to do a lot more running than I was used to, but in retrospect it's no more than I do now.

But when you said you had to do a lot more running, are you suggesting that there was some sort of deal that you had to deliver the goods?

Well, I think so. They pay for you to be there, you do what they say, if you can. But I think it is very wrong to say that they pressurize you into training really hard. They are quite willing to work out individual schedules for you and they don't push you any more. The coach knew I was running between twelve and twenty miles a week when I went out there and the girls that were running there already were running something like seventy miles a week. Well, he didn't put me onto seventy miles a week or anything like that, but he did increase my mileage quite substantially. But when I went out there I had just finished a track season and they were already into their cross-country training, so it was much more mileage anyway than they would do when they were competing and so I had to slot in there. But I think it was better that I slotted in than play the prima donna, wanting an individual training schedule or anything. I did feel that I owed them my training.

What about the academic side? You were met by people from the athletic department at the airport and they were the people who sorted out your residences and so on? What about contact with academic departments and counseling about courses you should follow?

They set you up with the courses initially because when they contact you, you tell them what you would like to do. Well, I didn't know anything about the universities there and I didn't understand what a major was and minor subjects and things like that. I had initially wanted to do geography and PE at Loughborough, so I was trying to do something along those lines there. But I found myself in classes I wasn't happy in — mostly in physical education because a lot of people, if they are in sports, automatically go into physical education. Well, I didn't really like that and after the first semester I was much more aware of how I should go about getting on the right courses for what I wanted to do eventually and so I sorted myself out. For the first term I did courses which were okay, but it wasn't really the right direction for what I wanted to do ultimately.

Did you find that there was any conflict between the training and the running and the academic side or that the two complement each other quite easily?

Not really, because you can schedule your own lectures. Certainly some lectures come in the evenings or the afternoons but the majority are in the mornings and they give all athletes priority of classes that fit in with their schedules. They might run the same course but with a different lecturer and three times in a day so you can take that course in a morning at 8:30 or 10:30 or whenever, rather than being slotted into a section which is mainly running at 3:00 in the afternoon. We used to have all our classes in the morning or the evenings and training was always at 3:45 until dinner time in the evening.

Why did you decide to stay in the States rather than come back to Britain as you originally thought you might?

Well, first of all, in the first couple of months I can remember writing home saying, "Well, it is all right for an experience but I would hate to live here." But by the end of that first three months, before I came home at Christmas, I really enjoyed the team spirit, having a coach that was on hand all the time, fantastic facilities to train, and I felt that the academic side of it was fine. I honestly didn't see that there was any point in coming back and starting a course here when I had done so much over there. All those factors made me want to stay there.

Did you find that while you were there, you spent most time with other athletes or non-athletes?

Definitely athletes. All of my friends really were based around the track team, and if they weren't on the track team at the time I was there, they had been. But you live in a resident hall too and you meet lots of people there as well. I lived in the halls for about nearly all of the four years I was there.

Was that an athletic hall?

No, they don't segregate you.

Some of the universities do have those, don't they?

I think they do.

Did you find there were a large number of other foreign students there with you or were you the only one?

There were quite a few other foreign people there but not from England. I was the only English person, and there was a few from Jamaica, some from Canada (if they are considered foreign), and I think there was a girl from Holland.

And do you think that the other foreigners there had the same kind of problems of adjusting as you did and did they all adjust satisfactorily in the way that you had, or did some of the other foreigners have different experiences from you?

I think some people had problems with the language because they didn't always speak English and that's really a barrier in itself. There was one girl from Norway and she found it really difficult. She couldn't speak American at all and she had to learn the language first before she could really do the academics. I think that really a lot of them go home after the first term because they can't manage the language.

Did you feel that you had any problems at all coping with the academic work? Did you find the academic work was a strain, did you find it easy, or was it just as you had expected?

I don't really know what I expected actually. I didn't really have a lot of time to ponder and think about it, but having been told it would be a cinch, the first year of the university there is very much like our "A"-level year and I don't think that it is much harder. But then as you move up the levels, going from 100-, 200-, 300-, to 400-level courses. The higher you get, the more difficult it gets, and I think that although the Americans might start out lower than us, by the time you get to the second year, things are about equal. The first year was okay but I didn't sail through, you know, score 100 percent; I never did anything like that. It wasn't dead easy and was probably more difficult than I thought.

How typical were you of the other foreign recruits in terms of graduating?

Well, I don't think a lot of them stayed over the whole four years. I think the majority probably dropped out before and went home, after a couple of years. For example, I know somebody who had been there for two years but has gone home for good now. So I don't think I was very typical of the foreign students, but it all depends on how adaptable you are and what you find for yourself there, how you make it work for you. Some people don't even go there with the intention of finishing; some people just take it as a break from study in our country. But I didn't see it like that, you know.

At the end of four years, you got your degree and you then had to decide what to do. Had you considered staying in America and capitalizing on the degree over there?

After the second year I did think I could live in America and I felt that I would stay there. But by the time I got to four years there I was really homesick and I wanted to come back and live in this country.

I was thinking then about where I was actually going to live and what I was going to do. It is very important for me to be close to my family, not in their back pocket but at least on the same continent. I just thought that there was no point in me living in America and never seeing them any more. So that was the major factor in my coming back; had it not been for my family I could quite easily loved to live in America. Also, work permits were a problem and I didn't think I would be able to get a work permit very easily.

What is the situation with work permits, then?

Well, as far as I know, you can have a job if an American can't fill it or if it is in a profession which is in demand and there is space for you. For example, an accountant can get a work permit, at least for a few years, maybe a temporary work permit. I was in teaching and I didn't think that I would find that very easy unless I wanted to go somewhere like Houston or California where they are having lots of problems recruiting teachers.

You mention that you wanted to go into teaching and you wanted, therefore, if you were coming back to England, to get the PGCE in Britain.[3] What was the situation about applying for a British PGCE course with an American degree?

Well, most places weren't interested. Two universities in England just turned me down flat.

What did they say?

That my qualification wasn't suitable for their course. The polytechnics were much more open to me.[4] I wrote to them before I completed the degree. They replied saying that if I took more courses in sociology and things like that, then I would be acceptable. But here the social science is much more based around sociology, so they wanted me to have a broader base in sociology; well, I didn't want to do that. Then Rummidge and Suffolk each offered me a place and I came to Suffolk.

There was a slight problem then in the sense that all institutions didn't recognize the US qualification. But were there other problems of adjusting back to the British system, having spent four years in the United States?

I don't think so. I haven't had any problems really this year, settling in with students here or anything. It is no different to how I expected it to be, and really I have settled in very well.

You say you didn't have any problems adjusting to the academic situation back in Britain and mixing with the students at Suffolk. What about the situation with the running? In the US you had a coach, you'd had the superb facilities, and then you come to a place like Suffolk with no facilities and no coach.

Well, I really missed it a lot, and I missed having the professionalism which they have there in their coaching. It's very good. You feel that they are being paid to do a job, so they are going to do it to the best of their ability. That's their life; whether it's a hobby in addition to being their job, it's still their life, and they put so much time and effort into it; it's incredible. There is so much available for you if you are sick or injured; the facilities are just fantastic. And you have a lot of faith in the coach. Now I'm back here, I don't even have a coach; I haven't had a coach all year. So it has been a real struggle and I think my running has suffered this summer because of that, although in the winter it was all right because anyone can go out and do a run and I just based my own training around what I did with them anyway. But you can only motivate yourself so far and on the track it is much more difficult. You get sick of running 'round timing yourself and having nobody to motivate you.

Now can you tell me if any foreign students in the United States, on athletic scholarships, have problems of leaving and subsequently re-entering the United States?

Yes, I certainly think they do because everyone is given an F1 duration-of-stay visa, or at least you are from Britain. I assume it's similar for other countries, and you have to have an I-20 form for every time you enter the country. This duration-of-stay visa lasts for four years (or mine was for four years), and then once that's up you have to have it renewed if you want to come back to the country and explain why; it's quite a lot of hassle. So I do think there is a tendency for students not to bother doing that because once they are in the country and as long as they don't leave, it would take a long time for anyone to catch up with them and to deport them. So quite a few students do tend to stay on without visas. In effect they are in the country illegally.

Do you think that would be more typical of students on athletic scholarships than other foreign students?

Yes, I do. Because usually other foreign students have got much more money—probably some grant from their own country. Also, athletics does sometimes interfere with your academic work. I know the baseball players have to go to the summer school sessions to make up their hours for the year, so that they are eligible to compete. So really there are certain sports where I do think the academics suffer because of it. Football and baseball are definitely two. But I don't think track is the same.

I was going to ask you about that, because one of the things that some sociologists say about American college sports is that student-athletes are exploited, by which they mean there is a lot of pressure put on them to perform in sports at the expense of their academic work. You didn't find that yourself though?

No, not at the expense of my academic work.

So what you would really say then is that, from your experience, it was in football, basketball, and baseball that the pressure was greatest.

Yes, because they seem to have games all through the week as well as the weekend. They would go away for three weeks at a time to play in tournaments and things like that. Anything which involves tournaments obviously takes up a lot of time and I really think the big-money sports like football float the university; they support the university and without their money, their track team wouldn't even exist. They wouldn't have any money at all. So really, them playing and drawing in the crowds and everything is very important for the university. And baseball, I don't know why that takes up so much time; I think it is because they have to go to so many places.

Can we talk about the situation with regard to the scholarship they gave you. Is it a one-year scholarship that is renewed annually or is it a four-year scholarship?

Well, there was a bit of confusion when I went there, really, because I was told that I would be offered a four-year scholarship at the time and nobody pointed out anything different to me. Well, when I get there, after the first year, I found out that it is reviewed every year and if you haven't performed up to a certain standard you would lose your scholarship. But you would have to do quite badly to get your scholarship revoked, but you do have to perform to a certain sort of standard. Otherwise you get cut, and of course that can really leave a foreign student out in the cold. I would have had to come home because there is no way I could have afforded to pay. I would need to have a scholarship which was about $8,500 to $9,000 a year. I could never have afforded to pay that sort of money.

What about if you had been injured as a result of training?

Injury doesn't affect your scholarship, not at the university where I was. But every university is autonomous in that sense and they all have their own rules. Some of the universities violate the rules and some don't. You are not supposed to pay for any kind of personal expenses for the students so they are not supposed to come and pick you up at the airports unless they have met you for the first time. But injury really does not affect it at all, so you would be safe there.

When you say some universities violate the rules, I think you'd probably say also that some departments and some sports are more likely to do so than other sports. Did you find that track and field at Nokowa was relatively honest in the way they operated?

From my own experience I never found them to be otherwise.

What about the drug situation?

I don't actually know of any drugs at my own university. I mean, you hear about it but I couldn't honestly say I would have any evidence of it, or evidence to say it happened. It's all over the place really. In my own part of the track team there was definitely none but I do think there might have been in other areas, but I don't know for sure.

But that would be based on some sort of circumstantial evidence—the fact that somebody had a meteoric improvement.

Yes.

Can we go back to talk about your relationship with the coach? Did you find the coach an authoritarian personality and how did you react in general to the coach?

He wasn't authoritarian at all. He was very well meaning. He was a very nice sort of person but he was quite religious to the point that he didn't really like anyone having a social life that I consider normal for a teenager. He didn't want me to go out to parties, to have boy friends, to drink at all, and all things like that. We really had a bit of conflict of personality. It was okay for the first two years, but gradually everything built up and we did have a rough patch in my third year when we had to have a long discussion about this. There were other girls there who were very much more dedicated to the sport than me and I was always compared to them. And yet I used to train with them and I used to perform as well, but for some reason he couldn't accept that I wanted to be young and normal, and running wasn't the be-all and end-all of my life. I didn't want to waste my youth just being so dedicated to sport.

Do you think that Americans with perhaps a similar background have a more traditional relationship with the coach? Would they have responded differently from a foreigner?

Yes. Where I was (and I am sure it is very different on the coast than in the center of America) the majority of people, if they are from in-state, come from farming communities or small towns and the drinking age is twenty-one. They would come to college for the first time — it's the first time they have been let loose so to speak — they either didn't drink at all or if they are athletes they tended not to get involved in that. On the other hand, people that weren't athletes used to go on binges of drinking and partying and having just a whale of a time, spending money, grants and everything, and blowing it all before the first term was over. It was almost like they had been under the thumb and then they had been let loose for the first time. Well, I wasn't really like that because in England it is much more, sort of, progressive from when you are younger. I mean your parents might introduce you to alcohol in a small way and then you'd go to the pub and you might have a few drinks. I felt that I wanted to just live a normal lifestyle, whereas some of the local people weren't interested in doing that because they were really dedicated to sport. From their high schools they had come through with the school coach and had just gone on. Here [in the UK] it is a club-based thing, very separate from your school.

Is this pride-in-school thing much stronger in America?

It is, and their standard of track in school in general, even in small towns, is much better than ours. Here you have to get to the English Schools Championships before you are really running at a high level.

I think you are saying that the American kids were much more in tune with the system.

Yes. But it was because my coach was particularly religious too.

Was it a sort of a fundamental Christian sect of some kind?

Yes, it was. I don't actually know what it was called now. He just happened to believe very strongly in his own beliefs and I felt that he was imposing them on me. But actually when we look back on it now, we really got on fine and it is just this misunderstanding. I was much too sensitive to what I thought he was thinking of me. He probably didn't really care as much as I thought he did.

Did other foreign athletes respond to him in the same way as you did?

I don't know. I know there were a few South Africans there that got on a lot better with him than I did. But they didn't want the same things in life as I did. They were dedicated to running and I think that's where it all went wrong really. I didn't have the dedication that many other athletes have and wouldn't run in the mornings. He thought that was awful, but I can't run in the morning and I thought that going from running three times a week to training twice a day was too much, so we compromised and I didn't do it. But I think he thought that because I wasn't doing it that I wasn't training as hard as them; but I was. I put everything into it.

What was the situation with other American students in both athletics and in academic work with respect to you as a foreign student? Did you find because you were English you were popular or did you find the opposite?

I think the Americans are very, very receptive to British people. Much nicer than the British are to the Americans. I got on very well, I think; it was an asset to me to have an English accent and that helped me quite a lot.

You mentioned the South Africans that were there. Was there any negative reaction to South Africans while you were there? These were white South Africans presumably?

Yes, they were all white South Africans. Well, I don't think there was any reaction on the team or anything. Really, half the team is black and half the team is white, and all the South Africans slotted in fine with the other people, but I remember there was bit of trouble with the white South Africans and the press in the town. At one time — it was probably to do with Zola Budd I should think — they were reporting about Zola in a local paper. Well, the white South Africans were really upset about this and they went and wrote to the paper to put in their point of view. So I think there was a little bit of trouble in that sense. Also, they wouldn't let some of the South Africans run in the local road races.

So South Africans could run in college meetings but not in open meetings.

Yes; not always though. It did get to be more like that after four years, but there is this strong "you mustn't let them compete" attitude in the road races. There was a road-running club with which the track

team were very close and it was run by separate persons, but we used
to get all our fees waived, we never had to enter the races or anything.
It was all because they were very friendly with the track team and
that was really good, but sometimes it caused a bit of a problem
because South Africans wanted to run and people complained; but
really, I liked them all very much and they weren't racist or anything
like that; it was really good.

What was the attitude of the local students to South Africans and foreigners?

I think there were some local people who disliked the fact that a lot
of people on the team were foreign.

Were the majority foreign?

At one time, yes. It changes and I was there for four years. At one
time I think nearly everyone in my section of the team, the distance
squad, was foreign. Then they form very close cliques with their own
in-state people. One year when the team won the Conference or
something, it was made up of almost entirely in-state athletes and they
were so proud of that. There was a bit of tension between the foreigners and the in-state people.

*So did you find that most of your friends were other foreigners rather than
Americans?*

Yes, they were, when I think back to it. Mostly they were Canadian.
But even if they are from Massachusetts or somewhere, they were
regarded as "foreign" by the in-state people. They had all come away
from home to stay at this university and I think that they held just
as much against those people as they did against me or anyone from
overseas. But it wasn't really very obvious, it was just sort of little
niggling.

*Do you think that in-state student-athletes reacted against foreign student-
athletes because they are basically taking scholarships away from local people?*

Well, I don't think they would mind if they got a full scholarship,
too, but you can't go over there unless you are on a full ride. You
see there was this big thing about, "Do you get the full scholarship?"
"Do you get a partial scholarship?" "How much is allotted to you?"

*The other thing I wanted to ask you was whether you found that being an
athlete helped you financially at all in a direct or indirect way. You had your
grant, your scholarship, which only paid for your tuition and accommodation.*

No, you never see any money. Everything is paid for so when your bills come through you just go and take it to the appropriate place, they sign whatever it is that needs signing, and you are paid for. When you get your books at the start of term or anything like that or for your classes you have to take along your schedule and they sign it and they say you can go to the bookshop and get the books that you need. It is all paid for you but you don't actually see any money. Or you shouldn't. If you do that it's illegal.

What about getting jobs on campus? Wasn't that necessary?

If you wanted to stay during the summer, they can sometimes get you a job on campus, which is okay. But during term time you are not allowed to have a job at all, although I am sure some people do. You really can't get in a job in a local pizza place or somewhere like that because you have to have a Social Security number and ours were always zero, zero, zero for the first three numbers, so they knew automatically that you were a foreign student, and so you couldn't really get a job. But it was very expensive. My parents paid for me to go home twice a year, which is £1000, but you'd go through that just to live there for a semester. That is quite a lot of money really. In some universities they do pay for them to go home and break the rules. If they didn't, athletes might not go there.

What about the qualifications you got from America? The degree that they gave you is sometimes thought of as second rate in this country and nobody told you when you went to the States what you could do with the degree. What are your reactions to that?

I think it is up to you, the responsible individual, to look into that yourself. Do they sit down and tell you what you can do with the degree here? I don't think so. I listened to a girl on the radio the other day saying that she had got a degree in history here but she can't get a job using her degree at all. I just don't understand why people prize the academics so much in this country and look down on US degrees when, in fact, Americans come out of university and can get really good, well-paid jobs and we can't.

So your observations are that the American degree in many respects has advantages and characteristics that the British degree doesn't have, that it is more broadly based and makes you more adaptable.

Well, I have learned a lot about subjects that I would never had touched on if I had lived in this country, because I would have done probably geography and PE. So I might know a wealth of knowledge about that but I wouldn't have done economics or sociology or child psychology, which I spent a lot of time doing there and it's all really interesting. Yes, it's much more superficial and not nearly as much in depth, but I don't think for practical everyday life it's essential to know so much depth about one area, because when you get out to the real world it doesn't count.

Can you include the athletic participation that you did as part of your degree qualifications in America? You know, if you compete for the cross-country team or the track team? Does that count toward your degree?

Well, what you have to do, you have to get a certain amount of credit hours. I had to get something like 125 credit hours and they specify which hours. You have to have a certain number in different areas. So I had to have so many professional teaching qualifications, a certain amount in my academic subject area, and then you have a few hours which are elective. The idea of that is to let you just take things that you are interested in to make up the last few hours. So you could count the track as one hour or something, hardly anything, and really that is all it counts for.

Earlier you mentioned that part of the reason for staying on in America was that you enjoyed the social life and the friends that you made. Do you want to develop that at all.

Well, I had a boyfriend there from the first year really, and he was a big influence on why I stayed in America, at the college I suppose. Well, of course, he would be. We're getting married in August.

Was he an athlete as well?

Yes, he was from Canada.

After you get married is he going to come back and live in Britain? Is he going to have any problems getting a job in this country with his American qualification?

No, he is going to transfer with his company and he will just come and work for them. But he has already had two years' experience of working, so he has got that to his credit. But has has done the CPA which is the Chartered Accountant exams for America and he has done his master's degree there as well. When he comes over here, if he wants to move around in the accounting profession, which he doesn't expect to have to do, he will have to go back and take his accountancy exams again.

So in the case of your fiancé, when he comes over here, if he wants to change jobs, he would have to get the British accountancy qualification?

Yes.

While you were in America you participated in lots of events, presumably all over the country. Where in America did you travel to compete?

Well, the majority of the races were based around the conference schools which were in the neighboring states. We went to Texas, Arizona, Nebraska, Iowa, and Oklahoma. But then they go much further afield too, so I spent some time in California. They'll fly you to lots of different places. We often went to Florida and over to the East Coast. I think they were very good about taking you all over the place. Money is no object, really. Well, I say it is no object; they will only take you if they think you are going to run well. You know they are a bit selective about who they take.

But that wouldn't apply to all meetings, would it?

No, they will take you to all of the local meetings; what they call local is the surrounding states.

Conference meetings?

Yes, but also when I first went there they took us down for a spring break trip which was a week in Texas. Then you run a meeting at the beginning of the week, you train all week, and you live in a hotel and then they take you to the meet at the end. But they have stopped doing that because of the expense involved.

What was the hotel accommodation like? What sort of standard of hotel did you stay in.

Not bad you know, quite nice hotels. I mean just basic enough.

But are we talking about Holiday Inn or Sheraton?

Quite often it was the Holiday Inn actually. But sometimes it is a bit less than that. Motels and things like that. Or Super 8. But they drive for miles and miles. I mean we drove for eleven hours in one day, and they drive the entire way and they stop off maybe twice and that's it. I found that unbelievable.

Can you give advice to anybody from Britain who might be considering going to America, or is it so much an individual thing that it really would be very difficult to advise anybody?

Well, what I'd tell them is that they shouldn't bank on using the degree in this country because it doesn't work for them, so they would need to understand that before they go. They should realize that the scholarship is a one-year deal and they renew it every year. They should also realize that there is no money given to you and that you really should have quite a fair amount of money at your disposal to do it. And that it is a very individual thing and that the academic side of it can be easy because of the variety of subjects you can take. I mean you can even get a degree in horticulture, I should think. I think it can be easy to get a degree but if you do the right subjects it can be just as challenging as doing a degree here.

What about someone who wasn't at all interested in the academic side and just wanted to go over for the sports? What should they look out for?

Well, if they just go for the sports and they don't care about the academic side of it, I think they should go somewhere where they are going to get taken to a lot of good-quality meets. I don't think there is any point in going to a small school where you don't get to compete with all the best runners. And I think you ought to go to a school which has got quite a lot of money; a small school doesn't have much money and they won't take you to as many places. I think you want to make the most of the experience, you want to be able to see as much as you can and to sample as much of the culture as you can. It really is a different place, and everyone in America is different as well. So if you go to the Midwest it won't be anything like going to California. I have a friend in the University of Southern California and I would think that would be entirely different.

You attended the University of Nokowa. Did they have trouble attracting Americans, out-of-state Americans, to that university?

Yes, because people who live in other parts of the United States didn't want to come to a place which has the reputation of being hick land and the middle of nowhere if they could get scholarships at other universities—if they were decent enough. Nokowa has a very good reputation as a track team and they probably wouldn't go for people who weren't able to maintain that reputation. So instead they look abroad.

You say that this was a sort of back-and-beyond part of the world and that it had a poor image for many Americans. Did you begin to discover that for yourself after you had been there any time and did you ever consider transferring to another institution, in a more pleasant climate for example?

I never really thought about transferring to a more pleasant place because I liked it so much where I was. The actual place is bland and it is very flat. It is a nice place to visit but you wouldn't want to live there. And that's really how it is. But well, I never wanted to go anywhere else, I was quite happy there.

Was the weather cold in winter?

Yes, freezing in winter and really hot in the summer. But the majority of the time when you are competing, say between September and November, and in the indoor season, it doesn't really matter. Then, in the outdoor season, it's nice. The climate is similar to our climate really. Just a bit hotter and a bit colder; I didn't find the weather too bad really.

One other thing I wanted to mention was the NCAA and the rules that it imposes. Did you find that the kind of rules that operate in United States colleges in any way prevented you doing anything you wanted to do? Did it constrain any races you could run in?

Not really, because I always came back here in the summer and any holidays I had I wasn't there. So all the rest of the time I was either training or competing and their rules didn't affect me. But I know that my roommate, who was a marathon runner, couldn't often compete in races that she wanted to or if she did she couldn't have the money that she could have earned. So I think those rules are a bit constraining.

Presumably not only the rules of the NCAA but the wishes of the coach as well dictated to some extent when you could compete.

Yes, but the road clubs that were in the city that I lived in often had races during the year and we would always go along and help, but we weren't allowed to compete because we had our loyalty to the track team.

Did you feel that was unfair in any way?

No, I don't think so, I don't think that you would expect to be able to compete. We got enough racing without needing to run extras, so that was okay.

There are Third World athletes at Nokowa. What did they do when they finished? Did they graduate, for example?

They have, in my experience, either married Americans, their families have emigrated to the States, or else they have lived there illegally. Some do graduate.

Johann

(This interview with Johann was held two years after he had finished six months' sojourn at a university in one of the mountain states.)

What level of athletic performance had you achieved before you went to the United States?

I was ranked about tenth in the 800 meters and about fifteenth in the 1,500 meters in my country for athletes of my age—which was seventeen.

Did you think about going into higher education in your own country?

Yes, but having had an offer from an American university, I thought it would be a good opportunity to see the States rather than stay at home.

How did you get to know about the university that you attended?

I saw an advertisement in a track magazine. I sent off details of my times and they wrote back and said that they were interested. I then got in touch over the phone.

Was that the only university you applied to?

Yes; it was the only one that I knew about, to be honest.

What were they offering you? A full scholarship?

Not really. They tried to offer me as little as possible over the phone. When I said that I couldn't really afford to go, they were happy to give me more. When I got to the US somebody told me that I could have got more if I'd been more pushy and that they had the money there. They were trying to hold back on what they were giving. The scholarship turned out to be okay but I also had about $2,000 saved up and my parents helped me because they saw it as an opportunity not to be missed. I had to pay the air fare and I had to find my spending money while I was out there. They did offer to get me work while I was there, but opportunities were very limited and what was available tended to be when we had classes.

When you were negotiating over the phone, was there any talk about the academic work involved?

I didn't feel that they were very interested in that. Of course, they had to ask me what academic background I had, but the main objective was to discover how fast you could run. I knew very little about the academic set-up. They said that their degree was as good as any I could get over here. All the time I was in the dark about what the university and the courses were like. I wanted a brochure or something like that. They sent nothing, so in the end I wrote asking for more information about the place because I was getting worried about whether I was being conned. I wondered even if there was a university there! If it had been now, I probably wouldn't have gone.

Why not? What's happened since then that would have changed your mind?

My track performances improved; I went to the world junior championships and since then I've had about five offers from other universities—including places like Notre Dame, Harvard, and Iowa State. They sent me all the literature, whereas I couldn't get it from the college I went to, no matter how hard I asked.

How old were you when you went out there?

I was seventeen, the youngest on the track team by far.

Did you intend to go out for four years and get a degree?

I'm not sure. When I went out I was pretty ignorant about how long it took to get a degree. They didn't really explain that to me because I was really going out there solely to run, not to get an education.

What were your first impressions when you arrived?

Nonstop living! The track coach picked me up at the airport and I stayed in his house the first night. He woke me at 8:00 the next morning and took me straight to the university to show me around.

Did you find the classes difficult to adjust to?

Some were easy but in PE classes I found it difficult to adjust to the theory of sports like football and baseball, which I had never come across before. Other courses had a lot of US content, too, which was new to me.

What was the athletic set-up like?

I had got the impression over the phone that the facilities were excellent but it turned out that it was the facilities that were one of the things that made me come home after six months. The track they had there was in a very bad state; I expected a synthetic track but it turned out to be worn down and virtually concrete. I was also expecting to find some really good runners on the team who I could train with, but it turned out that there was nobody better than me.

Then the coach turned out to be nowhere near as good as I'd expected. I soon started coaching myself! When I talked on the phone I asked about the facilities and though I didn't realize it at the time, it was clear that he was avoiding telling me about them. The coach kept saying they would get a synthetic track shortly—but it never materialized. All our races were at other colleges. Also he said that we would be flying to our track meetings but in fact we were cramped up in twenty-four-hour van journeys to our track meets!

Was there any tension between you and the coach when you decided to coach yourself?

Not really. He more or less let me do what I wanted, and after coaching myself I was running better so they were happy to let me carry on.

Did your track performances improve while you were out there?

Yes. I was pretty consistent over the season and I did a personal best for 800 meters. I peaked for the major championships but I was coaching myself.

Did you get good competition in the track meets?

Yes; we had races against some good West Coast schools like UCLA. The competition was good but there was nobody at my university for me to train with. There was also a problem with the high altitude; I got breathless very quickly.

Did you feel an obligation to go to classes? How important was that?

Messages would be passed on to the coach if we didn't do well in classes. He did remind us to keep up with our academics but it was mainly to get us to keep our GPA up so we'd be able to return next season. He wasn't really interested in my academic work.

You mentioned earlier some of the reasons for not going back after the summer break [the facilities, the coach and the lack of training companions]. Were there any other reasons?

When I came back in the summer I linked up again with my coach and started training with him and had a number of good athletes to train with. The US experience was expensive but I saw it as an opportunity to visit the US and see the place, but to go back would have meant repeating what I had already done unless I decided to stay for four years and get a degree.

Did you think about transferring to another college?

I had thought about it but I didn't really have any links with any other colleges. I didn't really think about it seriously.

Were there any other foreign recruits on the university track team?

Yes, there were a lot of foreigners there, mainly in the distance events. The only Americans in the team were the sprint and power guys. The Americans seem to lack distance runners.

Did you find that your experience of the university was also held by the other foreign recruits?

Not really. One of the guys from England had been out there for five years and really liked it. But a lot of the guys go out to the US when they're not running particularly well and just use the trip to see something of America. I think if you're at your best it's not really the place to be. A lot of the foreigners out there were not of a very high standard. They were not going to do much over here so going to the US was worth it for them, but I wanted to make more of my running, so I came back.

While you were over there was there any objection from US students to foreigners coming over and getting athletic scholarships?

Some US athletes were jealous of the kind of scholarship I was getting because there were lots of guys, who by European standards would be first-class sprinters, who were not on as good scholarships as us.

I wonder if the place you attended had a kind of negative image for kids from, say, California?

There are so many good athletes, especially in the sprints, that they can't all go to places like UCLA. So those just below the elite would come to our college because it provided better scholarships than they could have possibly got in the top California schools, where full scholarships would have gone to better athletes.

Did you find that a lot of the track team came from within the state?

Very few actually—only about two or three. Most were from California.

Who did you mix with while you were there, students or student-athletes?

Student-athletes, because when I went out there I was immediately put in accommodation with four English lads—so it was all track runners. So I did mix with runners; we didn't really mix with the others. Perhaps we would have been thought outcasts—being foreigners as well.

What was the situation about renewing your scholarship for a second year, had you wanted to?

The scholarships for the next year were entirely based on how you had performed in the championship meet. Right after the meet, following a long, tiring journey home, the coach had us in his office individually, asking us how we felt we had done. He was pretty pleased with me so he offered me the same scholarship the next year with free meals at a local casino. He tended to do that with a lot of the European athletes because the casino saw this as good publicity. Some people, who made the NCAA meet, were given two meals a day there. These were real good meals—steak, whatever you wanted. Unfortunately, one of my friends from Africa, who hadn't done too well at the championships, had his scholarship cut by more than half so he was going to have to fork out a couple of thousand dollars for himself. He wasn't very rich and was quite upset about it. He didn't know what to do, having been out there for two years, not knowing whether to carry on or to leave. The only option was for him to stay there and work all summer and make some money for the following year. It wasn't very easy because of the visa situation regarding work. So that he could stay on after he had finished at university, one guy there actually married an American girl—a sort of marriage of convenience. After he'd lived with her for a year or so he was going to get a divorce!

Did you experience any discrimination while you were over there?

Not at all really; in fact being European seemed to make me popular.

Was the coach upset when you said that you were not going back after the summer break?

I told him on the phone and he was rather surprised. I should add that he came over to Europe on a recruiting trip and I spent a week or so with him trying to recruit athletes. He came to some local meets and just asked people if they were interested in going over there. Also some lads had written to him and he arranged to meet them. I think he had done this before.

Have you found, since you got back, that the six months in America has had any advantages for you?

It's had a great effect on my running because when I was out there the day was centered around training; it was all very methodical. I used to fit my training around everything else I had to do but since coming back from the US I'm more organized and have done better for myself.

If a kid who was a good class runner wanted advice about going to the US, how would you advise him?

I would tell him to check out the university properly, to get in touch with people who had been there and what they thought of the place.

You talked earlier of the universities who wrote to you after the World Junior Championships. Have you reconsidered going back to the US, perhaps to one of the colleges that expressed interest in you?

I've always got the information if I decide to do so. But now that I've started at college here I want to finish it. When I was at high school nobody seemed very interested in me completing the course there, so I really want to get the diploma this time.

Dave

(This interview with Dave was held about six months after he had returned from two years at a junior college in the southwest. He was nearly thirty years of age at the time of the interview.)

When did you start sports seriously?

I started when I was eight; I was in the club system; my father was keen on track and cross-country. From there I went through the track and cross-country system and took part in the English Schools Championships, never winning but placing in the first five or ten. I was never a junior international. I spent some time out of athletics for health reasons (I had stomach ulcers when I was seventeen) but came back to it with the running boom.

Did you find that training for sports interfered very much with your school education?

Not really; it wasn't pressure or anything; at that time I would prefer to sit down and read track literature rather than pick up school books.

How did this interest in track influence your academic performance at school in terms of examination results?

I don't think it affected them. I think it was just that I was not bright!

I got eight "O" levels and went on to study for my "A" levels. I went on to do State Registered Nursing training but that didn't suit me and I got back into my running again. I went to a kibbutz for two years and then I was unemployed for three or four years and concentrated on my running.

What sort of standard did you reach in the period when you were concentrating seriously on athletics?

From being a good regional runner, I gradually improved and made a major breakthrough in 1984, reaching international level, and got inside the Olympic qualifying time for 5,000 meters. But I didn't make the Olympic team because I finished outside the first three in the trial. Then there were ups and downs with injuries. I did take part in one major international games, the European Indoor Championships.

During this period of high-quality track, were you approached by American universities?

No, because I was older than twenty-four or twenty-five. I had been approached in my [early] twenties when I had been doing some reasonable road performances, but at that time I wasn't interested.

How many colleges approached you?

About three, and I approached one college but that fell through.

How did you get to know about the one college which you approached?

I met an Irish coach at the British championships and he gave me a lot of addresses to write to, mainly junior colleges. I got responses from three of them. One of the coaches couldn't spell and write properly so I was put off by that straight away. Another sounded okay, but the third was the one I went to. It was a junior college in the southwest. They sent me a huge package full of information about the place. The coach there had a great deal of athletic experience— he wasn't a kind of converted baseball coach.

What sort of level had he coached at and performed at himself?

He had broken world indoor records and was an Olympic bronze medalist. Obviously that was too good to ignore.

When you say that the offer was too good to ignore, what criteria were you taking into account? You obviously considered the quality of his expertise, but were there also factors at home which encouraged you to go? Were they offering you anything over there?

At the time, I thought that I needed to go into higher education. If I was to do this in England it would mean getting "A" levels and that would mean working part-time. Then I thought about a US scholarship once I found out I was still eligible to do that. The other thing was that if I was going to go to college, I didn't want to sacrifice my running. I wanted it to be a positive experience. There was no big desire to go to America; it was just that I didn't have that many opportunities available to me.

What was the "package" they were offering you?

It was a full scholarship, tuition fees, and living expenses.

When you flew out to the southwest what were your initial impressions of the place? What did you think about the set-up, the college and so on?

I had been married a week; I had left my wife behind and she was following on in a month or so. It was a hell of a journey, having to change at Dallas, and when I got there I was very tired. It was very scenic. I was initially lifted by that. The coach was very friendly — he met me at the airport — and he was a lot younger than I expected. His big joke is that he brings his athletes in under cover of darkness, because we were driving out of the city in total desert. After driving for about forty-five minutes, we turned off into a dirt road and we were at the college. Then he took me to where I was staying, the dorm, which was desolate. There was nothing on the walls at all. I did feel depressed, but the coach, a redneck kind of guy, said that the best thing to do was to get up and go for a run and shake it off. He took me for a run straight away and it did make me feel better.

Were you put in an athletic dorm?

Yes.

Were there any other foreign students there, on the track team?

Yes; there were Jamaicans and two Irish boys had just left. There was a Venezuelan and a Puerto Rican.

What proportion of the men's track team was foreign?

About 40 percent.

This was before your wife arrived. You had a month to settle down. What was your reaction to the type of academic work you were doing?

It wasn't excessively hard. My main problem was that I hadn't done formal study for years. The structure was unusual. I was put in an

English class and when my paper was marked I was told I was using archaic language! I was using normal everyday English phrases, which gave me some difficulty with their use of the language. Once it was sorted out it seemed amusing.

Did you find being English was a novelty to the other students? Was there any discrimination?

It was a novelty—positive discrimination, really. Some of the Jamaicans had problems because the southwest is still, you know. . . . The word "nigger" was used a number of times. The other thing that I had difficulty with when I got there was the fact that they had a lot of Navaho Indians on the team. They recruited heavily from the reservations. This was intriguing to me—a bit of a culture shock. But it was really an uplifting experience for me—the whole time I was there, learning about the American natives.

What was the situation with regard to sports facilities at the college?

The facilities were of a high standard. They had just had a new track—stuck out right in the middle of the cotton fields; the baseball ground is next to it and a swimming pool. Everything's there but it's ridiculous—all out in the middle of the desert. It just looks completely out of place.

How many students are there in the college?

About two thousand.

Are the majority locals?

Yes. There were about seventy to eighty athletes and other people resident in the dormitories.

In your first month there did you mix mainly with other athletes or did you mix with non-athletes?

Mainly other athletes. The thing the coach tried to get going was team spirit. We were up every morning at 5:30 to 6:00, out on the road, training in a group. Those were the first people I would get to know. Because I was quite a bit older it was difficult for me. The others were just out of high school and a bit childish. Luckily the coaches took me under their wing a bit and I tended to mix with them rather more.

What about competing with high-school graduates? Did you find this to be an advantage or not? Was the level of competition in a JC meet high enough for you, compared with say, that at a big NCAA college?

At the JC the level was very low. It wasn't until I got to the national championship that I was tested in any way, apart from one invitational event we had involving NCAA Division I schools. I had a good battle with some very good runners. I was a bit arrogant going into this, perhaps because of the easy wins I had in the JC meets. At that level I had a difficult time shaking them off.

For most of the students in the JC, I presume that they were going to use the two years to qualify for entry into university, or were they going to leave after two years?

At the end of the two years they would hopefully have transfer credits so they could finish their degree. They would do two years in a four-year establishment.

Did you find that also applied to student-athletes? Would they get credits and go on to an NCAA school?

As long as they could keep their GPA at around 3.0 or above. Otherwise they wouldn't survive at a four-year school.

Were there any foreign students who had gone to the JC to develop language skills? Were there any athletes who could have gone to NCAA schools who went to the JC?

Yes, but more by accident than anything—bad recruiting by NCAA schools perhaps. Some of the Jamaicans were exceptionally bright and they were academically frustrated being at a JC initially, but I think it was probably the best thing for them because it fed them into the American culture more easily. If they had gone to one of the big four-year schools, they would have been completely swallowed. They came from small towns.

Did you have much contact with the town in which the college was sited? Or was the college the community?

For most of the student-athletes the college was the community. But for me, I was living outside of college eventually.

What about the furtherance of your athletic ability? What happened to your expectations regarding running?

With my running I was two years away from the Olympics when I first went. Having been inside the qualifying time previously, I was sure I could make the team this time because I was getting to my late twenties; I saw it as my last chance—though I don't see it like that now. So my main aim, having had two very good winters in the US in the right sort of climate. . . .

What was wrong with the British climate for you?

I had trouble with asthma in the winters. The moment I stepped off the plane in America to the time I came home I had no problems with asthma, but as soon as I got home it returned. The coach I was with was very fierce—what I needed at the time; he thought I'd gone soft, though it was just that I'd come from a more reserved training background. Anyway, I didn't make the Olympic team, the result partly of over-racing, perhaps on the US road circuit—but this had nothing to do with the college. Once I got on the road-racing circuit it was difficult to turn invitations down and as we came to the end of our stay we were running out of money and I didn't want to get into that situation again. Overtraining then, but I could have done that in England.

While you were in America did you have the chance to get into any big invitational meets? While you were there did you discover positive things about the US system or any negative things? What are the pros and cons of the US college sports set-up?

Because the college coach had so many contacts nationwide he was able to arrange for me to get open meetings on the track whenever I wanted. I had total trust in him; I never felt he was holding me back so that he could squeeze a few points out of me at the state championships. If anything, I felt I was taking advantage of them. The track seasons were so short and intense; I didn't see many people reaching their full potential because many would not continue into their late twenties, beyond the college set-up. I'm not saying they were burned out but simply that they didn't reach their potential.

In your case you didn't feel that the coach exploited you. Did you find that to be a common occurrence elsewhere in the US?

At some of the track meets—just dual meets against a neighboring college—they had people out there with knee braces on and bandages, just to get a few extra points. And the thing that was drummed into them was this thing about "no pain, no gain," "it's got to hurt if you want to do well," "no guts, no glory"—all that sort of crap. It was plastered all over the weight rooms and so on. I believe there's got to be some discomfort in training for any sport but when it comes to the possibility of major physical damage, that's too much. Some people over there saw struggling to finish in a state of pain as a positive thing—that someone would have the guts to do it—but I didn't see it that way.

What's interesting to me is that we normally think of the big American sports of football and basketball as reflecting the glory of the community, but what you're saying here is that even in a sport like track, the work ethic and glory-of-place syndrome are very prominent.

Yes, there was too much emphasis on getting them psyched up before a meet and not enough on actual physical warm-up. They had a trainer there who did the patching up; he was a kind of safety net, but if you're injured there's nothing anyone can really do about it. There's a lot of pressure on injured people to get back in the sport. They don't actually put people back on the track, they encourage peer pressure; so there are comments made at team meetings where the importance of winning is emphasized so that people get back in before they're ready. They don't discourage that.

Was the coach's attitude toward you anything other than an athlete to score points for the school? Coaches need survival; therefore they need points. How did you see your situation?

Well, I was something of an exception, but I saw with an English boy I helped recruit in my second year, that when he had injury problems, and problems in adapting to his college work, he got frustrated, and I noticed the difference in the way they treated him because he was younger, not such a good athlete. He was treated more as a points machine than a person.

When you say you were treated in a special way, is that because you were an international and the coach could appreciate your international aspirations?

Yes, and because in the first year I won the national for them. When you've done something for them you get positive feedback; it's as if you've got to earn their respect.

Did the guy you got out there have any wish to go to the States before you approached him?

Yes. He wanted to come out. He got his "A" levels but he hadn't got into the university or polytechnic of his choice in England so he was unemployed and a bit frustrated. When I rang him up, he was at a bit of a low ebb so he thought it was the best thing to come over. I wouldn't really encourage anyone to do this if they're feeling down, but in the event, it's turned out very well for him and he's very happy there. But I think it's a mistake to think it's going to solve your problems.

Will this guy go on to a four-year college?

Yes, he's done enough to be pestered by some of the top schools. He won the state championships and on the basis of that he will get some good offers. The coach's contacts with NCAA schools will also help him.

Did you find that among the foreign student-athletes you met there the majority stayed on in the short term after college?

I know a lot—especially the distance runners—who hit the road circuit; some come home and do really well in England. A lot like the idea of coming back and showing that the US experience has not done them any harm.

Was there the feeling that you—and other foreigners—were depriving local Americans of athletic scholarships that were rightly theirs?

There was that feeling but I have to admit that most people thought it was a positive thing, mainly because the lads on the team learned a lot from me athletically and in other respects. One of the big resentments was that they have this system of All-American status— you get that if you finish in the top twenty in the cross country or in the top five in the track national championships—and I was included in that. An American runner who was, say, twenty-first in cross-country wouldn't therefore get All-American status.

So was this All-American status a big thing for them?

Yes, especially for the college. They could say that we have so-and-so many All-Americans, and this does mean a lot to them. In the first national JC cross-country championship I won, there were five or six foreigners in the first twenty.

Now, when you got back to Britain you'd got an associate degree and you had to face the question of what to do next. You ended up going to a polytechnic. Did the American experience help at all, in a formal sense of having an extra qualification—because you only had the eight "O" levels—or in any other way?

As regards entry, I was okay because I was a mature student so I wouldn't have had any problems anyway. The associate degree was looked upon more as a curiosity really by the staff there. I don't really think it's worth the paper it's written on in this country. It is in the

US and it's worth something to me because it was two years of fairly hard work but not beyond my capabilities. The thing is that many of the subjects I did in America I am now going over again in more detail in my degree.

What sort of degree did you study in the college?

It was geared toward recreational administration. I did physiology and anatomy as two of my options.

In Britain at the moment we've got a lot of athletes of eighteen or nineteen who are unemployed and can't get into higher education. How would you advise them about going to the States on an athletic scholarship?

Certainly have a two-way ticket but don't use that as a cop-out. After all, in the first two or three weeks I was ready to come home, but looking back on it now it was a turning point in my life — very positive.

It must be more difficult to get into NCAA schools. Is it still worth going to a NAIA school or even a JC for an English kid of eighteen?

Yes, I think it is, so long as they realize that they are there to work and train hard. It's not a holiday camp. A lot of people go thinking that the American way of life is easy, but it's not. You've got to realize that they've got a different work ethic to us. They work in a very positive, enthusiastic way; once you get into their mode of thinking, it's okay, but while you think that they're trying to screw you, you're lost.

Insiders' Views of the Foreign-Athlete Experience

The above student-athletes were not selected at random, but this does not detract from the fact that, besides providing further empirical evidence of a number of themes discussed in earlier chapters, the interviews and personal histories move closer to an examination of the meaning of the college experience to foreign student-athletes themselves (i.e., "insiders"), rather than the meanings and interpretations attributed by academic researchers (i.e., "outsiders"). It can be argued that such commonsense views of the world are as "real" as the worlds created by sports journalists, historians, sociologists, and geographers.[5]

It would be possible to decode the preceding interviews in order to provide "evidence" of both exploitation and enjoyment of the American college sports experience for the foreign student-athlete. But limited evidence is found for college sport as a source of hegemony (page 34), and it could be argued that contrary evidence exists in some of the foreign student-athletes' stories to suggest that sport-hegemonic values have been resisted. That college sport has "manipulated" all the story-tellers appears unproven. At the same time, the possibility that "false consciousness" exists cannot be ignored. This chapter illustrates, therefore, the differentiated nature of the sojourn experience. Interpretation and opinion, however, will be reserved for the final chapter of this book.

EIGHT

Interpreting the Brawn Drain

In the opening chapters of this book it was shown how the sporting characteristics of the American higher education system emerged out of the nineteenth-century desire to boost one's place. In order to help defeat neighboring schools in sport, which is by far the most visible form of collective representation, the recruitment of foreigners has now become commonplace. The majority of the big-time sports universities have at least some foreigners on their rosters, as have many of the smaller institutions. This is quite consistent with the booster mentality. But while such boosterism, and foreign sports recruiting, is common throughout the world, it is only in America that the sport-place boosting nexus has become so evident in institutions of higher education. It is this, as much as anything else, that makes American higher education unique.

Because of the widespread presence of professional sports opportunities in North America, it can be argued that representing one's country is less of a goal for athletes than it is in, say, the Soviet bloc, where professional opportunities (in the Western sense) in sports have traditionally been unknown and where aspiring athletes have tended to view participation and success in the Olympic Games, rather than a salary via professional sports, as the ultimate goal.[1] In the United States, therefore, it can be argued that nationalism in sport is emphasized less than localism in sport; rather than concentrate on developing US Olympic athletes, a large number of college coaches concentrate on boosting local success, upon which their jobs depend, often with the help of foreign recruits. While such foreign student-athletes might absorb some national (American) cultural traits, they do remain foreign citizens; yet for much of their sporting careers they *represent* not the United States or their own countries, but an alien locality in its time-honored competition with other localities. American college sports, therefore, use global human resources to further local pride-in-place.

It is not surprising, perhaps, that the importation of foreigners has inspired controversy and debate both inside and outside the United States. This chapter seeks to explore some of these controversies. In doing so, several themes touched on in earlier chapters are related here to debates about foreign athletic recruiting which have been generated both in the United States and overseas. These controversies have assumed two basic forms, one "liberal," the other "ideological." In day-to-day speech, "ideology" is used in an "aware" sense, i.e., to refer to an explicitly recognized political stance. In this book, however, the word has frequently been used to refer to an "unaware" ideology in the sense that assumptions made about sport and society are not made explicit.[2] Such assumptions are taken for granted; until they are pointed out, they are rarely even recognized because they are often presented in what passes for a "scientific" or "value-free" approach. Several such unaware ideological stances are explored in what follows.

Controversies at Home

Stemming the Flood

One of the most popular views regarding foreign student-athletes is that the number of foreigners being admitted to American colleges should be reduced, or even stopped altogether. The desire to reduce numbers of foreigners often results from the fact that a finite number of scholarships are available and that a grant-in-aid awarded to a foreigner will mean that it cannot be awarded to a native-born American. In the mid-1970s, New Mexico track coach Hugh Hacket noted that "we are hurting our own program by recruiting too many foreign athletes. . . . We should be building up American track."[3]

Undoubtedly some native-born American high-school talent (though not the truly elite) will be deprived of athletic scholarships with the availability of grants-in-aid to foreigners, and several proposals to reduce the number of foreign student-athletes have been presented. For example, the publisher of the prestigious *Track and Field News* stated in the late 1970s that the number of foreigners in America's athletic departments should be proportional to the numbers of foreign students in the university as a whole, hence making the team representative of the school, at least in terms of foreigners.[4] Such a proposal is similar to that employed in American professional baseball and in sports such as cricket and ice hockey in Britain and rugby in France.[5] However, when applied to universities, it ignores two important considerations. First, some universities—notably, for example, the US International University in San Diego—is international by definition. Similarly, other universities have large numbers of foreigners as a result of their academic reputations (e.g., MIT, Columbia) or because of their geographic proximity to an international boundary (e.g., Texas Southern). In other cases, traditions of recruiting foreigners to particular departments because of academic specialties may also exist. If the above proposals were applied, such universities would be at an even greater advantage than those currently accused of over-recruiting foreign athletic talent.

Some critics go a stage further and advocate the banning of *all* foreign student-athletes. Such a view was articulated by Indiana coach Sam Bell who felt that "we should try to eliminate them from scholarship assistance."[6] A swim coach has argued that colleges are "overburdened to accommodate foreign swimmers" and that "many feel that a total ban should apply. In fact, there is a strong sentiment to the effect that foreign nationals should not be allowed in this country with US coaching."[7] Likewise, in 1977, a William and Mary coach suggested a limitation on the number of foreign student-athletes who could compete in championships, while a Long Beach State colleague was arguing for a limit on the number of foreign athletes on one squad.[8]

If such suggestions were implemented there undoubtedly would be uproar from civil rights groups and liberal politicians. It would run counter to the traditional accommodation of foreigners by the United States, part of the freedom-to-move ideology which has characterized American history. As Seton Hall basketball coach P. J. Carlesimo put it, when confronted by critics with the idea that foreigners should be banned from college basketball, "That's garbage. Tell them to take a walk to Jersey City and take a look at the Statue of Liberty."[9] Banning the athletes would also be contrary to the American tradition of projecting American values to an all-too-willing body of scholarship recipients, and it further ignores the ideological basis of American intercollegiate sports, i.e., the "win-at-all-costs" ethos characteristic of many institutions.

Training Their Talent

Linked to the above criticisms of foreign recruiting is a view that accuses US coaches of undermining American sports by training the talent of their opponents on the international sports scene. When, in the 1970s, the numbers of athletic scholarships for most sports were reduced, coach Gary Wieneke of Illinois hoped that this would lead to the curtailment of the foreign recruiting, adding that "we are under a heavy burden to provide educational opportunities and athletic development for our *own* athletes."[10] Such a view is also reflected in the rhetorical question of Mel Brodt, a Bowling Green State coach, who asked, "What are our institutions for? Are they to enhance the ready-made foreign athlete or are they to develop our own American athlete?"[11] This kind of criticism of foreign recruiting is duplicated by those involved in professional sports all over the world. It illustrates the strength of *national* feeling, as opposed to the feelings and aspirations of *individuals*. It is a view which at best fosters xenophobia and nationalism, and at worst, racism—which, as we have already seen, is viewed by some as part and parcel of the sojourn experience for some foreign recruits.

Solutions to the abuses of the recruiting game within the United States itself could, in theory, also be applied to the international migration of student-athletes. One idea, propounded by John Underwood, would be to curtail recruiting by imposing a "sphere of influence," based on the number of high school athletes available, around individual universities.[12] Coaches would be kept within that circle, with no personal recruiting trips outside it. If Underwood's suggestion stopped there, the foreign recruit would obviously be excluded altogether, except, arguably, in the case of institutions near the Canadian or Mexican borders. However, he suggests additionally that if remote prospects wished to attend universities of their choice, coaches and athletes could exchange letters and phone calls. Restricted to the domestic scene, this would still be cheaper than the national free-for-all; operated at the global scale, it would undoubtedly increase the importation of foreigners. Indeed, the international phone call, letter, or personal contact is already a cheap way to recruit, and if the restriction of a national sphere of influence were imposed (without restraint at the international level), foreign recruiting would likely boom.

Another suggestion is advocated by John Rooney who believes that the "recruiting game" should be played according to a fundamentally different set of rules.[13] He stresses the need to fully recognize big-time college sport as being out-and-out professionalized. By doing so, he argues, "both the distasteful aspects of recruiting and the unethical practices so often associated with maintaining athletes on campus would be eliminated." Rooney is talking particularly about the big-time football and basketball programs. However, he also argues that for sports in that foreigners are recruited—sports like ice hockey, soccer and track—collegiate professional leagues could be set up.

In other sports that recruit substantial numbers of foreigners, however, Rooney argues that "there is no conceivable justification for universities providing athletic scholarships." Such sports include golf, tennis, swimming, and gymnastics, and Rooney suggests that it should be the students in such sports who foot the bill for their presently "subsidized training facilities." If this suggestion were mandated, foreign migration would very likely decline, although the extent of the reduction of the foreign in-flow would be problematic, given that many foreign recruits in these sports are from relatively affluent families.

The Overage Advantage

It was pointed out in chapters 4 and 5 that the average foreign recruit tends to be somewhat older than US-born student-athletes. Despite the effective discrimination against "overage" foreigners resulting from the 1986 NCAA legislation, mature foreign athletes continue to be recruited, on the one hand under various NCAA clauses (e.g., the "military clause") and on the other by NAIA institutions and junior colleges. If someone in their late twenties, therefore, really wants to attend college in the United States, plenty of doors still remain open. Criticism of the "overage foreigner" was vociferous in the 1970s but has been somewhat muted since, partly as a result of the aforementioned legislation. The obvious point of criticism is that more mature foreigners competed at an unfair advantage over high school graduates, fresh into college. One American athlete responded typically: "The problem is that most foreign athletes turn out to be seasoned veterans and have several years' start on the athlete who's only had high school or JC meets to contend with."[14]

The unfair-advantage criticism has been countered, however, by the view that the mature foreign international athletes provided US collegians with motivation and enhanced competition which would otherwise be absent. Journalist Bob Hersh felt that "foreign athletes bring to our program more than they take from it. Both as teammates and as opponents, they provide a highly beneficial added dimension to training and competition."[15] A correspondent to *Track and Field News* stated in the context of long-distance running that the best way to improve US standards was "to bring in as many great foreign distance runners as possible and let the youth of America run against, or behind, them."[16] At the same time, it is worth remembering that the majority of foreign student-athletes are considerably inferior to the best of the US freshmen.

A somewhat radical solution to both the number and age of foreign recruits would be to de-emphasize team scoring in championship meets and concentrate instead upon individual athletes, US-born or foreign.[17] But such a view underestimates the strength of the place-boosting ideology which gave rise to much college sport in the first place and continues to sustain it to the present day. If we return to chapter 1 and figure 1, it is apparent that such a suggested reform ignores the national ideology within which local sports events are embedded. Cosmetic changes may be relatively easy; changes to long-felt and deeply entrenched national ideologies are well-nigh impossible in the short-to-medium term.

Just as there have been controversies in the United States, so too have their been debates and discussion overseas concerning the pros and cons of foreign recruiting. These are examined next.

Controversies Abroad

Poaching Our Athletes

The notion that the United States, in some way, deprives various nations of athletic "capital" by offering foreigners athletic scholarships is not new. Over thirty years ago, the International Amateur Athletic Federation, the world's governing body for track and field, rejected an Australian proposal to strip athletes of their amateur status if they accepted athletic scholarships in the United States.[18] This is a sure sign of the international stigma attached to athletic scholarships at that time. But rejection of this suggestion by the world governing body did not prevent criticism. In April 1961, when a trickle of British track-and-field athletes were migrating to American colleges, the editor of the UK track magazine *Athletics Weekly* noted that the British Amateur Athletic Board was, "quite rightly, taking a serious view of the scholarships offered to some of our leading athletes by certain universities in the USA."[19]

Two decades later an almost identical perspective was articulated in Canada where it was noted that an ever-increasing number of promising Canadian student-athletes were being lured to the United States. This was seen as being "distressing" to Canadian universities and their administrators. The federally funded objectives and program of the Canadian Interuniversity Athletic Union were seen as "being severely undermined through this exodus of highly qualified young Canadians, who envision a better educational-athletic experience in the US."[20] The growth of the Canadian student-athletic assistance program was the result.

Such perspectives see foreign recruiting as a form of poaching, another reflection of the deep ties binding sport to place. It views "them" taking "our" athletes, irrespective of the possibility of gains to both student-athletes and donor country.

In the case of Olympic gold medalists or world champions who have been educated in American universities, it is difficult to immediately see the validity of the "poaching" argument since college, athlete, and country each appear to have benefitted from the period of sojourn. It is in the shorter term that such an anti-poaching perspective appears to be valid; having peaked for, say, the NCAA championships in May or June, the athlete is burned out for the high points of the European championships in August and September.

The problem with the "poaching" argument is that it totally overrides the freedom of movement of students, or for that matter of athletes. It places national interest over individual interest, treating individuals as pieces of "human capital." It is certainly desirable for national sports bodies to advise young athletes about the wisdom of migrating to a US college, and, as we have seen (chapter 3), in some countries a watered-down version of the US model of scholarship assistance has been introduced and better facilities have been provided to encourage athletes not to migrate. But to *impose* bans on migration of students has too many overtones of totalitarianism.

The South African Connection

The subject of the recruitment of South African student-athletes was touched on in chapter 5 when it was noted that such athletes could act in opposition to global opinion, which favors non-contact with South African sports participants, by accepting athletic scholarships in the United States, thereby training and competing at the highest levels. Many countries of the world strongly discourage sporting contacts with South Africa, and offending athletes face the possibility of being barred from subsequent competition. Such isolationism, on the part of most of the world's nations, results, of course, from their intensely negative attitudes toward South Africa's *apartheid* policies.

Consequently, a number of South African athletes have, over the years, left the country as the only means of gaining top-class competition. The most famous was Zola Budd who, having suddenly arrived in Britain in 1984, was granted British citizenship within two weeks of her application (on the basis that her grandfather had been born in London), and, although the entire world perceived her as a

South African runner, represented Britain (somewhat ignominiously) at the Los Angeles Olympics. In doing so, she nevertheless became a heroine of South African sports. Other South African athletes have obtained Swiss, Israeli, and, in the case of former world 1,500-meter record-holder Sydney Maree, a *black* South African student-athlete who attended Villanova University, US citizenship.

Maree's sojourn at a US university did not seem controversial, though the participation of black South Africans in British sports has raised the question whether such participation contravened the Gleneagles Agreement which, in 1977, urged the witholding of any form of support for South African sports participants by members of the Commonwealth. An example of the problems inherent in the temporary Americanization of South African athletes is that of Annette Crowley, a *de facto* South African swimmer who was enrolled at the University of Texas in 1986. Claiming British antecedents and having a British passport (*a la* Budd), but with parents living in South Africa and not having lived in Britain in the previous year, she was selected for the 1986 England team for the Commonwealth Games in Edinburgh. The strong anti-South African feeling at the time was sufficient, however, to result in her being dropped from the team shortly before the games started.[21] While sojourn in the United States had enabled Crowley to train at the highest level, she discovered that the values adopted by the NCAA were far from emulated in the countries of the Commonwealth.

Clearly, the accommodation in US athletic departments of South African student-athletes *does* contravene the spirit of the Gleneagles Agreement (though the US is not a signatory to it). Yet, as was shown in chapters 3 through 5, South African student-athletes have been more than welcomed for the contribution they make to college tennis, golf, swimming, and other sports, and such movement to the United States will continue, irrespective of events in South Africa. In this context, the NCAA appears to be acting independently of world opinion, accepting athletes who masquerade as students, and implicitly colluding with *apartheid.* It should be stressed that the overwhelming majority of South African recruits are white.

American Cultural Imperialism
Viewed from one perspective, foreign student-athletes in the United States can gain access to both education and sport. In this way the US college experience is seen as advantageous to all parties. Viewed another way, however, student-athletes can be considered as pawns in the hands of the athletic department (i.e., they are exploited) or as

victims of US cultural imperialism. In other words, foreign athletic recruiting can be viewed as a kind of political phenomenon since talent of any kind temporarily settling in America is making an implicitly political gesture.

Cultural imperialism implies the erosion of regional cultures[22] and the absorption of the dominant global culture—that of the United States. The radical Canadian observer of US sports, Bruce Kidd, argues that foreign recruiting is a form of cultural colonialism of much of the world, recruits forming negative images of their own countries. He comments: "Have you tried to figure out what it does to their head [sic]? You know what it does, it tells them that what happens in this country really doesn't amount to very much. The big apple is where it is at, where things really count, is in the United States.[23]

This comment applies to Canada but it could be applied throughout the world. It has been argued elsewhere that nowhere is the threat of cultural imperialism or its results more evident than in the field of education,[24] and the American college athletic department provides an excellent milieu for the reinforcement of a particular set of values. The resulting adoption of American values and the (perhaps subconscious) negative attitudes toward their own nations may result despite the fact that rich forms of traditional body-cultures are found in their own nations. In many African countries, for example, a tension exists between joining the world sports system by adopting Western-style sports and the strengthening of traditional forms of body-culture.[25]

It has been shown that in extreme cases traditional cultural and religious values held by foreign student-athletes can be overruled in the interests of the university athletic department (see page 131). Similar infusions of Western ideas include the wisespread adoption of a large number of American values. It was noted in chapter 4 how many Kenyan athletes favored the money-orientated US road-race circuit, rather than return to Kenya and run there. In some tragic cases, foreign athletes adopt the worst kinds of American values, the decline of the once-great Henry Rono into alcoholism being the most well-known case. It has also been noted that the number of home-based role models decreases when athletes from countries with limited sports development remain in the United States.

A more deeply structural perspective would suggest that the American *values* inherent in competitive sports are basically undesirable in that they encourage competition at the expense of cooperation, emphasize place-bonding rather than class solidarity, and provide a puerile alternative to a focus on the pressing problems of late-twentieth-century society.

Related to cultural imperialism is sporting dependency, which results from long-term dependence on US scholarships and the resulting underdevelopment of sports facilities at home. The most graphic examples of dependency are found in the islands of the West Indies, notably Jamaica, Barbados, and Trinidad, where international athletes are almost totally dependent on US athletic scholarships (table 37). The sports system of such countries, especially in track and field, is systematically linked to colleges in the United States, well-established pipelines and contacts acting as conduits between much of the Caribbean and the United States. In Jamaica, members of the sports federations actively encourage athletes to seek American athletic scholarships, this being justified by the lack of resources at home.[26] It is not simply a phenomenon of the so-called Third World, however, as the long-standing dependence of Ireland on US track scholarships so clearly shows. The recruitment of Irish athletes to universities like Villanova has been described by the Irish national track coach as "a disaster for Ireland." He has stated that "the best Irish athletes go to America and most of them end up staying there. They often become crazy about money and lose their commitment to Ireland."[27] As a result of long-term dependence on American universities to develop its athletes, Ireland has been left with what are widely regarded as

Table 37. Caribbean dependency. Athletes from the former British West Indies who have won Olympic track-and-field medals since 1952. (All but one attended US universities.)

Event	Year	Medal	Athlete (Country)	College
100 m.	1968	Silver	Lennox Miller (Jamaica)	USC
	1972	Bronze	Lennox Miller (Jamaica)	USC
	1976	Gold	Haseley Crawford (Trinidad)	E. Michigan
	1976	Silver	Don Quarrie (Jamaica)	USC
	1984	Bronze	Merlene Ottey (Jamaica)	Nebraska
200 m.	1964	Bronze	Ed Roberts (Trinidad)	N.C. Central
	1984	Bronze	Merlene Ottey (Jamaica)	Nebraska
400 m.	1952	Gold	George Rhoden (Jamaica)	Morgan State
	1952	Silver	Herb McKenley (Jamaica)	Illinois
	1964	Silver	Wendall Mottley (Trinidad)	Harvard
800 m.	1952	Silver	Arthur Wint (Jamaica)	*
	1960	Bronze	George Kerr (Jamaica)	Illinois

* Arthur Wint did most of his running in England, representing the Royal Air Force and the University of London.

the worst sports facilities in Europe. In such cases the US college sport syndrome has unwittingly contributed to the underdevelopment of sport elsewhere in the world. Such occurrences are obviously analogous to those that have taken place in the world economic system. While it could be argued that, as part of a symbiotic relationship, the US colleges become equally dependent upon the long-established connections with donor states (fig. 26), the ownership and control of the athletic means of production (the athletic departments) is obviously in the hands of the United States. Genuine *interdependence* would require the establishment and realization of non-exploitive relationships in the production of athletes.[28]

The provision of US scholarships to foreign athletes, notably those from the so-called "Third World" is, however, far from necessary for international sports success. The most graphic example is of another Caribbean island, Cuba, which in recent decades has assumed primacy among Caribbean and Latin American nations, and has occasionally even challenged US sporting hegemony. Cuban success can be demonstrated by the country's improvement in the summer Olympics unofficial points totals. Ranked fifty-third in 1960, twenty-third in 1972, and eighth in 1976, Cuba was placed fourth in 1980. At the Pan-American Games in 1983 Cuba won more gold medals than Canada and the rest of Latin America put together.[29] In contrast to many other countries of the Third World, Cuba has been able to develop a highly diversified sporting "output," world-class athletes being "produced" across a range of events (exploding the "myth of supposed black physiological inferiority in aquatic and field sports"),[30] in contrast to the specialties of, say, Kenya (distance runners) or Ja-

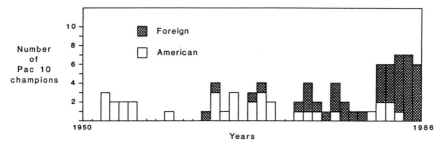

Figure 26. Washington State University's Pacific 10 track-and-field champions, 1950-86. It could be argued that WSU has become increasingly dependent on foreigners for track success, but the means of "athletic production" lies with the university, not the athlete. (Source of data: Washington State University)

maica (sprinters). In track and field in 1988, for example, Cuba produced sixty-one world-class athletes to Kenya's forty-four, despite the
fact that the population of Kenya was twice that of Cuba.[31] Whereas
Kenya produced one world-class athlete per 459,090 of its population,
the respective figure for Cuba was one per 165,570. Furthermore,
Cuba's "output" was much more diversified than Kenya's; while Kenya
had 72 percent of her world-class performers in one group of events,
the distances, Cuba's were distributed among the throws (34 percent),
the jumps (31 percent) and the sprints (34 percent). Of course, it is
possible to point to certain communist countries such as Albania and
China which have very low levels of per capita athletic output. It also
is possible to demonstrate that European countries whose athletes
have, in part, been trained in America have high levels of "production" (e.g., Finland). The point about Cuba is that it is the only Third
World country to have produced such a diversified and high level of
athletic output without the assistance of American athletic scholarships.

In the case of Cuba, the world sports system has operated in a
different way from that typified by the migration of student-athletes
to the United States. The Soviet sphere of influence has been felt by
the presence of Soviet coaches and trainers who have moved to Cuba
rather than have Cuban athletes train in the Soviet Union. Over fifty
Soviet coaches have helped train Cuban athletes for the Olympic and
Pan-American Games.[32] Since the mid-1970s, however, Soviet help
has declined and Cuba has increasingly developed its own "national
system" of athletic production. It has also assisted in the sporting
development of other Third World nations by sending coaches and
trainers overseas. Cuban athletes are therefore seen as products of a
domestic, rather than a foreign system, linking sports success with a
national regime, enhancing national pride, and contributing to nationalism. Countries that have had athletes in the United States, on
the other hand, cannot so readily recognize their sporting successes
as resulting from anything other than an alien system. The effect on
national self-perception is illustrated by the comments of Trevor Slack
and David Whitson:

> Although Brazilians are proud of the achievements of a Joaquim
> Cruz (Olympic 800-meter gold medalist in 1984), they know that he
> lived and trained in the United States. He is not, in other words, a
> product of any Brazilian track system, however much the authorities
> may seek to associate themselves with his successes. More importantly,
> any claim of a link between sporting success and a national regime
> must be judged on whether or not the development of elite athletes

takes place within a system of community sports provision and whether such development efforts exclude women or have a class distribution. The use of sport to promote nationalism among a population is unlikely to have an enduring or widespread effect unless all the people are touched by national development efforts. Cuba is well aware of this and has taken steps to address the issue.[33]

The distinction between such "national development efforts" and the training of foreign student-athletes in American universities should be obvious from such comments.

If it is assumed that the production of elite athletes is worthwhile, then the Soviet-Cuban model would appear preferable to the United States-Jamaican approach, especially if the performances of Cuban athletes in recent decades is used as evidence. Problems connected with the foreign student-athlete experience abroad are also negated when coaches go to the athletes, rather than vice versa. It remains to be seen, however, how many other socialist (or Third World, for that matter) nations follow the Cuban model at a time when East-West relations are changing and the international movement of athletic talent is intensifying. The signs are that Eastern European states may well be major suppliers of student-athletes to American campuses in the years ahead.

A Final Word on Exploitation

A recurring theme in this book has been the question whether foreign student-athletes have been exploited or not. Having outlined the problem of deciding what exploitation is in chapter 2, we explored students' perceived satisfaction with their time in the United States in chapter 6 and found that they did not appear to view their period of sojourn in America as exploitive. The decision to go to America in the first place, however, cannot be viewed in purely voluntaristic terms; and neither must we totally ignore the structures of serious sport and the US education system in any analysis of the foreign student-athlete experience. As Richard Gruneau has put it, "we must struggle to avoid one-sided considerations of players as voluntary agents acting in the absence of constraining structures which do not allow for creative and transformative capacities of players";[34] or, as Derek Gregory put it, people are not "puppets responding to the marionette movements of the systems and structures which bound them."[35] Sports can only be practiced meaningfully within the structures of international rule-making bodies and bureaucracies, which in turn define the social practices of intercollegiate athletics and the recruiting of athletes; however, it *is* possible for individuals not only to use the system to their own (sometimes perverse) advantage—as in the examples of cheating given on pages 119-20—but also to use the college experience for the creation of lasting friendships, to see the varied landscapes and regions of North America, and to have a once-in-a-lifetime adventure. Others, however, do feel dissatisfied and perceive the foreign student-athlete experience as alienating and exploitive, though from the evidence provided in this book their numbers are small. In other words what is seen in intercollegiate sports, as in other popular forms of culture and events involving "heroic consumption,"[36] is a "fractured" experience, providing education and creating memorable social and sporting events and lasting friendships for some while exploiting others who, for a time at least, may be stupefied by a diet of athletic illusion. Any generalization claiming that foreign recruiting per se exploits student-athletes is therefore an oversimplification.

It has been shown in previous pages of this book, however, that in a small number of areas something approximating exploitation undoubtedly does take place. The most obvious case is where no advice is given concerning cross-national comparability of academic qualifications. Athletic departments (or the universities of which they are notionally a part) could therefore avoid accusations of exploiting foreign recruits by explaining clearly, when they first offer a student-athlete a scholarship, exactly what that athlete can trade against the degree. Will it count for anything if the athlete returns home? Will it enable a student to go on to master's or doctoral degrees outside the United States? Will the American degree lead to salary differentials vis à vis a degree from the student's home country? These are the questions students need to ask and athletic departments need to answer.

Colleges involved in recruiting foreign student-athletes might also evaluate the extent to which they have identified specific situations which are known to provide problems (many of which were described in chapter 6) for foreign recruits. Having done so it may be possible, as with other temporary sojourners abroad, to "train the person in those specific skills that are lacking."[37] In other areas of the foreign student-athlete's experience, too, a greater awareness of what an athletic scholarship entails needs to be made more explicit. For example, all foreign recruits should be made aware of their "rights"—their freedom to compete outside of the collegiate circuit, their position with respect to the lucrative competitions outside intercollegiate sports, and the encouragement they will get to meet academic, as well as their athletic, potential. As with all student-athletes, foreign recruits should not feel that the university is getting more out of them than they are getting out of the university. An eminent British swim coach, David Bance, has therefore advised athletes contemplating going to the United States on athletic scholarships *not to* if they can continue their education *and* their sport at home.[38] On the other hand it could be argued that if they *could* combine both at home, one year in America could be an adventure and an experience they might not otherwise obtain.

Conclusion

This book has provided a framework for exploring the international recruiting of sports talent. The contexts in which foreign recruiting is practiced, the patterns of student-athlete recruitment that currently exist, and the experiences of foreign recruits while in the United States have formed the book's structure. Given the ideological background to US college sports, the widening global embrace of the achievement-sport ideology and its concurrent commodification, it is unlikely that foreign recruiting will cease. Indeed, as Gregory Sojka has put it, "when academic institutions labor under the pressure of credit-hour production quotas and the emphasis on victory remains strong in college athletics, [the number of] imported student-athletes will inevitably increase."[39] In addition, with the domestic pool of talent shrinking with the decline in the number of college-aged athletes, the recruiting process is likely to become even more competitive than it is at present[40] and consequently more international than ever. At the same time, demands by many universities, and demands by many foreign athletes, reflecting respectively the American desire to win at sport and the personal wish for success, will continue to feed the talent pipelines which crisscross the world's sporting stage. Any attempts to stop or even reduce such recruiting would therefore be simply tinkering with the system, not changing it. This book has provided evidence that foreign recruits, mainly in the non-revenue sports, tend *not* to see themselves as being exploited by the US sports system. That is not to say that none do, nor to ignore the fact that false consciousness is only recognized retrospectively. Given the global character of sports and the increasing permeability of national boundaries, international sports recruiting of all kinds is likely to intensify. The geographical margins of foreign athletic recruiting by American universities are likely to expand and to embrace Eastern Europe and Third World countries hitherto untouched by the "brawn drain." Such is the power and magnetism of the American way of sport.

Notes

Preface

1. Neil Amdur, "Texas-El Paso's Use of Foreigners Raises Questions," *New York Times*, 21 March 1982, section 5, p. 8.

2. Bruce Kidd, "Sport, Dependency and the Canadian State," in *Sport, Culture and the Modern State*, ed. Hart Cantelon and Richard Gruneau (Toronto: University of Toronto Press, 1982), 299.

ONE The Global Arena

1. Carl Ojala and Michael Gadwood, "The Geography of Major Baseball Player Production, 1986-1988," *Sport Place* 3, no. 3 (1989): 24-25. See also Mark Rupert, "A Geographic Analysis of Professional Baseball's First Year Player Signings, 1965-1977 (master's thesis, Oklahoma State University, 1980), and Alan Klein, "Baseball as Underdevelopment: The Political Economy of Sport in the Dominican Republic," *Sociology of Sport Journal* 6, no. 2 (1989): 95-112. That 90 percent of the players in the National Hockey League are Canadians is a well-known fact, but the NHL *is* an international league.

2. Data from *Rothman's Football Yearbook 1988* (London: Queen Anne's Press, 1988).

3. Joe Maguire, "The Commercialization of English Elite Basketball 1972-1988: A Figurational Perspective," *International Review for the Sociology of Sport* 23, no. 4 (1988): 305-23.

4. Data from *Wisden Cricket Monthly* 8, no. 12 (1987): 26-27. See also David Lemmon, *Cricket Mercenaries* (London: Pavilion Press, 1986).

5. Daniel Mathieu and Jean Praicheux, "L'espace mondial des grandes manifestations sportives internationales," *Mappemonde* 2 (1989): 7-13; Nicholas Jacquier, "D'ou viennent-ils?," *La Suisse*, 20 August 1987, 23.

6. Walter Adams, ed., *The Brain Drain* (New York: Macmillan, 1968), and

William Glaser, *The Brain Drain: Emigration and Return* (Oxford: Pergamon Press, 1978).

7. Adrian Furnham and Stephen Bochner, *Culture Shock* (London: Methuen, 1986). See also Stephen Bochner, ed., *Cultures in Contact* (Oxford: Pergamon Press, 1978).

8. Seth Spaulding and William Flack, *The World's Students in the United States* (New York: Praeger, 1976), and Otto Klineberg and William Hull, *At a Foreign University: An International Study of Adaptation and Coping* (New York: Praeger, 1979).

9. Respective examples include John Rooney, *The Recruiting Game*, 2nd ed. (Lincoln: University of Nebraska Press, 1987), and Tates Locke and Bob Ibach, *Caught in the Net*, (New York: Leisure Press, 1982). The latter genre is also well illustrated by Gary Shaw, *Meat on the Hoof* (New York: St. Martin's Press, 1972).

10. Spaulding and Flack, *The World's Students.* See also *Higher Education in International Perspective*, ed. Philip Altbach and David Kelly, (London: Mansell, 1985).

11. Marianthi Zikopoulos, ed., *Profiles: Detailed Analyses of the Foreign Student Population, 1985/1986* (New York: Institute of International Education, 1988). See also the Institute's annual publication, *Open Doors.*

12. Although international sports talent migration is an obvious element of international relations, it has been likewise noted that "sport struggles for a mention in international relations texts." See Trevor Taylor, "Sport and International Relations," in *The Politics of Sport*, ed. Lincoln Allison (Manchester: Manchester University Press, 1985), 28. It almost goes without saying that when geographical agendas have been made concerning studies of skilled talent migration, no mention is made of talented sports personnel; see Allan Findlay and W. T. S. Gould, "Skilled International Migration: A Research Agenda," *Area* 21, no. 1 (1989): 3-11.

13. Typical examples are John Rooney, *A Geography of American Sport: From Cabin Creek to Anaheim* (Reading, Mass.: Addison-Wesley, 1972); John Bale, *Sport and Place: A Geography of Sport in England, Wales, and Scotland* (Lincoln: University of Nebraska Press, 1982); and Daniel Mathieu and Jean Praicheux, *Sports en France* (Paris: Fayard-Reclus, 1987). For a review of geographical work on sport, see John Bale, "The Place of 'Place' in Cultural Studies of Sports," *Progress in Human Geography* 12, no. 4 (1988): 507-24.

14. John Bale, "Sport History as Innovation Diffusion," *Canadian Journal of History of Sport* 15 (1982): 38-63.

15. John Bale, "Towards a Geography of International Sport," *Occasional Paper* 8 (Loughborough, Eng.: Department of Geography, Loughborough University, 1985).

16. David Ley, "Cultural/humanistic Geography," *Progress in Human Geography* 9, no. 4 (1985): 415-23.

17. Rooney, *The Recruiting Game*, Ch. 4.

18. Allen Guttmann, Foreword to Bero Rigauer, *Sport and Work* (New York: Columbia University Press, 1982).

19. Taylor, "Sport and International Relations," 28.

20. John Hargreaves, "Sport, Culture and Ideology," in *Sport, Culture and Ideology*, ed. John Hargreaves (London: Routledge, 1982), 30-61.

21. Ron Johnston, "The World Is Our Oyster," *Transactions of the Institute of British Geographers* n.s. 9, no. 4 (1984): 443-59.

22. Johann Galtung, "Sport and International Understanding: Sport as a Carrier of Deep Culture and Structure," in *Sport and International Understanding*, ed. M. Illmarinen (New York: Springer-Verlag, 1984), 12-19.

23. Alan Hay, "The World as a Spatial Economic System," *Geography* 70, no. 2 (1985): 97-105.

24. Henning Eichberg, "Body-culture as Paradigm: the Danish Sociology of Sport," *International Journal for the Sociology of Sport* 19, no. 1, (1989): 43-63.

25. Henning Eichberg, "Olympic Sport: Neocolonialism and Alternatives," *International Review for the Sociology of Sport* 19, no. 1 (1984): 97-105.

26. Ibid.

27. Allen Guttmann, *From Ritual to Record* (New York: Columbia University Press, 1978).

28. Ali Mazrui, *A World Federation of Cultures: An African Perspective* (New York: Free Press, 1976), 411.

29. Hargreaves, "Sport, Culture and Ideology."

30. John Hoberman, *Sport and Political Ideology* (London: Heinemann, 1984), 222.

31. William Good, *The Celebration of Heroes: Prestige as a Control System* (Berkeley: University of California Press, 1978), 167n.

32. John Wreford Watson, "Image and Geography: The Myth of America and the American Scene," *Advancement of Science* 27 (1970): 71-79.

33. Michael Argyle, "Inter-cultural Communication," in *Cultures in Contact*, 61-80.

34. Peter Taylor, *Political Geography* (London: Longman, 1985).

35. Hoberman, *Sport and Political Ideology*, 20.

36. Andrew Kirby, "Leisure as Commodity: The Role of the State in Leisure Provision," *Progress in Human Geography* 9, no. 1 (1985): 64-84.

37. Taylor, *Political Geography*, 29.

38. Ibid., 28-33.

39. Anthony Giddens, *The Constitution of Society: Outline of the Theory of Structuration* (Cambridge: Polity Press, 1984), 17.

TWO Sport in the American University

1. Good reviews of American sports history are provided in Benjamin Rader, *American Sports: From the Age of Folk-Games to the Age of Spectators* (Englewood Cliffs, N.J.: Prentice Hall, 1983), and Mabel Lee, *A History of Physical Education and Sport in the USA* (New York: Wiley, 1983). The history of American education is well reviewed in Richard Wynn, Chris De Young, and Joanne Wynn, *American Education*, 8th ed. (New York: McGraw-Hill, 1977).

2. Guy Lewis, "The Beginning of Organized Collegiate Sport," *American Quarterly* 22, no. 2 (1970): 222-29.

3. James Frey, "Boosterism, Scarce Resources and Institutional Control: The Future of Intercollegiate Athletics," in *Sport and Higher Education,* ed. Donald Chu, Jeffrey Segrave, and Beverley Becker (Champaign, Ill.: Human Kinetics, 1985), 115-29.

4. Lewis, "The Beginning," 224.

5. William Beezley and Joseph Hobbs, " 'Nice girls Don't Sweat': Women in American Sport," *Journal of Popular Culture* 16, no. 4 (1983): 42-53.

6. Ibid., 43.

7. Lee, *History of Physical Education,* 70-71.

8. Jesse Steiner, *America at Play* (New York: McGraw-Hill, 1933), 91.

9. Daniel Boorstin, *The Americans: the Democratic Experience* (New York: Random House, 1972).

10. Rader, *American Sports.*

11. Rooney, *The Recruiting Game,* 14.

12. Wilbur Zelinsky, "Where Every Town Is Above Average: Welcoming Signs Along America's Highways," *Landscape* 30 (1988): 1-10.

13. Boorstin, *The Americans,* 155.

14. Ibid., 153.

15. Frey, "Boosterism, Scarce Resources," 116.

16. Edwin Cady, *The Big Game: College Sports and American Life* (Knoxville: University of Tennessee Press, 1978), 165-66.

17. Rader, *American Sports,* 214.

18. Rooney, *The Recruiting Game,* 18.

19. William Baker, *Jesse Owens: An American Life* (New York: The Free Press, 1986), 33.

20. Lee, *History of Physical Education,* 245.

21. Robert Stern, "The Development of an Organizational Control Network: The Case of Intercollegiate Athletics," *Administrative Science Quarterly* 24, no. 2 (1979): 242-66.

22. R. A. Smith, "Preludes to the NCAA: Early Failure of Faculty Control of Intercollegiate Athletics," *Proceedings of the North American Society for Sports History,* 1981, 27.

23. Stern, "Organizational Control Network," 247.

24. *NCAA Directory 1987-1988* (Mission, Kans.: NCAA, 1987).

25. Beezley and Hobbs, "Nice Girls Don't Sweat." For a more recent view, see Susan Birrell, "The Woman Athlete's College Experience: Knowns and Unknowns," *Journal of Sport and Social Issues* 11 no. 1/2 (1987-88): 82-96. See also K. F. Dyer, *Catching Up the Men* (London: Junction Books, 1982), 113-14.

26. Joann Rutherford, "Women's Intercollegiate Athletics in the United States: A Geographical Examination, 1971-1977" (Ed.D. diss., Oklahoma State University, 1977), 84.

27. Birrell, "Woman Athlete's College Experience," 84.

28. Geoff Winningham and Al Reinert, *Rites of Fall: High School Football in Texas* (Austin: University of Texas Press, 1979), 8.

29. Robert Lynd and Helen Lynd, *Middletown* (New York: Harcourt, Brace and World, 1929), 435.

30. Roger Jenkinson, "The Geography of Indiana Interscholastic and Intercollegiate Basketball" (Ed.D. diss., Oklahoma State University, 1974), 73-74.

31. Miller Brewing Company, *Miller Lite Report on American Attitudes Towards Sports* (New York: Miller Brewing Co./Research and Forecasts, Inc., 1983), 128.

32. UNESCO, *Statistical Yearbook, 1989* (Paris: UNESCO, 1989), 225-31.

33. U.S. Bureau of the Census, *Statistical Abstract of the United States* (Washington, DC.: U.S. Bureau of the Census, 1988), 140.

34. Central Statistical Office, *Social Trends* (London: Her Majesty's Stationery Office, 1989), 94.

35. Boorstin, *The Americans*, 481.

36. E. B. Fiske, *Selective Guide to Colleges* (New York: Time Books, 1982), 45.

37. Brian Shapiro, "Intercollegiate Athletic Participation and Academic Achievement," *Sociology of Sport Journal* 1, no. 1 (1984): 45-51. See also H. L. Nixon, "The Athlete as Scholar in College," in *Studies in the Sociology of Sport*, ed. A. L. Dunleavey, A. W. Miracle, and L. R. Rees (Fort Worth: Texas Christian University Press, 1982).

38. John Rooney, "America Needs a New Intercollegiate Sports System," *Journal of Geography* 84, no. 4 (1985): 139-43.

39. K. Henschen and D. Fry, "An Archival Study of the Relationship of Intercollegiate Athletic Participation and Graduation," *Sociology of Sport Journal* 1, no. 1 (1984): 52-56.

40. NCAA, *Guide to International Academic Standards for Athletic Eligibility* (Mission, Kans.: NCAA, 1984).

41. Jean Guiton, *From Equivalence of Degrees to Evaluation of Competence* (Paris: UNESCO, 1977), 9.

42. B. Mellor, *The American Degree* (Hong Kong: Hong Kong University Press, 1962). For a more recent commentary, see Department of Education and Science, *Aspects of Higher Education in the United States* (London: Her Majesty's Stationery Office, 1989).

43. Mellor, *The American Degree*, 43. The lack of international equivalence works both ways. Hence, American students are admitted to a French university "if they produce a certificate from a recognized accrediting agency that they have completed two years of college" (W. D. Halls, *International Equivalences in Access to Higher Education* [Paris: UNESCO, 1971], 26).

44. NCAA, *Manual 1985-86* (Mission, Kans.: NCAA, 1986), 70.

45. Rooney, *The Recruiting Game*, 160.

46. Ibid.

47. Mitchell Raiborn, *Revenues and Expenses of Intercollegiate Athletic Pro-

grams: Analysis of Financial Trends and Relationships, 1981-1985 (Mission, Kans.: NCAA, 1986), 13, 32.

48. Donald Chu and Jeffrey Segrave, "American Intercollegiate Sport: The Search for Rationalization" (paper read at conference of the International Association for the History of Physical Education and Sport, Edmonton, Alberta, 1983).

49. Cady, *The Big Game,* 70-71.

50. Theodore Goudge, "A Geographical Analysis of Major College Football Programs: The Parameters of Success" (Ed.D. diss., Oklahoma State University, 1984), 87.

51. E. Brady, "Foul Shots in the Land of 'Who Shot JR,' " *USA Today,* 28 March 1986.

52. Nand Hart-Nibbrig and Clement Cottingham, *The Political Economy of College Sports* (Lexington, Ky.: Lexington Books, 1986), 33.

53. John Koval, "American Contemporary Festival: A Case Study," (paper read at conference on "Sport and Culture," Clemson University, 1984), 4.

54. Johann Huizinga, *In the Shadow of Tomorrow* (New York: Norton, 1936).

55. James Coleman, "Athletics in High School," *Annals of the American Academy of Political and Social Science* 338 (1961): 3-43.

56. Goudge, *Major College Football Programs,* 10.

57. Joseph Arbena, "Funding Big-Time Intercollegiate Athletics: Fifty Years of the Clemson IPTAY Club" (paper read at the thirteenth meeting of the North American Society for Sports History, La Crosse, Wis., 1985). For a more detailed, more descriptive account, see Arbena, *IPTAY: the First Fifty Years* (Clemson, S.C.: Clemson IPTAY Club, 1984). For an excellent review of the "economic base" of collegiate sports, see Hart-Nibbrig and Cottingham, *Political Economy,* Ch. 5.

58. Lee Sigelman and Robert Carter, "Win One for the Giver? Alumni Giving and Big-Time College Sports," *Social Science Quarterly* 60, no. 2 (1979): 284-94.

59. Rooney, *The Recruiting Game,* 21.

60. NCAA, *Manual,* 9.

61. Rooney, *The Recruiting Game* and *A Geography of American Sport.*

62. Rooney, *The Recruiting Game,* Ch. 4.

63. Quoted in *Track and Field News* 34, no. 3 (1981): 60.

64. Rooney, *The Recruiting Game,* 149-50.

65. George Sage, "The Intercollegiate Sport Cartel and Its Consequences for Athletes," *Arena Review* 3, no. 3 (1979): 2-8.

66. Stanley Eitzen, "How Can We Clean Up Big-Time College Sports?," *Chronicle of Higher Education* 31, no. 22 (1986): 96.

67. Allan Sack, "Big-time College Football: Whose Free Ride?," *Quest* 27 (1977): 87-96.

68. Quoted in Neil Isaacs, *Jock Culture USA* (New York: Norton, 1978), 185. See also Shaw, *Meat on the Hoof.*

69. Steven Figler, "Measuring Academic Exploitation of College Athletes

and a Suggestion for Sharing Data," *Sociology of Sport Journal* 1, no. 4 (1984): 381-88.

70. Ibid., 128.

71. Ibid.

72. Harry Edwards, "The Collegiate Athletics Arms Race: Origins and Implications of the 'Rule 84' Controversy," *Journal of Sport and Social Issues* 8, no. 1 (1984): 7.

73. James Michener, *Sports in America* (New York: Random House, 1976), 52-60.

74. Earle Ziegler, *Issues in North American Sport and Physical Education* (Washington, DC: American Alliance for Health, Physical Education, Recreation, and Dance, 1979), 161.

75. Ibid.

76. Edwards, "Athletics Arms Race," 5.

77. Philip Boshoff, "Keep the World of Sport Hermetically Sealed," in *Sport and Higher Education*, ed. Chu, Segrave, and Becker, 61-67.

78. Ibid., 63.

79. Jack Scott, *The Athletic Revolution* (New York: Free Press, 1971).

80. Hart-Nibbrig and Cottingham, *Political Economy*, 56.

81. Boshoff, "Keep the World of Sport," 63.

82. Quoted in *Track and Field News* 42, no. 1 (1989): 73.

83. Sack, "Big-time College Football," 96.

84. Jay Coakley, *Sport in Society: Issues and Controversies* (St. Louis: Mosby, 1982), 149.

85. Wilbert Leonard, "Exploitation in Collegiate Sport: The Views of Basketball Players in NCAA Division I, II and III," *Journal of Sports Behavior* 9, no. 1 (1986): 11-30.

86. Hans Lenk, *Social Philosophy of Athletics* (Champaign, Ill.: Stipes, 1979), 108.

87. Eldon Snyder and Elmer Spreitzer, "Sport, Education and Schools," in *Handbook of Social Sciences and Sports*, ed. Günter Lüschen and George Sage (Champaign, Ill.: Stipes, 1981).

THREE Dimensions of Global Recruiting

1. The best source is *Open Doors*, published annually by the Institute of International Education, Washington, D.C.

2. It is true that sports scholarships are available, though on a very modest basis, in other countries. See Bruce Bennett, Maxwell Howell, and Uriel Simri, *Comparative Physical Education and Sport*, 2nd. ed. (Philadelphia: Lea and Febiger, 1983), 143-44. In addition, purists might argue that Oxford and Cambridge universities in England have regularly recruited American oarsmen for their rowing (crew) teams over the years. This is true, but compared with the American set-up the numbers involved are infinitesimal and the notion of athletic scholarships is not formally recognized. In Germany (and perhaps elsewhere in Europe), it has been shown that American sports personnel enroll at universities in order to enter the country with

the intention of representing professional sports teams there. It may be difficult for foreign workers to enter the country, and enrolling at a university (but hardly ever attending classes) is an expedient way of getting around the red tape. I am grateful to Dieter Lucht of the University of Bamberg for this point.

3. Halls, *International Equivalence*, 28.

4. *Open Doors*, 1986/87, 29.

5. UNESCO, *Statistical Yearbook, 1951* (Paris: UNESCO, 1951), 250.

6. *Open Doors*, 8.

7. Klineberg and Hull, *At a Foreign University*.

8. *Open Doors*, 65.

9. Ibid., 29.

10. Dick Bank, "Idaho Is First PCC Champ," *Track and Field News* 10, no. 10 (1957): 3.

11. Larry van Dyne, "Bring Me Your Strong, Your Fleet . . . ," *Chronicle of Higher Education* 12, no. 5 (1976): 1.

12. John Loy, Barry McPherson, and Gerald Kenyon, *Sport and Social Systems* (Reading, Mass.: Addison Wesley, 1978), 103-4.

13. John Manners, "African Recruiting Boom," in *The African Running Revolution*, ed. Dave Prokop (Mountain View, Calif.: World Publications, 1975).

14. Ibid.

15. Quoted in "NCAA Overage Rule Claims Victims," *Track and Field News* 34, no. 5 (1981): 45.

16. Quoted in "Forcing Foreign Recruitment," *Track and Field News* 30, no. 5 (1977): 56.

17. Quoted in "14 Grants a Boost to the Little Guys?," *Track and Field News* 31, no. 2 (1978): 62.

18. NCAA, *Manual*.

19. Personally communicated by the Athletic Department, University of Richmond.

20. NCAA, Participation Surveys.

21. Jean Harvey, "Sport Policy and the Welfare State: An Outline of the Canadian Case," *Sociology of Sport Journal* 5, no. 4 (1988): 315-29. See also Jean Harvey and Roger Proulx, "Sport and the State in Canada," in *Not Just a Game*, ed. Jean Harvey and Hart Cantelon (Ottawa: University of Ottawa Press, 1988), 89-92, and Bruce Kidd, "The Elite Athlete," ibid., 287-307.

22. Gregory Sojka, "Evolution of the Student-Athlete in America," *Journal of Popular Culture* 16, no. 4 (1983): 54-67.

23. NCAA, Participation Surveys.

24. Tom Hollander, "A Geographical Analysis of Foreign Intercollegiate Track and Field Athletes in the United States" (master's thesis, Eastern Michigan University, 1980), 72.

25. John Bale, "Alien Student-Athletes in American Higher Education:

Locational Decision-Making and Sojourn Abroad," *Physical Education Review* 10, no. 2 (1987): 81-93.

26. Harold McConnell, "Southern Major College Football: Supply, Demand and Migration," *Southeastern Geographer* 23, no. 2 (1983): 94.

27. Sojka, "Evolution of the Student-Athlete."

28. van Dyne, "Bring Me Your Strong"; Kwane Fitzjohn, "Big Guy on the Block," *West Africa* 3791 (1990): 668.

29. Ibid.

30. John Rooney and James McDonald, "Sports and games," in *This Remarkable Continent,* ed. John Rooney, Dean Louder, and Wilbur Zelinsky (College Station: Texas A & M University Press, 1982), 265.

31. Amdur, "Texas-El Paso's Use of Foreigners."

32. Roy Johnson, "A Charming Nigerian Giant Grows a Bit More at Houston," *International Herald Tribune,* 31 March 1983, 15.

33. These and other data relating to women student-athletes in this chapter are previously unpublished and have been obtained from university athletic department rosters.

34. van Dyne, "Bring Me Your Strong," 7.

35. Unpublished data provided by Andy Smith, Geography Department, Oklahoma State University.

36. Ibid. See also John Bale, "Foreign Student-Athletes in NCAA Division I Universities: An Empirical Study of Six Men's Sports," *Journal of Comparative Physical Education and Sport* 10, no. 1 (1988): 21-31.

37. Personally communicated by the Athletic Department, Texas A & M University.

38. Quoted in *The Guardian* (London), 1 April 1989.

39. van Dyne, "Bring Me Your Strong," 7.

40. Quoted in *The Times Educational Supplement* 556, 1 July 1983.

41. Bale, "Foreign Student-Athletes," 27. Schools other than those indicated here which have a strong foreign presence include Trinity, Hawaii, and Weber State. See Theodore Goudge and Peter Meserve, "Intercollegiate Tennis, the American Game: A Spatial Analysis of Player Origins" (paper read at the annual meeting of the Association of American Geographers, Phoenix, Arizona, April 1988).

42. Ibid.; Bale, "Foreign Student-Athletes," 27-28.

43. Goudge and Meserve, "Intercollegiate Tennis."

44. Bruce Kidd, "Canada's 'National Sport,' " in *Close the 49th Parallel etc. The Americanization of Canada,* ed. Ian Lumsden (Toronto: University of Toronto Press, 1970), 258-74.

45. Quoted in *Swimming World and Junior Swimmer* 21, no. 12 (1980): 44.

46. Bale, "Foreign Student-Athletes."

47. Ibid.

48. Neil Amdur, "Is College Recruiting of Foreigners Excessive?," *New York Times,* 15 March 1977, 46.

49. "Kentucky Basketball: Made in the USA," *Chicago Tribune,* 28 Oc-

tober 1988. I am grateful to Howard Stidwill, Department of Physical Education, Northern Illinois University, for this reference.

50. Amdur, "College Recruiting of Foreigners."

51. Peter Alfano, "Sports and Elite US Colleges," *International Herald Tribune,* 18/19 February 1989, 22.

52. Nigel Thrift, "Flies and Germs: A Geography of Knowledge," in *Social Relations and Spatial Structures,* ed. Derek Gregory and John Urry (London: Macmillan, 1986), 366-403. Regional variations in knowledge about the US collegiate sports set-up were graphically brought home to me during a visit to Fiji in 1986. While in the capital, Suva, I talked with one of the best runners in the islands, who was interested in enrolling as a student-athlete but, being "overage," thought he would not be admitted. He was unaware of the existence of NAIA and junior colleges for which he would have been eligible.

FOUR Track and Field: The International Recruiting Game

1. Howard Stidwill, "Motives for Track and Field Competition of Foreign and Domestic Grant-in-aid Student-Athletes in NCAA Division I Colleges and Universities" (Ph.D. diss., Oregon State University, 1984). See also Howard Stidwill and Arnold Flath, "The Internationalization of Track and Field at American Universities," *Journal of Comparative Physical Education and Sport* 7, no. 2 (1985): 26-42.

2. The *Track and Field News* annual ranking lists are made up of the top fifty US athletes per track and field event. Foreign residents were included until 1988 and were designated by their country of origin and their college or university affiliation. Such lists have been published since the early 1950s, and an athlete's inclusion on the lists is used to define "elite" or "superior" status in this chapter.

3. van Dyne, "Bring Me Your Strong," 1.

4. Hollander, "A Geographical Analysis of Foreign Athletes," 14.

5. Ibid.

6. John Bale, "The International Recruiting Game: Foreign Student-Athletes in American Higher Education," in *Education and Society: Studies in the Politics, Sociology and Geography of Education,* ed. Liz Bondi and Hugh Matthews (London: Routledge, 1988), 178-212.

7. Quoted in John Rodda, "Kenyan Mountain Men at Peak," *The Guardian* (London), 23 March 1984. Oddly, there is virtually no mention of US college recruiting of African athletes in *Sport in Africa: Essays in Social History,* ed. William Baker and James Mangan (New York: Africana Publishing, 1987). The only comment alludes to the unlikely possibility of the development of the All Africa University Games (in the mid-1970s) leading to the diminution of what Baker terms the "muscle drain" of African athletes to American universities (ibid., 240).

8. Ewald Nyquist, "The Immorality of Big-Power Intercollegiate Athletics," in *Sport in Higher Education,* 101-13.

9. Quoted in *Track and Field News* 36, no. 9 (1983): 52.

10. Terrence Monnington, "The Politics of Black African Sport," in *The Politics of Sport*, 163-64.

11. Ibid.

12. Theodore Goudge, "Interscholastic Athletic Participation: A Geographical Analysis of Opportunity and Development," *Proceedings*, U.S. Olympic Academy, vol. 7 (1983), 165-202.

13. The notion of regional place-preferences is described in Peter Gould and Rodney White, *Mental Maps* (Harmondsworth: Penguin, 1974).

14. Manners, "African Recruiting Boom," 65.

15. Quoted in Larry Middlemiss, "Some Hard Lessons for U.S. Track," *Track and Field News* 27, no. 5 (1974): 30-31.

16. Hollander, "A Geographical Analysis of Foreign Athletes," 69.

17. Quoted in Paul Geneson, "Track's Winningest Coach," *Track and Field News* 33, no. 4 (1980): 15.

18. Stidwill, "Motives for Track and Field Competition," 29.

19. Ibid.

20. Amdur, "Texas-El Paso's Use of Foreigners."

21. Nyquist, "The Immorality of Big-Power Athletics." The athletic role of the junior college is described in Albert Figore, "The 'Cooling Out' Function of Junior Colleges for the Student-Athlete," *Arena Review* 12, no. 2 (1988); 97-104.

22. Jeff Hollobaugh, "Kenya's Collegiate Connection," *Track and Field News* 41, no. 12 (1988): 26-31.

23. Beezley and Hobbs, "Nice Girls Don't Sweat," 44-45.

24. Birrell, "Women Athletes' College Experience."

25. NCAA Participation Surveys.

26. See *Track and Field News* 42, no. 1 (1989): 63.

27. Alice Andrews, "Towards a Status of Women Index," *The Professional Geographer* 34, no. 1 (1982): 24-31. See also Joni Seager and Ann Olson, *Women in the World: An International Atlas* (London: Pan Books, 1986).

28. Edwards, "Collegiate Arms Race."

29. *Open Doors*, 1988, 14.

FIVE Recruiting Tactics and the Migration Decision

1. Quoted in *Track and Field News* 30, no. 4 (1977): 56.

2. Ted McLaughlin, "One Coach's View of Foreigners," *Track and Field News* 33, no. 3 (1980): 43.

3. Geneson, "Track's Winningest Coach."

4. Hollander, "A Geographical Analysis of Foreign Athletes," 69.

5. Quoted in *Track and Field News* 30, no. 4 (1977), 56.

6. Quoted in Richard Jablonski, "Ibrahim taking NCAA 'Final Exam' Once Again," *The News and Courier* (Charleston, S.C.), 13 December 1984.

7. Quoted in "Forcing Foreign Recruitment."

8. Carole Breitenbucher, "Wisconsin's Homegrown Formula," *Track and Field News* 35, no. 11 (1982): 45.

9. Quoted in Stidwill and Flath, "Internationalization of Track and Field," 32.

10. Quoted in Hollander, "A Geographical Analysis of Foreign Athletes," 70.

11. Quoted in Kari Brackett, "Ehrlich's Team Dotted with Worldwide Talent," *Northern Star* (DeKalb, Ill.), 12 November 1987, 19.

12. Manners, "African Recruiting Boom."

13. "The Dutch Basketball Goldmine," *International Herald Tribune*, 19 May 1989, 27.

14. Quoted in Jim McLaurin, "Clemson Soccer Has American Look in NCAA Soccer Final," *The Columbia Record*, 14 December 1984.

15. Breitenbucher, "Wisconsin's Homegrown Formula."

16. Author's research.

17. David Connett, David Leppard, and Charles Oulton, "Verdict on the Fat Profits of Tennis," *The Sunday Times* (London), 28 June 1987, 9.

18. Quoted in *Athletics Weekly* 36, no. 25 (1982): 14. Contrast this comment with Connor's view of the sporting facilities at SMU (page 133).

19. Brian Mitchell, "An Emigrant British Athlete," *Athletics Weekly* 27, 22 (1973), 4-5.

20. Quoted in *Athletics Weekly* 31, no. 10 (1977): 9.

21. Quoted in *Track and Field News* 32, no. 10 (1979): 34.

22. George Pachovsky, "Canada's High Jump Superstar," *Athletics Weekly* 37, no. 5 (1983): 29-30.

23. Wallace Lambert and Otto Klineberg, *Children's Views of Foreign People* (New York: Appleton-Century-Crofts, 1967), 120-22.

24. William Buchanan and Hadley Cantril, *How Nations See Each Other* (Urbana: University of Illinois Press, 1953), 50-51.

25. D. J. Walmsley and Gareth Lewis, *Human Geography: Behavioural Approaches* (London: Longman, 1984), 141-42.

26. Quoted in *Track and Field News* 32, no. 5 (1979): 34.

27. Hollander, "A Geographical Analysis of Foreign Athletes," 67.

28. Bale, "Alien Student-Athletes," 83.

29. Steve Berkowitz, *International Herald Tribune*, 17 February 1989, 18.

30. Quoted in Hollander, "A Geographical Analysis of Foreign Athletes," 67.

31. Middlemiss, "Hard Lessons," 300.

32. Roy Johnson, "A Charming Nigerian Giant."

33. Bill Bell, "Debbie Rudd: A Britisher and a Trojan . . . for Life," *Swimming Times and Junior Swimmer*, 20, no. 3 (1979): 41-43.

34. Curtis Roseman, "Migration as a Spatial and Temporal Process," *Annals of the Association of American Geographers* 61, no. 3 (1971): 589-98.

35. Quoted in Rick Riley, "Ngeno: Courting Stardom," *Track and Field News* 27, no. 5 (1974): 7.

36. Bill Jauss, "Recruiters Zero in on Kankakee," *Chicago Tribune*, 20 January 1989.

37. Manners, "African Recruiting Boom," 64.

38. "The Mainline's Irish Pipeline," *Track and Field News* 27, no. 8 (1974): 26.

39. Melvyn Watman, "Will Coghlan Fulfill His Potential This Year?," *Athletics Weekly* 35, no. 19 (1981): 28.

40. Jumbo Elliott and Thomas Berry, *Jumbo Elliott: Maker of Milers* (New York: St. Martin's, 1983), 68.

41. Sally Jenkins, "Somalian Finds Winning the Easiest Thing in the USA," *International Herald Tribune*, 24 March 1985.

42. John Hendershott, "Brigham Young University: Foreign Depot Amid Unusual Standards," *Track and Field News* 24, no. 9 (1971): 22.

43. *Track and Field News* 41, no. 1 (1988): 22.

44. Pat Bucher, "Interview with Nick Rose," *Athletics Weekly* 34, no. 17 (1980): 38.

45. Quoted in Bill Kemenjar, "Track Coach Hemery Still Learning," *Athletics Weekly* 35, no. 25 (1981): 30-32.

46. John Bale, "Athletic Aliens in Academe," in *Sport, Culture, Society: International Historical and Sociological Perspectives*, ed. J. A. Mangan and R. B. Small (London: Spon, 1986), 6-13.

47. Quoted in Tom Lobaugh, "British Runner Gives Lesson in 800 Meters at OSU Meet," *Tulsa World*, 3 April 1988.

48. Letter to *Athletics Weekly* 23, no. 50 (1969): 6.

49. Stidwill, "Motives for Track and Field Competition," 57-58.

50. Hollander, *A Geographical Analysis of Foreign Athletes*, 68.

51. Tony Kornheiser, "Australia's Lesson for US Basketball," *International Herald Tribune*, 13 March 1989, 17.

52. Quoted in "The Lure of the Quick Buck," *South* 95, 1988, 15.

53. Allan Pred, *Behavior and Location*, 2 vols. (Lund, Sweden: Gleerup, 1967 and 1969). It is doubtful if students make objective, rational decisions about choice of universities in their own country; see W. A. Reid, "Applicants' Images of Universities," *Educational Review* 26 (1973): 16-29.

54. Bale, "Athletic Aliens."

55. John Goodbody, "The Brazilian Cruz Missile," *Running*, March 1985, 50-53.

56. Author's research.

57. Quoted in *Track and Field News* 35, no. 10 (1982): 41.

58. Author's research.

59. Stidwill, "Motives for Track and Field Competition," 59.

60. "Koskei's Age Still Undefined," *Track and Field News* 34, no. 6 (1981): 51. See also "Koskei Now Ineligible," *Track and Field News* 35, no. 3 (1982): 60.

61. Quoted in *Track and Field News* 26, no. 9 (1973): 23.

62. Quoted in *Track and Field News* 37, 4 (1984), 68.

63. Sojka, "Evolution of the Student-Athlete," 65.

64. Quoted in *Track and Field News* 35, no. 3 (1982): 30.

65. NCAA, *International Academic Standards*, 19, 27.

66. Rooney, *The Recruiting Game*, 160.

67. Cited in *Track and Field News* 40, no. 4 (1987).

68. Quoted in *The Guardian* (London), 4 April 1989.

69. Bale, "Foreign Student-Athletes," 27-28.

70. Robert Archer and Antoine Bouillon, *The South African Game: Sport and Racism* (London: Zed Press, 1982), 281.

SIX The Student Experience

1. Spaulding and Flack, *The World's Students.*

2. Ronald Taft, "Coping with Unfamiliar Environments," in *Studies in Cross Cultural Psychology*, vol. 1 (London: Academic Press, 1977), 121-53.

3. Peter Adler and Patricia Adler, "From Idealism to Pragmatic Detachment: The Academic Performance of Student-Athletes." *Sociology of Education* 58, no. 4 (1985): 245.

4. Peter Adler and Patricia Adler, "Intense Loyalty in Organizations: A Case Study of College Athletics," *Administrative Science Quarterly* 33, no. 3 (1988): 401-17.

5. Quoted in *Athletics Weekly* 24, no. 7 (1970): 2.

6. Nigel Whitefield, "Nat Muir—Prepared for a Good 10,000m," *Athletics Weekly* 39, no. 21 (1985): 26-34.

7. Steve Newman, "The Good and the Not So Good," *Coaching Review* (1980): 24-27.

8. Quoted in R. Weekes, "Fighting Back from the Deep End," *Times Educational Supplement* 560, 29 July 1983, 8.

9. David Wilkie, Pat Besford, and T. Long, *Wilkie* (London: Kemp, 1976), 31.

10. Bell, "Debbie Rudd," 410.

11. Quoted in *Athletics Weekly* 29, no. 38 (1975): 20.

12. Quoted in Hollander, "A Geographical Analysis of Foreign Athletes," 7.

13. Quoted in John Kingston, "Bradstock Still on Course for 80m," *Athletics Weekly* 38, no. 31 (1984): 43-44.

14. Quoted in Manners, "African Recruiting Boom," 68.

15. Bale, "Athletic Aliens,"

16. Ibid. But note Adler and Adler, "From Idealism."

17. Nort Thornton, "A Case for Foreign Swimmers," *Swimming World and Junior Swimmer* 28, no. 7 (1987): 5.

18. Quoted in Stidwill, "Motives for Track and Field Competition," 38.

19. Joseph Mihalich, *Sports and Athletics: Philosophy in Action* (Totowa, N.J.: Rowman and Littlefield, 1982), 117.

20. Bale, "Alien Student-Athletes."

21. Neil Amdur, "Politics Has Created a Painful Obstacle Course for African Runners," *The New York Times*, 29 May 1977, v. 8.

22. Bruce Ogilvie and Thomas Tutko, *Problem Athletes and How to Handle Them* (London: Pelham, 1966).

23. Letter to *Athletics Weekly* 23, no. 44 (1969): 25.

24. Sally Jenkins, "Somalian Finds Winning Races the Easiest Thing in the USA," *International Herald Tribune,* 24 June 1985.

25. Letter to *Athletics Weekly* 27, no. 34 (1973): 14.

26. Quoted in John Rodda, "An Upwardly Mobile Young Man from the Palace," *The Guardian* (London), 8 August 1987, 13.

27. Quoted in *Athletics Weekly* 31, no. 10 (1977): 9.

28. Quoted in David Davies, "Parkin's Finest Amateur Hour," *The Guardian* (London), 7 April 1984, 13.

29. Rigauer, *Sport and Work.* Taylor was the founder of "time and motion" studies, applied to industrial efficiency.

30. Stidwill, "Motivation for Track and Field Competition."

31. Bale, "Alien Student-Athletes," 88.

32. Quoted in John Cobley, "Lynn Williams: Canada's L.A. Bronze Medalist," *Athletics Weekly* 39, no. 18 (1985): 30.

33. Bale, "Alien Student-Athletes," 86.

34. Quoted in Chris Sigley, "Swedish Lieutenant Adjusts to Transfer," *The Northern Star* (DeKalb, Ill.), 28 September 1988, 19.

35. Klineberg and Hull, *At a Foreign University,* 76.

36. L. Ballinger, *In Your Face! Sports for Love and Money* (Chicago: Vanguard, 1981), 60.

37. Quoted in *Track and Field News* 30, no. 4 (1977): 56.

38. Letter to *Track and Field News* 30, no. 1 (1977): 62.

39. Quoted in *Track and Field News* 30, no. 4 (1977): 56.

40. Scott, *The Athletic Revolution.*

41. Bale, "Alien Student-Athletes," 89; Klineberg and Hull, *At a Foreign University,* 77-79.

42. Bale, "Alien Student-Athletes," 89.

43. Klineberg and Hull, *At a Foreign University,* 79.

44. Ibid.

45. Bale, "Alien Student-Athletes."

46. Klineberg and Hull, *At a Foreign University.*

47. Nyquist, "Immorality of Big-Power Athletics," 105.

48. Amdur, "Texas-El Paso's Use of Foreigners."

49. Ibid.

50. Robert Reinhold, "Has Big-Time Track Program Gone Too Big?," *New York Times,* 29 April 1984, sec. 5, 1-7.

51. John Hendershott, "Konchellah Has Choice of Events," *Track and Field News* 33, no. 11 (1980): 5.

52. Quoted in Hendershott, "Brigham Young University."

53. Ibid.

54. Quoted in Chris Moulton, "Interview with Carey May," *Athletics Weekly* 37, no. 16 (1983): 84-87.

55. Seymour Sudman and Norman Bradburn, *Asking Questions* (San Francisco: Jossey Bass, 1982). See also Bale, "Alien Student-Athletes."

56. Quoted in Hollander, "A Geographical Analysis of Foreign Athletes," 79.

57. Roy Moor, "Purvis Gives Up U.S. Scholarship," *The Times* (London), 24 February 1987, 37.

58. Monnington, "Black African Sport."

59. Letter to *Athletics Weekly* 27, no. 38 (1973): 7.

60. *Athletics Weekly* 39, no. 29 (1985): 40.

61. Quoted in Whitefield, "Nat Muir," 33.

62. T. Young, "The Sociology of Sport: Structural Marxist and Cultural Marxist Approaches," *Sociological Perspectives* 29, no. 1 (1986): 3-28.

63. Wilbert Leonard, "Exploitation in Collegiate Sport," 27.

64. Quoted in Manners, "African Recruiting Boom," 65.

65. Ibid., 69.

66. Hollander, "A Geographical Analysis of Foreign Athletes," 76.

67. Spaulding and Flack, *The World's Students.*

SEVEN Being There

1. I was assisted in the interviewing by Howard Stidwill. In each case the transcript of the interview was read and edited by the interviewee. On depth interviewing, see *Applied Qualitative Research*, ed. Robert Walker (London: Gower, 1985), chs. 3 and 4.

2. Anne Buttimer, "Introduction," in *The Practice of Geography*, ed. Anne Buttimer (London: Longman, 1983), 8.

3. After an undergraduate degree course, British students usually follow a one-year post-graduate certificate of education (PGCE) course in order to qualify for teacher status.

4. Polytechnics and universities are two strands in the British educational system. Although the former were originally intended to be more vocationally oriented, in reality, there is little difference between them.

5. David Smith, "Towards an Interpretive Human Geography," in *Qualitative Methods in Geography*, ed. John Eyles and David Smith (Cambridge: Polity Press, 1988), 256-67.

EIGHT Interpreting the Brawn Drain

1. James Riordan, "Elite Sport Policy in East and West," in *Politics of Sport*, 66-89. The effects of *perestroika* are explored in Jim Riordan, "Playing to New Rules: Soviet Sport and Perestroika," *Soviet Studies* 42, no. 1 (1990): 133-45, and in Manfred Gärtner, "Socialist Countries' Sporting Success before Perestroika—and after?" *International Review for the Sociology of Sport* 24 (1989): 283-97.

2. Andrew Kirby, "An Approach to Ideology," *Journal of Geography in Higher Education* 4, no. 2 (1980): 16-26.

3. Quoted in Middlemiss, "Hard Lessons," 30.

4. Bert Nelson, "Of People and Things," *Track and Field News* 31, no. 4 (1978): 54.

5. John Bale, *Sports Geography* (London: Spon, 1989), 107-8.

6. Tom Jordan, "These Are 'All Americans'?" *Track and Field News* 28, no. 4 (1975): 56.

7. Letter to *Swimming World and Junior Swimmer* 28, no. 7, (1987): 85.

8. Quoted in "Forcing Foreign Recruitment?," *Track and Field News* 30, no. 4 (1977): 56.

9. Quoted in Kornheiser, "Australia's Lesson for US Basketball."

10. Quoted in "Forcing Foreign Recruitment?," 56.

11. Quoted in Manners, "African Recruiting Boom," 62.

12. John Underwood, *Spoiled Sport* (Boston: Little, Brown, 1984), 185.

13. Rooney, *The Recruiting Game*, Ch. 12.

14. Quoted in Jordan, "All Americans?," 56.

15. Bob Hersh, "Keeping Track," *Track and Field News* 31, no. 4, (1978): 56.

16. Quoted in *Track and Field News* 30, no. 1 (1977): 62.

17. Hersh, "Keeping Track."

18. *New York Times*, 26 August 1958, 38.

19. Editorial, *Athletics Weekly* 15, no. 14 (1961), 3.

20. Government of Canada, *A Challenge to the Nation: Fitness and Amateur Sport* (Ottawa: Ministry of Supply and Services Canada, 1981), 29.

21. Quoted in *The Times* (London), 31 May 1986, 38. For a succinct review of the sport situation in South Africa, see Adrian Guelke, "The Politicization of South African Sport," in *Politics of Sport*, 118-48.

22. Richard Peet, "The Destruction of Regional Cultures," in *A World in Crisis? Geographical Perspectives*, ed. Ron Johnston and Peter Taylor (Oxford: Blackwell, 1986), 150-72. The Americanization of European culture (excluding sports) is well described in *Superculture: American Popular Culture and Europe*, ed. Christopher Bigsby (London: Paul Elek, 1975).

23. Bruce Kidd, "Athletics and the Big Dollar," in *Sports or Athletics? A North American Dilemma*, ed. J. Murphy (Windsor, Ontario: University of Windsor, 1973), 134-41; see also Klein, "Baseball as Underdevelopment."

24. Keith Buchanan, *Reflections on Education in the Third World* (Nottingham: Spokeman Books, 1975), 36-37.

25. Neils Larsen and Lisbet Gormsen, *Bodyculture: A Monography of the Bodyculture among the Sukuma in Tanzania* (Slagelse, Denmark: Bavnebanke, n.d.).

26. Michael Coleman, " 'Athletes Were Tougher in My Day'—Herb McKenley," *Athletics Weekly* 37, no. 41 (1983): 27-29.

27. Quoted in *Athletics Weekly*, 21 April 1989, 17.

28. Roger Lee, "Interdependence," in *The Dictionary of Human Geography*, ed. Ron Johnston (Oxford: Blackwell, 1981), 172-73. See also Joon-Mann Kang, "Sports, Media and Cultural Dependency," *Journal of Contemporary Asia* 18, no. 4 (1988): 430-43.

29. Riordan, "Sport in East and West."

30. Ibid. For an analysis of national differences in athletic diversification, see John Bale, "The Geography of World Class Track and Field Athletes," *Sports Exchange World* 4 (1979): 26-31.

31. Data from *Athletics: The International Track and Field Annual 1989/90*, ed. Peter Matthews (London: Sports World, 1989).

32. Riordan, "Sport in East and West."

33. Trevor Slack and David Whitson, "The Place of Sport in Cuba's Foreign Relations," *International Journal* 53, no. 4 (1988): 596-617.

34. Richard Gruneau, *Class, Sport and Social Development* (Amherst: University of Massachusetts Press, 1983), 51.

35. Derek Gregory, "People, Places and Practices: The Future of Human Geography," in *Geographical Futures,* ed. Russell King (Sheffield: The Geographical Association, 1985), 56-76.

36. David Ley and K. Olds, "Landscape as Spectacle: World's Fairs and the Culture of Mass Consumption," *Society and Space* 6 (1988): 191-212.

37. Furnham and Bochner, *Culture Shock,* 243.

38. David Bance, "The American Coaching System," *The Swimming Times* 16 (1984): 14-20, and ibid. 16, no. 12 (1984): 38.

39. Sojka, "Evolution of the Student-Athlete," 63.

40. Hart-Nibbrig and Cottingham, *Political Economy.*

Index

A Note on the Author

John Bale is Lecturer in Education in the School of Human Development at the University of Keele, Staffordshire, England. He is the author of *Sport and Place* and *Sports Geography,* and is international editor of *Sport Place: An International Magazine of Sports Geography.* Bale has published numerous articles on the geographical and historical dimensions of sports.